Critical Perspectives on Private Authority
in Global Politics

Critical Perspectives on Private Authority in Global Politics

Edited by

Hans Krause Hansen
Department of Intercultural Communication and Management,
Copenhagen Business School, Denmark

Dorte Salskov-Iversen
Department of Intercultural Communication and Management,
Copenhagen Business School, Denmark

First published in 2008 by
PALGRAVE MACMILLAN
Houndmills, Basingstoke, Hampshire RG21 6XS and
175 Fifth Avenue, New York, N.Y. 10010
Companies and representatives throughout the world.

PALGRAVE MACMILLAN is the global academic imprint of the Palgrave Macmillan division of St. Martin's Press, LLC and of Palgrave Macmillan Ltd. Macmillan® is a registered trademark in the United States, United Kingdom and other countries. Palgrave is a registered trademark in the European Union and other countries.

ISBN-13: 978–1–4039–8946–8 hardback
ISBN-10: 1–4039–8946–X hardback

This book is printed on paper suitable for recycling and made from fully managed and sustained forest sources. Logging, pulping and manufacturing processes are expected to conform to the environmental regulations of the country of origin.

A catalogue record for this book is available from the British Library.

A catalog record for this book is available from the Library of Congress.

10   9   8   7   6   5   4   3   2   1
17   16   15   14   13   12   11   10   09   08

Printed and bound in Great Britain by
CPI Antony Rowe, Chippenham and Eastbourne

Contents

Part III   The Mediation of Authority

List of Table and Figures

Table

Figures

Preface

The intellectual journey that led to this book goes back quite some time, as do most such journeys. When people – and their work – travel, creative encounters take place, in particular if you venture into unknown territory or if your work is washed ashore in unexpected places. Today, such dynamics are routinely referred to as 'innovation'. Whether this volume is innovative in its approach is for the reader to judge. Meanwhile, the editors will like to thank the group of distinguished scholars and colleagues who signed up for this journey, bringing with them tons of expertise, ideas, curiosity, courage and, importantly, humour.

The project was formally launched in late 2005. In March 2006, all the contributors got together at an intensive and highly stimulating two-day workshop at Copenhagen Business School, discussing first drafts and thrashing out the conceptual framework. Second, third, and fourth drafts were debated in virtual space, at various conferences and in the corridors at CBS. Crucial insights have been generated in the process of editing the volume, exchanging views and clarifying positions together with our co-authors.

We would also like to express our gratitude to the *International Studies Association Workshop* on 'Accomplishments and Challenges on Private Authority and Private Governance', Chicago 27 February 2007, convened by Tony Porter, Virginia Haufler and Claire Cutler for sharing with us their reflections on emerging themes in the scholarly field of private authority.

We would also like to thank Berlin Partner Gmbh for the permission to use the illustration in Chapter 9, and the Copenhagen Business School for the permission to use 'Desargues' as the cover illustration. Created by the Danish artist Steffen Joergensen, the figure 'Desargues' is named after the French mathematician, G. Desargues, the creator of projective geometry.

Finally, we would like to thank Gudlaug Thora Stefansdottir and Arthur Mühlen-Schulte for their timely assistance and careful work.

HANS KRAUSE HANSEN AND DORTE SALSKOV-IVERSEN

Notes on Contributors

Sven Bislev is a political scientist and has been Associate Professor at Department of Intercultural communication and Management, Copenhagen Business School, in comparative societal analysis since 1988. His research and publications revolve round European welfare states, globalization, comparative culture, new public management and governance. Sven is currently CBS Vice Dean for education.

Maribel Blasco is Associate Professor of Spanish American Studies at the Department of Intercultural Communication and Management, Copenhagen Business School. She has a PhD in International Development Studies from Roskilde University, Denmark, and an MA in Latin American Politics from the London School of Economics, UK. Her research focuses on social welfare in Latin America: schooling, housing and corporate social responsibility, with a particular interest in family and generational dynamics.

Lilie Chouliaraki is Chair in Media and Communications at the Department of Media and Communications at the LSE. She has published extensively on the moral implications of the media in contemporary public life, particularly on the link between mediation and social action. She is the author 'The Spectatorship of Suffering' (Sage, 2006), 'Discourse in Late Modernity' (1999, with N. Fairclough) and the editor of 'The Soft Power of War' (Benjamins, 2007); she is currently working on 'Violence and the Media. Virtue Ethics and Public Life', Polity Press.

John Clarke is Professor of Social Policy at the Open University, UK, where he has worked for more than twenty five years. His research and teaching have centred on the social, cultural and political struggles around the remaking of welfare states. These concerns have ranged from the impact of managerialism and consumerism on state policy and practice, through to wider questions of globalisation, neo-liberalism and the reworking of alignments between nations, states and welfare. He is currently working with colleagues on the unsettled relationships between changing publics and changing public services.

Mikkel Flyverbom is Assistant Professor at University of Southern Denmark. His research focuses on the role of private and non-state organizations in the global governance of new communication technologies, such as the Internet. In particular, the focus is on 'multi-stakeholder' networks – comprising members of business, government and civil society groups – and the form of social coordination they perform. His theoretical perspective draws on interpretive and critical approaches to communication as well as theories about global governance, globalization and networks. Mikkel Flyverbom teaches courses on globalization, communication in a globalized world and intercultural communication in cross-disciplinary programs.

Hans Krause Hansen is Associate Professor at the Department of Intercultural Communication and Management and presently Director of the Business, Language and Culture Studies Programme, Copenhagen Business School. His research revolves around private authority in global governance, public management and political communications, corruption and Latin American Studies. Recent publications include articles in Alternatives, Corporate Reputation Review, Gestión y Política Pública, Global Society, Critical Quarterly and Citizenship Studies. Hans is also the co-editor (with Jens Hoff) of *Digital Governance: // Networked Societies Creating Authority, Community and Identity in Network Society*, 2006.

Wendy Larner is currently Professor of Human Geography and Sociology at the University of Bristol, United Kingdom. She has previously worked and/or held fellowships in New Zealand, Canada and the United States and has published widely in the fields of political economy, governmentality, economic geography and social policy. She is also co-editor (with William Walters) of *Global Governmentality: New Perspectives on International Rule* (Routledge 2004).

Janet Newman is Professor of Social Policy at the Open University. Her research and publications focus on analyses of governance, policy and politics in trying to understand new social and cultural formations. This approach spans work on the managerial reforms of the 1990s, analyses of the politics and policies of New Labour, and changing configurations of power associated with the 'modernisation' of European welfare states. Recent research projects include an ESRC study 'Power, Participation and Political Renewal: Case Studies in Public Participation' (with M.Barnes and H.Sullivan); and an AHRC/ESRC study 'Creating Citizen-Consumers: Changing Relationships and Identifications' (with J.Clarke et al.).

Hans Peter Olsen is a doctoral candidate at the Department of Intercultural Communication and Management, Copenhagen Business School. He has written 'Fra idé til institutioner. Ombudsmandsinstitutioners globale udbredelse' ('From Idea to Institutions. The Global Diffusion of Ombudsman Institutions') (Copenhagen Political Studies Press, 2006). He is currently completing his Phd thesis on the transnational regulation of government auditing.

Tony Porter is Professor of Political Science at McMaster University in Hamilton, Canada. He has published *States, Markets and Regimes in Global Finance* (Macmillan, 1993); *Technology, Governance and Political Conflict in International Industries* (Routledge, 2002); *Globalization and Finance* (Polity, 2005); and co-edited with A. Claire Cutler and Virginia Haufler, *Private Authority and International Affairs* (SUNY Press, 1999). In recent years his single and coauthored articles have appeared in *Business and Politics, Global Governance, Global Society, New Political Economy, Policy Sciences, Review of International Political Economy*, and *Review of Policy Research*.

Dorte Salskov-Iversen is Associate Professor at Copenhagen Business School and Head of the Department of Intercultural Communication and Management plus currently Vice President. Her research is located at the interface between management and organizational change and international political economy, with (co-authored) publications in journals like International Journal of Public Sector Management, Alternatives, Corporate Reputation Review, Global Society, Critical Quarterly, Discourse and Society and in anthologies like Barbara Czarniawska and Guje Sévon (eds) (2005) 'Global Ideas' (Liber); Morten Ougaard and Richard Higgott (eds) (2002), *Towards a Global Polity* (Routledge).

Birgit Stöber is Assistant Professor at the Department of Intercultural Communication and Management, Copenhagen Business School (since 2004). She is born and educated in Berlin with an MA in Geography, Political Sciences and Media and Communication Studies (Technical University Berlin, 1996). She received her PhD at the Department of Geography, University of Copenhagen (2004). Her research focuses on Place Branding, New Urban Governance and the socio-economic organisation of the Cultural and Creative Industries with particular focus on mass media. She has also worked for three years as a foreign correspondent for various German newspapers and public service radio with residence in Copenhagen.

Mette Zølner has been Associate Professor in French Studies at Copenhagen Business School since 2002. She holds a PhD from the European University Institute in Florence. She has published on national identities, on values and identities of French managers and on policy networks. She is currently working on French managers in small and medium-sized companies in the era of globalization.

1
Investigating the Disaggregation, Innovation, and Mediation of Authority in Global Politics

Hans Krause Hansen

Distinctions between the public and private, and the national and international, have fashioned modern political institutions and practices, as well as social theory. Contemporary conceptions and understandings of globalization challenge these distinctions, leading the social sciences to ask questions like the following: *How* are the boundaries between the public and private, and national and international, being reconfigured? *How* do these redrawn boundaries shape power and authority and vice-versa in an increasingly interconnected world? This book investigates some of the mechanisms, processes, and practices involved in the production and contestation of authority in global politics as these boundaries are being redrawn. It explores the emergence of new, hybrid arrangements of authority that do not easily fit into conventional accounts of what authority looks like under such circumstances.

Obviously, we are not the first to venture into this complex terrain. In fact, scholars of international political economy and international relations in particular have recently explored how the conventional epitome of public authority – the state – is facing complex global forces. It is under these challenging conditions, as Cutler, Haufler and Porter (1999) point out, that *private* authority takes on great significance in international affairs. For example, corporations exert governance functions when they set up rules and standards that are adhered to by themselves and others, often without directly involving governments. Hall and Biersteker (2002) take a broader approach and argue that there are different types of private authority, including those of a moral kind exercized by social and religious movements, and those of an 'illicit' kind, exercized by transnational organized crime, whose activities violate legal norms. Other recent research deals with the role of non-state actors and rule-making under headings such as private organizations in global politics (Ronit and Schenider 2000), non-state actors and authority (Higgott, Underhill and Bieler 2000), non-state actors in world politics (Josselin and Wallace 2001), corporate social responsibility and self-regulation (Haufler 2001), private governance (Mattli and Büthe 2005), private power in global governance, transnational business civilization (Cutler 2003; 2006), business power (Fuchs 2005), business regulation (Braithwaite and Drahos 2000), new modes of governance (Koenig-Archibugi and Zürn 2006), to mention just a few. This research includes studies of very different non-state actors operating in a wide variety of issue areas ranging from global finance and accounting standards to international security (e.g. Aykens 2002; Porter 2005; Leander 2007).

Authority: An extended view

Drawing on some of the research quoted in the above, and inspired by other approaches to the investigation of power, authority, and governance to be spelled out in the below, this book takes an 'extended' view of authority. It argues that states represent only one historically specific manifestation of authority. Other manifestations exist concurrently, suggesting that, at any one time, multiple forms and dimensions of authority are at play. It furthermore contends that authority relates to the public and the private, the national and the international, and to a variety of other binary distinctions, in ways that can only be grasped by looking into the specificities and dynamics of social practice and contexts, including the particular knowledges and institutions that shape them. Obviously, there are complex problems inherent to the concept of authority and to the binary distinctions in question. These problems cannot be resolved theoretically once and for all, but will have to be dealt with in relation to concrete empirical analyses and from several perspectives, which is also why the authors of this book draw on several understandings of authority and of the distinctions in question. However, across the differences, these understandings nevertheless revolve around two particular traditions.

The first tradition has dominated much of the recent discussion of private authority in international studies. It relates authority to the concepts of legitimacy and consent, establishing a distinction between authority and power: 'What differentiates authority from power is the legitimacy of claims of authority (...) Having legitimacy implies that there is some form of normative, uncoerced consent or recognition of authority on the regulated or governed' (Hall and Biersteker 2002: 4–5). The presence of legitimacy, consent, and a sense of obligation on the part of the subject is what makes relations of authority a particular instance of relations of power. Relations of authority have several dimensions of which two are particularly important (Aykens 2002: 362–4): a 'formal' dimension that originates in an entity – e.g. an 'office' – based on con-stitutions, by-laws, and other formal and procedural techniques. This dimension roughly corresponds to be *in* authority, that is, to have a 'right of command'; and a 'substantive' dimension that results from the ascription of respect and credibility to an entity – a person, organization or an office – this dimension roughly corresponds to be *an* authority. Importantly, the substantive dimension may include those cases where authority is acquired through subjects' recognition of knowledges, practices, and other activities that are not necessarily 'formal' in the above sense, and these include instances of 'private' or 'non-state' authority. In other words, we may comply with what a person or an organization instructs us to do because we acknowledge them as *an* authority. They may have particular knowledge and expertise, but no 'right of command'.

This understanding of authority, briefly sketched here but debated at great length in the relevant literatures, simultaneously echoes and struggles with conceptualizations from classic political theory con-cerned with sovereignty, compliance, and the 'consent of the governed', as well as Weber's theory of domination and legitimacy (e.g. Flathman 1980; Raz 1987; Connolly 1987; Beetham 1991; O'Kane 1993; Conway and Romijn 2004; Mulligan 2004; Lukes 2005). Current scholarly work in this tradition is directed towards investigating the processes that question and functionally undermine or complement public authority. Such processes include the rise of *private* authority – or, by way of apply-ing the above vocabulary, the proliferation of substantive authority. The *de facto* recognition of private authority in political spaces and publics across borders challenges the claim in conventional political theory that only elected and representative governments 'ought' to be capable of exercizing authority. As is forcefully argued in studies of private authority, this normative position should not be confused with the 'empirical fact' that non-state actors seem increasingly to be functioning authoritatively in ruling themselves and others (Cutler 2002: 33).

One challenge in this conceptualization of authority is the casting of authority as *public* in nature and based on a *public sphere*, which allows actors being accountable through political institutions. But few actors endowed with private or non-state authority as suggested by the literature are accountable through formal political institutions. Nor are they necessarily participants in one, single, public sphere, but are rather participants in a wide variety of sub-publics or micro-spheres that constitute the public realm (Sheller and Urry 2003; Chouliaraki 2006; Hansen and Hoff 2006). As a consequence, their authority may be very partial and only recognized, legitimate and complied with in some publics, while contested and rejected in others.

The above conceptualizations of authority are different from the tradition grounded in Foucault's understanding of power and authority, which includes the concept of governmentality (Foucault 1991: Rose and Miller 1992; Hindness 1996; Rose 1999; Dean 1999; Larner and Walters 2004). In these studies, there is a stronger focus on the rationalities, techniques, and practices of power and authority than on their 'intrinsic' features and functions, whether defined as public or private. Here, authority is not a concept to be defined in advance by means of models of domination, legitimacy, compliance, and consent, and it is even less to be attached to particular social actors or predefined territories. Instead of conceptualizing the state – and in principle also non-state actors – as having specific features, maintaining certain functions, and being involved in particular kinds of governance, it is understood within the larger question of 'government' and 'self-government', that is, the methods and practices through which we shape the conduct of others and ourselves in everyday life, in institutionalized practices, and in spaces that are not reducible to the state or to the coordinates of the interstate system. This position implies a view of power and authority as inherently productive and shaped by knowledges and discourses. Consequently, 'government' refers to a much wider range of activities than the making and enforcement of laws through the state. This takes the study of power and authority beyond and across the spheres and dichotomies of conventional political thought.

In fact, the very notion of public or private authority as based on legitimacy, compliance, and consent appears from this perspective as just one among a number of influential rationalities and techniques of government, tied to a specific discourse on the formation of the modern state. Unlike many theories pertaining to the first tradition, studies of governmentality and similar approaches do not see the intensified regulation of modern societies ultimately as a result of the historical penetration of public authority by the state. In governmentality inspired studies, the formation of the modern state in the shape of an ensemble of more or less authoritative institutional forms is viewed as contingent upon the general 'governmentalization' of societies, including the specific ways in which social practices have become objects of knowledge. In this way, the state is one among many effects of a wide range of disciplinary practices – practices that allow it to appear as standing apart from, and above, society. On closer inspection this appearance and its institutional manifestations are to be unpacked if we are to understand the dynamics of political practice and the registers of authority on offer. Like the first tradition, the Foucauldian approaches to power and authority, including studies of governmentality, have been challenged. Some scholars argue that these approaches have great difficulty in accounting for the significance of more durable and constraining forms of 'structural' economic or political power (e.g. Reed 1998: 207). Others have found a tendency in studies of governmentality to present an 'excessively coherent view of governance' and to conflate 'strategy and outcome' (e.g. Clarke 2004b: 114).

Can theories of private authority and studies of governmentality be synthesized in the study of how authority is made in global politics? No, these two strands cannot be readily reconciled – except in the very broad sense that states represent only one historically specific manifestation of authority, that multiple forms and dimensions of authority are operating at any one time, and that the making and contestation of authority are basically relational, socially constituted, and challenge conventional social distinctions more than ever. However, it may not be necessary or even desirable to synthesize the two perspectives. In fact, it may prove more productive to acknowledge and creatively harness the tension between the two. Thus, in most chapters we can identify traces from both strands of thinking about authority, though a majority of the contributors draw their arguments from the Foucauldian tradition.

As both perspectives combine and mix throughout the book, the making of authority in specific social and political arenas is explored by simultaneously looking into the force of socially operating distinctions between 'state' and 'non-state', 'public' and 'private', and 'national' and 'international'. Conceptually, these distinctions are, in a sense, mutually defining and make up opposing categories or ideal types. The important task here, however, is not to investigate these distinctions for the sake of theoretical interest as this as been done at length elsewhere (e.g Walker 1993; Shapiro and Alker 1996; Weintraub and Kumar 1997; Sheller and Urry 2003; Barnett 2003; Barnett and Low 2004), but rather to explore the ways in which they are constituted and, at the same time, muddled by the dynamics and complexities of social practice and context. When we unravel the dynamics and practices of specific environments, we meet a variety of differences in terms of what is deemed public and private, what is envisioned as pertaining to the national, international or transnational realms, and not least, what counts as authoritative. We also encounter important differences regarding the strategies deployed by the actors who operate in these contexts. Such strategies often defy existing accounts of new forms of authority.

Demonstrating how these distinctions are historically constructed, mobile and negotiable is important. To be defined in public law as a state agency, for example, is to be given 'special access to legal, economic and military resources, as well as to a special form of authority and a network of supporting organizations' (Garland 1997: 95). In other words, such a demarcation between state and non-state is expressed institutionally, and in most parts of the world it will have important ramifications for both state and non-state authorities. Regarding the historicity and contextuality of the distinction between public and private, '[i]t makes a big difference whether President Carter kisses the Empress Farah Dibah in private or in public' (Van Gunstern 1979, quoted in Pollitt 2003: 4). In other words, identical actions have different meanings according to the location, domain or institutional context in which they take place, and the socially operating distinctions underpinning them involve a division of institutions, practices, and dispositions, as well as an allocation of positions and identities (Clarke 2004a: 28).

These distinctions, divisions, and allocation patterns are not fixed, however. Their particular forms and stability are challenged by the continuing production, dissemination, and appropriation of technical devices and technologies in contemporary politics and social life (Barry 2001). This book, therefore, also explores what the proliferation of modern information and communication technologies and the global circulation of media discourse prompted by these developments mean for the above mentioned distinctions and the making and contestation of authority. This includes a particular attention to some of the technical devices and technologies which are a *sine qua non* for the creation of connections and linkages between human beings across boundaries. There is an important public, mediated, and discursive dimension to authority construction in global politics. Examining this dimension may help us understand why and how a variety of actors can become recognized as being invested with authority, and maintain it, and how particular processes or rules are de facto accepted, seen as right, met with indifference and apathy, or outright rejection.

If investigating the contingency and dynamics of arrangements of authority in a globally mediated environment generates new ways of understanding them, then it also opens up new ways of acting upon these arrangements. Since the 1990s, research on private authority and global governance more generally has offered a series of approaches highlighting the polycentric character of contemporary power and authority (e.g. Scholte 2005). Most accounts underscore how public authority, as the site of representative democracy that channels citizen interests and legitimizes governmental actions, is challenged by the formation of cross-boundary political spaces in which alternative forms of authority, in particular private, are produced, negotiated, legitimized, and contested. These spaces may open up new ways in which people participate in politics (Benner et al. 2002). But they may also significantly magnify already existing asymmetries because of the absence of mechanisms to ensure a sufficient degree of transparency and accountability (Ottoway 2001). In any case, before we judge whether and in which way such spaces might be democratic or not, we need to know more about their creation, including the mechanisms of authority being enacted by and through them. This is interesting since many of the emerging arrangements of authority do not possess the hard coercive capacities of states, but rely on soft techniques and modes of governance – credibility, reputation, image, informality, and collaboration – in order to assert their authority. This observation, of course, does not imply that states do not also rely significantly on these techniques, or that non-state actors are not hierarchical and in many cases equipped with coercive powers (Rosenau 2002; Nye 2004; Risse 2004).

This book, then, explores the variety of ways in which authority is made in a globally mediated environment. In addition to the focus on specific practices and actors – 'public' and 'private' and 'in-betweens', including what in many cases turns out to be a complex, hybrid, and fluid constellation of differences and identifications – we scrutinize specific arenas and issue areas in which these processes take place. We also take a look at the ways in which these processes are redrawing and contesting taken for granted boundaries between the public and the private, and between the national and the international. The common methodological thread linking the different chapters is the case study, which allows us to focus on authority making in specific settings and domains, including on the discursive moments of social practices involved in the making and contestation of authority. By way of complementing previous research, mostly conducted in the fields of international relations and international political economy, this book includes scholars with roots in cultural and organization studies, media and communication studies, human geography, ethnography, and area studies. This naturally leads several contributors to question some of the assumptions on previous research on private authority, but it also opens up fresh perspectives on the issue of authority making in global politics.

Three conceptual lenses

Below we will briefly introduce three conceptual lenses in order to shed light on important dynamics of contemporary authority making: the disaggregation of authority, the innovation of authority, and, the mediation of authority. While they introduce a series of themes that run across the entire book, these lenses also provide the reader with an overview of its basic structure. In the conclusion of the book, we reflect on the strengths and weaknesses of the volume and draw out the key themes that have emerged against the backcloth of the findings of each chapter.

The disaggregation of authority

Debates on globalization, governance, and private authority often start from the assumption that major shifts in the spatial and social organization of power and authority are taking place: from public to private, from national to global, from government to governance. These debates have led to critical discussions of the relevance of state-centric understandings of politics, and in particular, to the claim that political authority cannot today in any meaningful way be envisioned as congruent with a clearly bounded territorial space. Often, these discussions are underpinned by the idea that the dispersion of power and authority is a novelty – a process that is closely related to the contemporary phase of globalization. Others have maintained that national governments remain critical as strategic sites for tying together the different infrastructures of governance and, not least, for legitimizing 'regulation beyond the state' (for accounts of these debates, see Held and McGrew 2002; Scholte 2005). While many of these recent attempts in international relations theory to move beyond state-centrism have provided us with important insights into the dynamics of global governance, they have told us less about the dynamics of authority formation in specific social contexts and political arenas. By presenting the dispersion towards the 'private' or 'non-state', the 'inter' or 'trans', and more fundamentally the movement from 'government' to 'governance' as a historical shift, some of these accounts remain within the parameters set by state-centrism.

Rather than taking these categories for granted, we propose to approach the realms delineated by the categories in question as historically produced fields of action produced by complex discourses and practices 'that help constitute subjects and objects of governance in particular forms' (see Larner Chapter 7: 130; Newman and Clarke Chapter 6; Newman 2005). Such a focus makes it possible to explore authority formation in a way that elicits its mechanisms in what strikes some as very ordinary, everyday activities. It may allow us not only 'to understand the operation of authorities in a disaggregated manner and to deemphasize the state as the ultimate seat of power', but also 'to examine the dispersed institutional and social networks through which rule is coordinated and consolidated, and the role that non-state institutions, communities, and individuals plays in the mundane processes of governance' (Sharma and Gupta 2006: 9; see also Hansen and Stepputat 2001).

In this vein, we find it apposite to use the term 'disaggregated authority' to denote not only the mutually constitutive character of arrangements of authority that rely upon or reinforce one another, but also to enable a view on such arrangements as heterogeneous, entangled, multi-layered, mobile and porous. Specifically, arrangements of authority can refer here to actors, processes, practices or rules that are de facto accepted or seen as right by one or more sub-publics, frequently involving hybrid mixes of public, private, technical, and popular authority (see Porter Chapter 2; Flyverbom and Bislev Chapter 4). Institutions and organizations – and in particular states and corporations – typically represent themselves as unitary and coherent, but on closer inspection, they bear witness to a variety of contradictions and fractures. It is by focussing on these contradictions and fractures that we begin to see the fundamentally disaggregated and often relatively fluid character of these arrangements, and, by implication, question something that is often taken for granted: the cohesion and unitariness of institutions and organizations in general and of the state in particular – the epitome of public authority. If the state can be conceived of as a unitary actor in theory it is and remains to a large extent disaggregated when studied in practice. In this lens, thus, the notion of 'state' makes sense as little more than a 'convenient stenographic label' for highly complex practices, coalitions and interactions that take place between a wide variety of actors in different positions (Abrahms 2006 [1977/1988]; Bourdieu and Wacquant 1992: 122; Bourdieu 1984).

The notion of the state as a 'unitary actor' has long dominated international legal and political analysis. Recently however, the concept of the 'disaggregated state' has been proposed to counter the tendency – inherent in the view of states as unitary actors – to focus only on the traditional, formal and functional aspects of states. By thinking of the state as disaggregated, the heterogeneous and highly complex landscape of networks, organizations and communicative practices that tie together state organizations and actors across boundaries becomes visible (Slaughter 2004a). The concept of the disaggregated state has also been complemented by the concept of disaggregated sovereignty – or 'new sovereignty' – which, as opposed to 'old sovereignty', is claimed to be relational, connected, interacting, and engaged rather than separated, or insular (Slaughter 2004b).

At first sight, the concepts of the disaggregated state and disaggregated sovereignty provide an interesting corrective to the approaches that portray the state as a clear, territorially bounded institution, distinct from society and in possession of the supreme authority to regulate populations within its territory. But this approach also carries with it a number of problems, in particular, the claim that states can change from disaggregated to unified actors under specific circumstances, such as going to war (Slaughter 2004a, 2004b). This claim assumes that states under special circumstances and not others do, in fact, have a single identity and a single set of interests, leaving aside the internal dynamics, potential fractures, and conflicts that shape those individuals acting in the name of the state. By downplaying the actual disunity and incoherence of political authority and political practices more generally, this stance is also at odds with the otherwise celebrated concept of network which usually eschews treating entities and organizational forms as a 'black box'. In spite of this caveat, the concept of disaggregation has the capacity to frame a broader analysis of the interaction and exchanges within and between a different forms of authority, potentially enriching studies of the practices of power at stake in different issue areas (see Porter Chapter 2). Furthermore, even if the concept of disaggregation in some previous research appears to be reserved for the study of government-to-government networks (Slaugther 2004ab), it provides an interesting entry point for investigating the cross-cutting arrangements that organize public, private, and civil society actors around issues of common concern (See Olsen Chapter 3; Flyverbom and Bislev Chapter 4; Salskov-Iversen and Hansen Chapter 8).

As already indicated, an important dimension of disaggregated authority is entanglement (Porter Chapter 2), which emphasizes the linkages and connectivity between different arrangements of authority, including the forms in which action and control at a distance can take place. The focus on entanglement, which may take the shape of cross-cutting networks, partnerships, institutional entrepreneurship, and other forms of intermediating activity (Olsen Chapter 3; Flyverbom and Bislev Chapter 4; Larner Chapter 7; Salskov-Iversen and Hansen Chapter 8), leads us to examine the practical ways in which arrangements of authority intermingle with one and other, and, importantly, on their mutually constitutive and relational character. In this lens, arrangements of authority, for example, in the form of state agencies and companies, appear not as preconstituted institutions that perform pre- and well-defined functions. Rather, they are seen as assemblages produced through everyday practices, discourses and non-human objects and technologies that facilitate action and control at a distance – the operation of which is irreducible to one single logic, but which nevertheless links these arrangements together (Collier and Ong 2005; Sharma and Gupta 2006).

In Part I of the book, *The Disaggregation of Authority*, three chapters are specifically concerned with these issues. Tony Porter, in Chapter 2, argues that the disaggregation of authority can involve the transformation of authority from more state-centric public forms to increasingly mediated private, technical, or popular forms of authority that are entangled with one another and with public authority. Porter explores the variation in the degree and character of the disaggregation of authority across issue areas with reference to three cases: airline and border security, global financial regulation, and the unauthorized downloading of songs. While the disaggregation of authority poses a challenge to traditional mechanisms of democratic accountability and legitimacy, it also creates new opportunities for citizens to influence or challenge authority. For Hans Peter Olsen, in Chapter 3, the standardization of government auditing is a case particularly rich in insights that can shed light on the wider phenomena of disaggregation and authority making on a transnational scale. Olsen explores the process through which various actors ranging from national supreme audit institutions to international financial institutions, accountants' associations and firms are becoming increasingly involved in standard-setting as a way of regulating the field of auditing. As such, this is a case of how new and 'soft' modes of governance manifest themselves in the form of voluntary standards produced by a network that spans both the public and private sectors and also beyond national boundaries. In Chapter 4, Mikkel Flyverbom and Sven Bislev investigate the emergence of Internet regulation as a global, political issue area in the context of the United Nations initiated discussions about the global information society. They explore how the disaggregation of authority is played out in the global governance of the Internet. And they show how the involved actors – governments, business, civil society groups, and international organizations – are constituted as 'stakeholders' in an emergent mode of governance which aligns multiple authorities and may have far-reaching consequences for issues such as development, gender, and human rights: 'multi-stakeholder participation.'

The innovation of authority

Contemporary scholarship on organizations and organizational change often emphasizes the role and impact of ideas and conceptions of modernization and innovation. The processes whereby changes are launched have been referred to as 'reforms', which revolve around two basic activities: 'attempts at convincing people that new forms should be installed and attempts at getting them to influence practice, getting them implemented' (Brunsson 2000: 150). We might add, quoting Connolly (1987: 14), that such attempts potentially enable organizations 'to realize an anticipated future more than to maintain or restore a pure condition located in the past'. In other words, projects of modernization and innovation can be a key driver in generating authority, because their 'futuristic orientation' provides the fuel for making a difference, for becoming visible, for being recognized as having something useful and valuable to offer, at least in some contexts.

In the public sector in most parts of the world, processes of modernization and innovation have been inspired by supra-national organizations and networks and, particularly, by the world of private corporations, and in a broader sense, by neoliberal discourses of modernization that underscore initiative, self-reliance, and the capacity for assuming responsibility for oneself (e.g. Salskov-Iversen et al. 2000; Hansen et al. 2002; Hansen and Salskov-Iversen 2005). In many ways the commercial enterprise has become the preferred model for the institutionalized reorganization, reinvention and innovation of public services, articulating the purported imperative of moving away from a traditional bureaucratic mindset and towards more entrepreneurial and flexible forms of organizing, so that public sector organizations become better equipped to provide the 'public goods' expected by demanding citizens (Hartley 2005; Newman and Clarke Chapter 6; Salskov-Iversen and Hansen Chapter 8).

In turn, debates on the survival and growth of private organizations and companies refer to the capacity to renew what they offer in increasingly competitive markets, with a specific attention to the particular ways in which that offering is created and delivered. The issue here is not only whether, for example, the adaptation of new technologies and organizational models, such as the so-called 'network enterprise' (Castells 2000), will improve production processes and increase sales, eventually leading to higher profits. It is also a question of the broader relationship between business and society, including how and to what degree corporations accept to integrate social demands, and to assume social and ethical responsibilities (Haufler 1999: 212; Haufler 2006; Cutler 2006), frequently but not always against the backdrop of a receding or impoverished state (Garriga and Melé 2004; Blasco and Zølner Chapter 5).

The notion that organizations – public, private or civil society – are being subjected to increasing demands for efficiency, effectiveness, performance, responsiveness, and responsibility towards the variety of 'publics', 'citizens', and 'consumers' that are seen as characterizing 'globalization', the 'information age', 'knowledge economy' and 'consumer society', is a key element in organizations' representations of themselves and their surroundings. These positions, epochal forms, and societal contexts are presented as unstable and competitive. The actors who populate them are portrayed as highly heterogeneous and diverse, their wants and needs as complex and volatile, expressed primarily through the market. The identification of such demands can prompt organizations to initiate innovation – discursive, organizational and technologically mediated processes of renewal that revolve around actors defined as nodal figures in political and economic spaces, such as citizens, customers and consumers (Newman and Clarke Chapter 6).

Innovation refers not just to a new idea – an invention – but to a new practice. In addition, it may include the reinvention and adaptation of a particular practice to another context. Conditioned on new combinations of new or already existing ideas, capabilities and skills, innovation does not take place in isolation. It depends on the connection to, and relationships with, the external world, which inspires, facilitates and makes possible the appropriation of ideas and practices (Salskov-Iversen and Hansen Chapter 8). According to this line of argument, the capacity for innovation rests on entanglement: it is by working with external relations and identifications that institutions and organizations – public, private, and hybrid forms – can emerge, become legitimate, carve out new niches. Alternatively, if they fail to engage with external identifications – they may risk being contested and even de-legitimized or destabilized, and, as a result, their claim to authority may be undermined.

At a first glance, the complex combination of these forms and contexts – and in particular the ubiquity of the entrepreneurial rationale – appears to effectively blur the traditional distinctions between the public and the private, the national and the international: the entrepreneurial rationale ensures the optimal functioning of all social sectors and spheres. But a different perspective is also possible: rather than erasing the boundaries between these domains per se, this rationale is reconfiguring them according to different principles, such as when the citizen is re-articulated as a consumer or a customer: 'A focus on the customer is conceived of as a crucial device for making organizations act in ways that most fully express the qualities of free enterprises and market competitiveness' (Du Gay 1997: 310). Furthermore, the focus on the customer or consumer is not necessarily expressing a tough, performance-oriented image of public sector organizations, but can in fact be completed with a soft-focus image, in which government appears as a

> good neighbour – someone who informs you about new developments that might affect you, cooperates with you, enables you to realize your own projects, supports you when you are in difficulty, learns from your experience – but hardly ever, it seems, orders you about or invokes the law to force you to do something you don't want to do. Further, this good neighbour has a computer. Networking, partnering, 'joining-up', involving the public and other 'relational' approaches can all be lubricated by the wonders of modern information and communication technologies. (Pollitt 2003: 52)

In Part II of this book, *The Innovation of Authority*, we contend that tracing the contradictory and multilayered processes through which arrangements of authority are being made and becoming entangled is inseparable from exploring the ways in which new ideas and forms of identification are introduced, assembled, and contextualized and contested within and across contexts – such as when corporate social responsibility becomes a vehicle for enhancing private sector legitimacy, or when consumer orientation becomes a driver for innovation in public section organizations. We therefore look at attempts at, and processes of, innovation and their implications for the authority and legitimation of organizations and practices in their various forms, as these take place in a variety of settings at the interface between the public and the private, the national, the international and the transnational.

Four chapters are particularly devoted to an investigation of these issues. What they have in common is that the actors examined – business associations, government units at different levels, and citizens – each in their own way are involved in and shaped by projects or processes of reform and innovation. In Chapter 5, Maribel Blasco and Mette Zølner use the globalizing narrative of Corporate Social Responsibility (CSR) as a prism through which to examine the types of appeals that private market actors make to public recognition in present day France and Mexico – two non-Anglo countries where the legitimacy of private actors has traditionally been low. This study offers an account of how business constructs itself as a legitimate actor and points to the necessity of investigating the normative and cultural-cognitive terrains that shape the particular ways in which this work of authority-building amongst private market actors may take place. That generalizing narratives often mask institutional variation and localized meanings concerning the public and private distinction is also an underlying theme in Chapter 6 by Janet Newman and John Clarke. This chapter analyses how the reform of public services in the UK has been driven – in part – by a conception of citizens as consumers of public services. This conception has been lodged in globalizing narratives about the transition to a consumer society and consumer culture, and, by implication, about the constitution by non-state actors – including citizens – of new forms of authority alongside self-responsibility and self-rule. Critical of such conceptions in policy discourse, and of their treatment in strands of the scholarly literature, the authors analyse the changing relationships and identifications at the interface between the reform of public services and the public. They question generalizing understandings of the constitution and remaking of public and private authority, realms, sectors as simple transitions from state to non-state, from state to market, and from citizen to consumers.

While Chapters 5 and 6 focus on national and sub-national settings, Chapters 7 and 8 take us out into transnational and translocal spaces. In Chapter 7, Wendy Larner explores how governments have started thinking about their expatriate populations in new ways and how these new understandings have become central to development strategies premised on increased participation in the globalizing economy. Empirically, she examines recent attempts to link expatriate networks to national development projects through a case study of New Zealand. Her argument is that diaspora strategies not only represent a new geographic imaginary and political-economic field, but that they also involve the active constitution of new spaces and subjects with distinctive characteristics. According to Larner, diaspora strategies not only disrupt conventional distinctions between the domestic and the international. They also contribute to the reconfiguration of public and private authority since new understandings of nation, state, and governance emerge.

Signs of such new understandings also appear in Chapter 8. Here, Salskov-Iversen and Hansen are particularly concerned with a number of processes that together can be seen to contribute to the innovation of (local) public authority. The chapter examines how local governments in Peru and Canada proactively use transnational networks to implement e-government. It posits that networked arrangements can hold out interesting opportunities for local governments intent on reinventing and consolidating their authority, and thus their legitimacy, in their local and national contexts. At the same time, some of these transationally networked arrangements are becoming recognized as forms of authority in very practical ways. The constitution and dynamics of 'private' authority in contemporary local and global politics can also flow from the public sector's translation of a number of private sector mentalities, notably managerialization and marketization. Finally, the authors draw attention to the crucial role of technologies in innovation processes. This aspect is further accentuated by the empirical backdrop to their discussion, namely the ascendance of digital tools in present-day reform projects, 'e-modernization', in the public sector and its interaction with citizens and other 'stakeholders.'

The mediation of authority

As already indicated, several chapters mention and discuss the role of technical devices, and media and communication technologies in the making of authority, be it in regard to the disaggregation of authority as such, to the regulation of media, or as part of innovation projects. This book's final part, *The Mediation of Authority*, contains two chapters that deal more specifically with these issues. Exploring authority in relation to processes of global mediation, these chapters demonstrate that the divide between the 'global' and the 'local' is not fixed once and for all but continuously negotiated. They similarly challenge fixed definitions of the 'public' and the 'private' by pointing out how mediation constantly blurs and reconfigures the two spheres.

It is difficult to understand what the framing, dissemination, appropriation, editing, recognition, and rejection of ideas and knowledge mean for the creation of authority without paying attention to the technological and discursive processes involved. In this book we use the concept of mediation to refer to both dimensions. Discourse reflects and shapes objects, mindsets, identities – individual and collective – and relationships. In addition to its constitutive role, discourse has both functional and strategic dimensions, that is, it can be designed to achieve certain ends. It can also be organizing, if not governing, as the activity of producing shared meaning requires and produces organizational forms, which, in turn, lie at the heart of the formation of institutions (Black 2002; Phillips 2003). Discourse is contingent upon all sorts of technological devices, as well as media technologies more narrowly speaking, such as the Internet and television. Such media have specific functional characteristics and relational potentialities – *affordances* (Hutchby 2001: 444–447) – which frame the possibilities for human action. In terms of their affordances, the different media technologies make certain forms of communication easier than others, offering us a horizon of opportunities with ramifications for social life and political organization. In a more general sense, thus, technical devices and technologies can be seen as an integral feature of the contemporary public sphere(s) and politics: 'If we regard the public sphere as a set of spaces within which matters of truth and justice can be raised in public, then there is always a technical dimension to the specific forms that the public sphere can take, and the connection between the realms of "public" and "private" politics' (Barry 2001: 9). As a consequence, instead of viewing human beings and material artefacts as worlds apart, it may prove more productive to view them as somehow interwoven or tied together (Latour 1991; Law and Hassard 1999). This may open up new ways of understanding the chains and networks that make possible the enrolment of social actors into, as well as their alignment with, particular societal projects. This, in turn, can provide us with insights into the dynamics of action at a distance, and by implication, the formation of authority (Law and Hetherington 2000; Dicken et al. 2001).

In discussions about global governance and the rise of new forms of authority the role of mediation is an emergent theme (see Deibert 1997 and 2003; Rosenau and Singh 2002; Latham and Sassen 2005; Choliararki 2006; Hansen and Hoff 2006), and it merits more scholarly attention. As Sing (2002) has pointed out, global politics is inherently relational and interwoven with the media and their derivatives: information networks. Information networks 'not only impact existing actors and issues but, as an increasing body of knowledge notes, networked interaction itself constitutes actors and issues in global politics' (Singh, 2002: 18–19). Thus, media technologies and information networks are crucial for political politics in a globalized world in at least two ways. First, the management and governance of any issue area – ranging from the reform of the public sector (Salskov-Iversen and Hansen Chapter 8) over city branding (Stöber Chapter 9), airport security, financial regulation and the downloading of music (Porter Chapter 2), to the mobilization and enrolment of expatriates in national projects (Larner Chapter 7) – imply the application of media technologies and the use of information networks. These are all pivotal to the successful enrolment and mobilization of persons, procedures, and artifacts in the pursuit of specific goals (Barry 2001). The creation of more durable and authoritative alliances – sectorial or criss-crossing – would be unthinkable without devices to coordinate activities and to act strategically. Second, media technologies and information networks are themselves the objects of governance and management, including the codes and rules that regulate media technologies and information networks at any given moment. In fact, one important and emerging issue area in global politics is global media governance – specifically the issue of Internet governance – to which a wide range of new actors and hybrid constellations devote considerable attention (Spar 1999; Siochrú and Girard 2002; Perri 6 2002; Deibert 2003; Flyverbom and Bislev Chapter 4). In short, mediation is deeply implicated in the processes of disaggregation and entanglement of authority described in the above, and has itself become a site of political contestation.

The proliferation of media technologies and information networks does not only imply that distant sites of political decision making and action can become linked and entangled, and that new modes of action and control at a distance have become possible, contributing to the complex and hybrid mixes of authority examined by Porter in Chapter 2. These technologies and networks also make possible the reframing of politically and ethically sensitive issues. From being essentially localized, such issues are stretched out across conventional boundaries, raising new questions about the potentialities of 'global civil society' and 'cosmopolitanism' while accommodating the 'moral' voices and actions of private authority, such as political and business personalities, celebrity activists, and NGOs. Moreover, they are shaped, appropriated, and contested in thematically and functionally highly diversified and geographically variable communicative spaces that operate on different yet increasingly converging media platforms (Barnett 2003; 2004: 195; Hansen and Hoff 2006). So, if processes of mediation address the role of media technologies in shaping arrangements of authority, then there is an important complementary, discursive aspect that should be taken into account: the capacity of the media to facilitate contemporary articulations of the 'public' and the 'private', the 'local and the 'global', including the shaping of public dispositions towards issues of public concern, towards various types of authority and subsequent political action (Chouliaraki Chapter 10).

In Part III of this book, *The Mediation of Authority*, we take a specific look at the role of mediation in the making of authority. In Chapter 9, Birgit Stöber explores an issue which can be seen as an example of this kind of articulation and the role of mediation herein: place branding. The practice of branding has it roots in business, particularly marketing and public relations. But in recent years it has begun to pervade other domains, including the activities of governments on different scales. Stöber examines some of the ideas, processes, and mechanisms that have made the branding of places an increasingly important feature of urban politics, using the city of Berlin as a case example. More than being a simple and rational adaptation to the demands of globalization, place branding rests on particular beliefs and governance techniques, which differ from previous modes of place marketing and promotion. Such beliefs and techniques do not only involve the entanglement of public and private authority, but they also assign a pivotal role to media and discursive processes.

Lilie Chouliaraki, in Chapter 10, focuses on how mediation links global and local politics to private authority. She argues that the cosmopolitan attitude of a 'global civil society' depends on more than the technological capacities and institutional powers of media, namely the discursive politics of mediation. These refer to the processes by which media technologies draw on language and image and, thereby, shape public dispositions. Using a number of news broadcasts in western European media on distant suffering, she shows that such dispositions encompass a number of ethical proposals for audiences. Crucially, the way in which the news broadcast accommodates the voices and actions of private authority, such as human rights NGOs, political personalities or celebrity activists to motivate local interest for a distant cause among diverse media publics, influences the disposition of responsibility and care vis-à-vis the sufferer. The presence of private authority in media discourse can thus introduce social solidarity in the everyday life of the spectator, potentially making a difference in the sufferer's conditions of existence.

References

Abrahms, P. (2006 [1988]) 'Notes on the Difficulty of Studying the State', in A. Sharma and A. Gupta (eds) *The Anthropology of the State. A Reader*. Malden: Blackwell Publishing, 112–130.

Aykens, P. (2002) 'Conflicting authorities: states, currency markets and the ERM crisis of 1992–93', *Review of International Studies*, 28: 359–380.

Barnett, C. (2003) *Culture and Democracy*. Tuscaloosa: The University of Alabama Press.

Barnett, C. (2004) 'Media, Democracy and Representation: Disembodying the Public', in C. Barnett and M. Low (eds) (2004) *Spaces of Democracy. Geographical Perspectives on Citizenship, Participation, and Representation*. London: Sage Publications, 185–207.

Barnett, C. and M. Low (2004) *Spaces of Democracy. Geographical Perspectives on Citizenship, Participation and Representation*. London: Sage Publications.

Barry, A. (2001) *Political Machines: Governing a Technological Society*. London: The Athlone Press.

Beetham, D. (1991) *The Legitimation of Power*. Basingstoke: MacMillan.

Benner, T., W. Reinicke, and J.M. Witte (2002) 'Shaping Globalization: The Role of Global Public Policy Networks', in Bertelsmann Foundation (ed) *Transparency: A Basis for Responsibility and Cooperation*. Gütersloh: Bertelsmann Foundation: 21–47.

Black, J. (2002) 'Regulatory Conversations', *Journal of Law and Society*, 29(1):163–196.

Bourdieu, P. (1994) 'Rethinking the state: genesis and structure of the bureaucratic field', *Sociological Theory*, 12(1):1–18.

Bourdieu, P. and L.J.D. Warquant (1992) *An Invitation to Reflexive Sociology*. Polity Press: Cambridge.

Braithwaite, J. and P. Drahos (2000) *Global Business Regulation*. Cambridge: Cambridge University Press.

Brunsson, N. (2000) 'Standardization and Fashion Trends', in Brunsson, N. and B. Jacobsson (eds) *A World of Standards*. Oxford: Oxford University Press, 151–173.

Castells, M. (2000) 'Materials for an explanatory theory of the network society', *British Journal of Sociology*. Special millennium issue 1: 5–24.

Chouliaraki, L. (2006) *The Spectatorship of Suffering*. London: Sage Publications.

Clarke, J. (2004a) 'Dissolving the Public Realm? The Logics and Limits of Neoliberalism', *Journal of Social Policy*, 33(1):27–48.

Clarke, J. (2004b) *Changing Welfare, Changing States. New Directions in Social Policy*. London: Sage Publications.

Collier, S.J. and A. Ong (2005) 'Global Assemblages, Anthropological Problems', in A. Ong and S. Collier (eds) *Global Assemblages. Technology, Politics, and Ethics as Anthropological Problems*. Malden: Blackwell Publishing, 3–23.

Connolly, W. E. (1987) 'Modern Authority and Ambiguity', in J.R. Pennock and J.W. Chapman (eds) *Authority Revisited: Nomos XXIX*, New York: New York University, 9–27.

Conway, M. and P. Romijn (2004) 'Introduction', *Contemporary European History*, 13(4): 377–88.

Cutler, A.C. (2002) 'Private international regimes and interfirm cooperation', in R.B. Hall and T. Biersteker (eds) *The Emergence of Private Authority in Global Governance*. Cambridge: Cambridge University Press, 23–40.

Cutler, A.C. (2003) *Private Power and Global Authority: Transnational Merchant Law in the Global Political Economy*. Cambridge: Cambridge University Press.

Cutler, A. C. (2006) 'Transnational Business Civilization', in C. May (ed) *Global Corporate Power*. Boulder: Lynne Rienner Publishers, 199–225.

Cutler, A.C., V. Haufler and T. Porter (eds) (1999) *Private Authority and International Affairs*. Albany: State University of New York Press.

Dean, M. (1999) *Governmentality: Power and Rule in Modern Society*. London: Sage Publications.

Deibert, R.J. (1997) *Parchment, Printing and Hypermedia*. New York: Columbia University Press.

Deibert, R.J. (2003) 'Black Code: Censorship, Surveillance, and the Militarization of Cyberspace', *Millennium. Journal of International Studies*, 32(3):501–30.

Dicken, P., P.F Kelly, K. Olds and H.W-C. Yeung (2001) 'Chains and Networks, Territories and Scales: Towards a Relational Framework for analysing the Global Economy', *Global Networks. A Journal of Transnational Affairs*, 1(2):89–112.

Du Gay, P. (1997) *Production of Culture/Cultures of Production*. London: Sage Publications.

Flathman, R.E. (1980) *The Practice of Authority: Authority and the Authoritative*. Chicago: Chicago University Press.

Foucault, M. (1991) 'Governmentality', in G. Burchell, C. Gordon and P. Miller (eds) *The Foucault Effect: Studies in Governmentality*. London: Harvester Wheatsheaf, 87–104.

Fuchs, D. (2005) *Understanding Business in Global Governance*. Baden-Baden: Nomos Verlagsgesellschaft.

Garland, D. (1997) 'Governmentality and the problem of crime', *Theoretical Criminology*, 1(2):173–214.

Garriga, E. and D. Melé (2004) 'Corporate Social Responsibility Theories: Mapping the Territory', *Journal of Business Ethics* 53: 51–71.

Hall, R.B. and T. Biersteker (eds) (2002) *The Emergence of Private Authority in Global Governance*. Cambridge: Cambridge University Press.

Hansen, H.K. and Hoff, J. (eds) (2006) *Digital Governace;//Networked Societies. Creating Authority, Community and Identity in a Globalized World*. Frederiksberg: Nordicom/Samfundslitteratur Press.

Hansen, H.K. and D. Salskov-Iversen (2005) 'Remodelling the Transnational Political Realm: Partnerships, Benchmarking Schemes, and the Digitalization of Governance', *Alternatives. Global, Local, Political*, 30(2): 141–164.

Hansen, H. K., D. Salskov-Iversen and S. Bislev (2002) 'Discursive globalization: transnational discourse communities and New Public Management', in M. Ougaard and R. Higgott (eds) (2002) *Towards a Global Polity*. London: Routledge, 107–124.

Hansen, T.B. and F. Stepputat (eds) (2001) *States of Imagination. Ethnographic Explorations of the Postcolonial State*. Durham: Duke University Press.

Hartley, J. (2005) 'Innovation in Governance and Public Services: Past and Present', *Public Money & Management*, 25(1): 27–34.

Haufler, V. (2006): 'Global Governance in the Private Sector', in C. May (ed) *Global Corporate Power*. Boulder: Lynne Rienner Publishers, 181–197.

Haufler, V. (2001) *A Public Role for the Private Sector: Industry Self-Regulation in a Global Economy*. Washington D.C: The Brookings Institution.

Haufler, V. (1999) 'Self-Regulation and Business Norms: Political Risk, Political Activism', in C. Cutler, V. Hauffler and T. Porter (eds) *Private Authority and International Affairs*. Albany: State University of New York Press, 199–222

Held, D. and A. McGrew (eds) (2002) *Governing Globalization. Power, Authority and Global Governance*. Cambridge: Polity Press.

Higgott, R., G. Underhill and A. Bieler (eds) (2000) *Non-State Actors and Authority, in the Global System*. London: Routledge.

Hindness, B. (1996) *Discourses of Power. From Hobbes to Foucault*. Oxford: Blackwell Publishers.

Hutchby, I. (2001) 'Technologies, Texts, and Affordances', *Sociology*, 35(2): 441–456.

Josselin, D. and W. Wallace (eds) (2001) *Non-State Actors in World Politics*. Basingstoke: Palgrave Macmillan.

Koenig-Archibugi, M. and M. Zürn (eds) (2006) *New Modes of Governance in the Global System. Exploring Publicness, Delegation and Inclusiveness*. Basingstoke: Palgrave Macmillan.

Larner, W. and W. Walters (eds) (2004) *Global Governmentality. Governing International Spaces*. London: Routledge.

Latour, B. (1991) 'Technology is Society Made Durable', in J. Law (ed) *A Sociology of Monsters: Essays on Power, Technology, and Domination*. London: Routledge, 103–131.

Law, J. and J. Hassard (eds) (1999) *Actor Network Theory and After*. Oxford: Blackwell Publishers.

Latham, R. and S. Sassen (eds) (2005) *Digital Formations. IT and New Architectures in the Global Realm*. Princeton: Princeton University Press.

Law, J. and K. Hetherington (2000) 'Materialities, spatialities, globalities', in J.R. Bryson, P.W. Daniels, N. Henry and J. Pollard (eds) *Knowledge, Space, Economy*. London: Routledge.

Leander, A. (2007) 'The Impunity of Private Authority: Understanding PSC Accountability', paper presented at the International Studies Association Annual Conference, Chicago, 28 February–3 March 2007.

Lukes, S. (2005) *Power. A Radical View*, 2nd edition. Basingstoke: Palgrave Macmillan.

Mattli, W. and T. Büthe (2005) 'Accountability in Accounting? The Politics of Private Ruling in the Public Interest', *Governance: An International Journal of Policy, Administration, and Institutions*, 18(3):399–429.

Mulligan, S. (2004) 'Questioning (the Question of) Legitimacy in IR: A reply to Jens Steffek', *European Journal of International Relations*, 10(3): 475–484.

Newman, J. (2005) *Remaking Governance. Peoples, politics, and the public sphere*. Bristol: Policy Press.

Nye, J. (2004) *Soft Power: The Means to Success in World Politics*, Public Affairs.

Perri 6 (2002) 'Global digital Communications and the Prospects for Transnational Regulation', in D. Held and A. McGrew (eds) *Governing Globalization – Power, Governance and Global Governance*. Cambridge: Polity Press.

O' Kane, R.H.T. (1993) 'Against Legitimacy', *Political Studies*, XLI: 471–487.

Ottaway, M. (2001) 'Corporatism Goes Global: International Organizations, NGO Networks and Transnational Business', *Global Governance* 7(3) (July–September 2001): 265–292.

Phillips, N. (2003) 'Discourse or Institution? Institutional Theory and the Challenge of Critical Discourse Analysis', in R. Westwood and S. Clegg (eds) *Debating organization: point-counterpoint in organization studies*. London: Blackwell Publishing, 220–231.

Pollitt, C. (2003) *The Essential Public Manager*. Maidenhead: Open University Press.

Porter, T. (2005) 'Private Authority, Technical Authority, and the Globalization of Accounting Standards', *Business and Politics*, 7(3):1–30, Article 2, available at http://econpapers.repec.org/article/bepbuspol/

Raz, J. (1987) 'Government by Consent', in J.R. Pennock and J.W. Chapman (eds), *Authority Revisited:Nomos XXIX*. New York: New York University

Reed, M. (1998) 'Organizational Analysis as Discourse Analysis: A Critique', in D. Grant, T. Keenoy and C. Oswick, *Discourse + Organization*. London: Sage Publications, 193–213.

Risse, T. (2004) 'Global Governance and Communicative Action', *Government and Opposition*, 39 (2): 288–313.

Ronit, K. and V. Schneider (eds) (2000) *Private Organizations in Global Politics*. London & New York: Routledge.

Rose, N. (1999) *Powers of Freedom: Reframing political Thought*. Cambridge: Cambridge University Press.

Rose, N. and P. Miller (1992) 'Political power beyond the state: problematics of government', *British Journal of Sociology*, 43(2):173–205.

Rosenau, J. N. (2002) 'Governance in a New Global Order' in Held, D. and A. McGrew (eds) (2002) *Governing Globalization. Power, Authority, and Global Governance*. Cambridge: Polity Press, 70–86.

Rosenau, J.P. and J.P. Singh (eds) (2002) *Information Technologies and Global Politics*. New York: State University of New York Press.

Salskov-Iversen, D., H.K. Hansen and S. Bislev (2000) 'Governmentality, Globalization, and Local Practice: Transformations of a Hegemonic Discourse', *Alternatives* 25: 183–222.

Scholte, J.A. (2005) *Globalization. A Critical Introduction*. Basingstoke: Palgrave Macmillan.

Shapiro, M.J. and H.R. Alker (eds) (1996) *Challenging Boundaries. Global Flows, Territorial Identities*. Minneapolis: University of Minnesota Press.

Sharma, A. and A. Gupta (eds) (2006) *The Anthropology of the State. A Reader*, Malden: Blackwell Publishing.

Sheller, M. and J. Urry (2003) 'Mobile Transformations of "Public" and "Private" Life', *Theory, Culture & Society*, 20(3): 107–125.

Singh, J.P. (2002) 'Introduction: Information Technologies and the Changing Scope of Global Power and Governance', in J.N. Rosenau and J.P. Singh (eds) *Information Technologies and Global Politics*. New York: State University of New York Press.

Siochrú, S.Ó. and Girard, B. (2002) *Global Media Governance*. Lanham: Rowland and Littlefield Publishers.

Slaughter, A-M. (2004a) *A New World Order*. Princeton: Princeton University Press.

Slaughter, A-M. (2004b) 'Disaggregated Sovereignty: Towards the Public Accountability of Global Government Networks', *Government and Opposition*, 39(2): 125–55.

Spar, D. L. (1999) 'Lost in (Cyber)space: The Private Rules of Online Commerce', in A.C. Cutler, V. Haufler and T. Porter, *Private Authority and International Affairs*. New York: SUNY Press.

Walker, R.B.J. (1993) *Inside/Outside: International Relations as Political Theory*. Cambridge: Cambridge University Press.

Weintraub, J. and K. Kumar (1997) *Public and Private in Thought and Practice*. Chicago: University of Chicago Press.

Part I

The Disaggregation of Authority

2
Disaggregating Authority in Global Governance

Tony Porter

This chapter has three main goals. The first is to examine this book's claim that there is a disaggregation of the state such that private authority and mediated discourses become more important in governance, including at the global level. The second goal is to explore and explain variation in the character of this disaggregation. Are some governmental activities more private and mediated than others, and if so why? The third and related goal is to examine the implications of this disaggregation for legitimacy, democracy, and resistance to the negative effects of power, consistent with the *critical* emphasis of this book.

The chapter starts with a conceptual discussion of the above issues. It then explores these issues with reference to three cases. The first case, which is most closely related to the traditional functions of the state, is the privatization of airline and border security. Of the three cases this one, since it is the least likely to exhibit disaggregated authority, will be examined in most detail. The second case, in which private authority can be expected to be most prominent, is the regulation of global finance. The third, in which mediation can be expected to display an especially significant role, is the unauthorized downloading of songs. It will not be possible, in the context of a single chapter, to examine these second and third cases more than briefly in order to draw out some comparisons. The degree to which authority in general, and public authority in particular, is being disaggregated will be explored in each case. Disaggregation in such different issue areas will testify to its general relevance, and variation in the character and pace of this disaggregation should provide clues to its mechanisms.

We may expect that the three cases also vary in the degree to which they involve public challenges to authority and in the way that authority seeks to legitimize itself in response. Airline and border security are likely to remain the most closed, hierarchical, and secretive – or in other words, as noted above, the least disaggregated – and the most reliant on traditional state-centric forms of legitimization. Finance can be expected to be more disaggregated and to rely much more on non-traditional forms of legitimization that are more private-sector and less state centric. The downloading of songs is likely to be the most disaggregated of the three and to display the strongest resistance to authority – and the legitimization of authority can be expected to involve mechanisms that are more popular and mediated than in the other two cases. Overall, the chapter hopes to convince the reader of the value of considering disaggregation in analysing the role of states and other actors with regard to governance and authority.

Disaggregated authority: Conceptual issues

The disaggregation of authority refers to a process in which authority is distributed, delegated or decentralized such that the instances of authority that operate at a distance from the original source rely upon, reinforce, or supplant the original source. This may have the effect of strengthening or weakening the authority of the state. Disaggregation differs from disintegration or fragmentation, since the decentralized instances of authority, in these other cases, only relate to one another as independent actors. These independent actors may affect one another, but their authority is not inherently interdependent. Relatedly, it differs from approaches that see the power of the state as weakening due to the independent emergence or growth of new competing sources of authority. The concept of *disaggregation* highlights the degree to which different types of authority can reinforce one another. Alternatively, the growth of competing types of disaggregated authority to that of the state can be associated with a decline in state authority while maintaining close links to or dependence on state authority.

In this chapter *authority* is used to refer to the degree to which rules are followed because they, or their source, are seen as right. This reason for compliance can be distinguished from coercion, on the one hand, or from bargains based solely on interests, on the other. The use of the concept of authority suggests that rules themselves have some autonomous significance, and are not just indicators of underlying configurations of power and interests. This concept is closely related to legitimacy, which refers to the *acceptance* of authority as right, and thus it is important for the discussion of legitimacy below. However, distinguishing carefully between authority and other sources of compliance goes beyond the scope of this chapter and is not its purpose. Moreover often elements of coercion, bargaining, and authority are intermingled. Thus in this chapter, authority and rules will be used interchangeably and rules will be assumed to have some autonomy. While it is not possible to decisively prove such autonomy to sceptics, it is hoped that the discussion that follows will support the plausibility of this assumption.[1]

In this section the significance of disaggregation will be discussed theoretically in three steps. The first step involves a *where* question: to *where* is public authority being disaggregated? One possible answer is that the change is primarily occurring within forms of public authority, such as when the emphasis of the European Union's member states on subsidiarity leads them to delegate some authority downward to local governments and some upward to the EU. However, it is also possible that other forms of authority than public authority are becoming more important. The second question is a *how* question: what are the processes through which authority is disaggregated from centralized states outward? Does it involve a type of deliberate delegation, as the subsidiarity example might suggest, or does it involve more profound alterations in social structures? The third step involves specifying some specific propositions about why disaggregation may vary by issue area.

To where might authority be disaggregated?

Three types of authority can be identified in addition to public authority, which is often seen as the only type. These others include private authority, created by business; technical authority, created by experts; and popular authority, created by social movements or other political activism. Each form of authority inspires compliance differently. Public authority draws upon traditional respect for the law, and increasingly upon the legitimacy conferred by democratic practices. Private authority draws upon a widespread belief in the inherent superiority of the market and other private-sector ways of doing things. Technical authority draws on respect for the scientific method. Popular authority evokes the inherent righteousness of a populace mobilized to create its own future. In each case the authoritative effect is strengthened by a coercive element. For public authority this is the armed force that the state can wield; for private authority it is market forces; for technical authority it is forces of nature that experts claim to reveal; for popular authority it is the threat of widespread civil disorder, or revolution.

Having provided an answer to the *where* question, it is now time to turn to the *how* question: how are these alternative forms of authority linked to public authority and one another.

How is authority being disaggregated?

A first step in answering this how question is to look at some general explanations for disaggregation that could be drawn from existing literatures. These include technological change, which enhances the authority of experts who can claim to be the masters of it, but also of market actors (for instance, who can use electronic networks to evade and undermine the control of public authorities), and of popular authority (for instance when new technologies such as the internet or mobile phones are used to mobilize the populace). A long historical trend of popular empowerment, accompanied by a growth in popular knowledge and competence, can also be seen as a source not just of popular authority, but of private and technical authority as well, to the extent that these two are driven by a popular demand for alternative forms of social organization, daily practices, and legitimizing reasons to those traditionally provided by public authorities. Some theorists have traced the changes in authority to generalized properties of late or post-modernity, including the destabilization of hierarchies, identities, and all forms of political, linguistic, and visual representation. The work of Luhmann suggests that the changes may be traced to an ongoing process of functional differentiation (Porter 2005b).

All of these explanations suggest that the process of delegation involves more of a social transformation than the EU model of delega-tion.[2] In part this may involve an independent growth of alternative forms of authority to the state's public authority. When we examine par-ticular cases below it will be apparent how rare independent instances of competing forms of authority are. However, the processes mentioned in the previous paragraph already suggest that these types of authority are more likely to be entangled with one another. Moreover, they suggest that new linkages and mechanisms involving knowledge are important in these processes of disaggregation and entanglement among types of authority, an idea that is consistent with the emphasis of this book on mediation. Two bodies of theory provide useful insights into the way these processes may work: the literature on *governmentality* and *actor-network* theory. I look briefly at each in turn.

The concept of governmentality, initially developed by Foucault, refers to the tendency of state power to be transformed over time from detailed and direct control of the behaviour of citizens (a type of control which Foucault called *police*) to 'control at a distance' involving the establishment of self-regulatory mechanisms that lead citizens to regu-late their own conduct in a way that aligns their behaviour with more general relations and systems of power, of which the state is a part. This is closely linked to Foucault's concept of power/knowledge, in which systems of knowledge and regimes of truth produce relations of power and the subjects involved in these relations. Power is therefore not only prohibitive, but productive as well (Foucault et al. 1991).

Actor-network theory (ANT) sees society as composed of networks of human and non-human 'actants' (Saldanha 2003). Actants include human and social actors, but also non-human objects or life-forms, such as machines or viruses, which have a capacity to affect behaviour in the network in a way that is similar in effect to human and social actors. Networks, then, are characterized by hybridity, in which human and non-human elements are mixed and inseparable. ANT eschews the agent/structure dualism for a focus on practices, especially socio-technical ones. Political change, including democratic initiatives, is interpreted as struggles within networks, and the 'enrolling' of human technological artifacts and other objects into programmes of action – processes in which the mobilization of 'objects of politics' become important (Marres 2004: 133). The exercise of power can be large-scale or small and mundane, as in an example provided by (Latour 1991) of a European hotel owner who modifies the behaviour of guests by weighting keys so that they don't walk off with them.

Both governmentality and ANT draw our attention to the way in which knowledge, in the form of relatively immaterial discourses or as embodied materially in technological systems and artifacts, has the capacity to shape conduct and draw one actant into a relationship with others. As such these approaches provide a very useful way to understand processes of disaggregation of public authority. Both concepts are the focus of large literatures and scholarly debates which are too extensive to consider in this chapter. For instance, while both have been criticized for overstating the power of systematized knowledge at the expense of individual agency, the approaches are sufficiently varied to include work that does not display this problem, and there is no reason that their general insights into the role of knowledge cannot be drawn upon for understanding the disaggregation of the state.

Some propositions about variations in disaggregation by issue area

Having now suggested that the disaggregation of the state involves a shift away from centralized public authority and direct top-down commands towards the creation of more decentralized networks of power in which the state plays a key but not all-powerful role, we can now turn to the question of how this disaggregation might vary by issue area. Three possibilities can be identified and formulated as propositions.

One possibility, which was suggested at the outset of the chapter in discussing the three cases that will be explored below, is that some issue areas, like airline and border security, may be closer to traditional public authority than others, and thus are likely to be less disaggregated. This is a common idea in realist international relations theory, where it is often assumed that states will tightly control security matters that they have always seen as central to their survival, while they are prepared to let other actors, such as international institutions, take care of more mundane, technical tasks, like postal rules. We can formulate this as a proposition: *disaggregration of public authority will be more pronounced the more it involves functions that are distant from the state's traditional preoccupation with security and violence.*

A second possibility is that the pace of disaggregation is affected by the presence and absence of the material prerequisites for the type of actor-network identified by ANT. Although ANT stresses the degree to which objects are changeable and constituted by the networks in which they exist, its materialist emphasis suggests that these objects cannot simply be dreamed up, and there may be occasions where they are not feasible. Existing technologies can be easily used to facilitate the delegation of some government functions and not others. For instance standard blank tax forms can easily be placed on a remote third-party website for citizens to download. In contrast, inspection of a crime scene and the interviewing of witnesses may require the use of all the human senses, and is likely to require the direct personal involvement of a representative of the state since current technologies do not allow such complex inspections to be carried out using the internet or other such forms of electronic mediation.

What makes some activities better suited to being disaggregated through mediated networks than others? Sensory complexity, as with the crime scene example, is likely to be one factor. Even large bandwidths, while allowing the capture of visual complexity through video, cannot yet capture touch or smell effectively. Externalities, which can be defined as the effects of activities that cannot be easily delimited by those engaged in them, are likely to be another factor, since such activities are not well suited for the property rights that are a precondition of any network involving market exchanges. For instance, it is relatively easy to price and sell a book on-line since it is clear what is being bought and sold. In contrast, a less well-defined exchange of knowledge, such as an agreement between two firms to jointly develop a new technology, can have unforeseen costs and benefits that cannot be captured in a price that is agreed in advance of the exchange. This more complex type of exchange requires a trusting working relationship and more complex long-range commitments for which the Internet alone is not well suited. We can formulate this as a proposition: *disaggregation of public authority will be more pronounced when it involves activities that lend themselves to mediation through networks, such as activities that have low sensory complexity and low externalities.*

A third possibility is that disaggregation is affected by the demand of non-state actors that the state share its power over the issues that concern them. This points to political struggles which may be highly contingent and thus not easily summed up as a proposition with relevance across issue areas. Nevertheless, social movement theory suggests that the propensity of an issue to lend itself to 'strategic framing' (Zald 1996) and the organizational capacity of civil society actors, along with the presence or absence of sympathetic or divided elites, can help explain why social movements might successfully push for authority to be disaggregated in some cases and not others. Strategic framing refers to the ability of social movements to provide interpretations of problems that resonate with existing widely held feelings, such as anger at violations of bodily integrity or denial of equality of opportunity (Keck and Sikkink 1998: 27). Television's affinity for dramatic visual events with emotional appeal is an important consideration in strategic framing (see also Chouliaraki this volume). The notion of regulatory 'capture', where a powerful industry gains control of a regulatory process, may also help in understanding the role of the private sector in demanding disaggregation. One therefore can formulate the following proposition: *disaggregation of public authority will be more advanced in issue areas in which the factors that explain successful cases of citizen activism, such as easy strategic framing, citizens' organizational capacity, and elite support, are present, or in especially concentrated industries.*

I now turn to an examination of the three cases in order to assess the merits of the above propositions, as well as of the concept of disaggregated authority more generally. As noted above, the primary focus will be on airport and border security, with the other cases only briefly presented for purposes of comparison. In each case I will start by assessing the degree of disaggregation that is evident, addressing both the *where* and *how* questions discussed above: does the dissaggregation involve an increased importance of private, technical or popular authority, and does it involve delegation or a more profound mediated dissemination? In the conclusion to the chapter, I will consider what each case has to say about the above three propositions.

Border and airline security

Traditionally border security has involved direct state control of the well-defined perimeter of its territory. Considering the centrality of control of territory to the security, identity, and authority of the state it is not surprising that states took particular care to police border entry and exit points.

The events of September 11, 2001 highlighted the degree to which this traditional picture was changing. The destruction was framed by the hijackers and the US government as a foreign attack on the authority of the US state, and yet the attack had originated from inside the US, carried out by people who had previously appeared to be going about their daily activities in a way that did not especially set them apart from others living in the country. The weapons used in the attack – box cutters and the airplanes themselves – were also ones that would not have been thought of at all as the types of traditional weapons that could be used to threaten a state's security and authority. While military technology such as nuclear-armed intercontinental ballistic missiles and radar-evading stealth fighters have also dramatically challenged traditional border defenses, 9/11 pointed to the challenge posed not just by high-tech hardware, but by individual people and the ideas that inspired them.[3]

An initial response of the US government to 9/11 was to centralize authority in its own hands. A key problem that was seen as having contributed to 9/11 was the degree to which airline security had been delegated to private firms who had failed to maintain adequate standards. Screeners were failing to catch more than 20 per cent of dangerous objects in tests (US Government Accountability Office 2005). Pay was low, training was poor, and turnover was high. In response to these problems the US government created a new federal agency, the Transport Safety Administration, which was given direct responsibility for airport security. For critics, the funding and operational model was far too centralized, and poorly suited to the great diversity across airports in their physical layouts, and the risks they needed to manage, such as seasonal differences in traffic volumes between northern and southern airports (Poole 2005b: 3; *Airport Security Report* 2005).[4] A small exception to complete federal control was five airports that were selected as experiments in allowing greater private-sector involvement, but each of these airports was assigned a particular contractor, allowing them no autonomy in this choice.

Despite this centralization there are two main other ways in which this case displays evidence of disaggregation. The first is the degree to which the US response is an aberration, since most governments have headed in the opposite direction and have delegated much more authority to private firms, a trend that is also evident in other changes that are more directly related to border control. The second is the degree to which state responses to this type of problem emphasize technologies, such as biometrics, that heavily involve private firms and technical experts in surveillance and control of the flow of bodies. I will briefly consider each of these in turn.

Contrary to the US initiative to federalize airport security, the overwhelming trend that began in the 1980s in other jurisdictions was to move towards contracting the implementation of passenger and baggage screening to private firms, with governments setting and enforcing performance standards for those firms. As of late 2001, 33 large European airports followed this model, and the two that didn't, Zurich and Lisbon, were moving in this direction (Poole 2005b: 6). Canada is following a similar pattern (*Airport Security Report* 2004). El Al has also operated this way for years. A high profile example of such delegation in a high-security case controlled by the US government was Baghdad airport, which was closed for 48 hours in June 2005, and a day in September 2005, as a result of a dispute between a British private security firm and the Iraqi government.[5] Critics of the US Transportation Security Administration (TSA) have urged it to move towards delegating more authority to the private sector, including the privately run airports and security services. Privately owned airlines continue to play an important role in security, both individually, through their checking of passenger ID, and collectively, through their self-regulatory International Air Transport Association standards (Kunreuther et al. 2002). By 2005 the US TSA was moving to privatize its Registered Traveler programme, which would give preferential processing to travellers with a special card (*Wall Street Journal* 2005).

With respect to border control more narrowly defined, there are many other examples of delegation as well. Some is delegation within the public sector. For instance the US has been eager to push the control of those seeking entry from its land borders out to its embassies, consulates, and ports abroad, in part because intercepting a terrorist with an active nuclear bomb in a border station on US territory may be too late to prevent the intended destructive act (Koslowski 2005: 1). This shift has been linked to the idea of the 'virtual border' by the CEO of the Bermuda-based technology consulting company Accenture, which, in coordination with a private-sector consortium called the Smart Border Alliance has a US government contract, valued at US$ 10 billion, in the context of the system called US Visitor and Immigrant Status Indicator Technology (US VISIT) to keep track of US border crossings electronically through the use of digital photos and fingerprints (*Business Week* 2004; Accenture 2005). Canada has been pursuing similar policies to reduce the ability of foreigners to make the type of refugee status claims that require them to be on Canadian territory.

In the case of trade, there is also a trend towards authorizing some firms to take responsibility at their own site for the security of the packages or vehicles they send across borders in exchange for expedited treatment at the actual border, as is the case, for instance, with the Fast and Secure Trade (FAST) program used at the US–Canada border, one of the most active borders in the world.[6] The Customs-Trade Partnership Against Terrorism offers expedited processing to firms engaged in trade if they meet certain security standards (Bodenheimer 2003), and the US Container Security Initiative puts US customs inspectors in foreign ports and requires those ports to have X-ray and radiation scanners (*Financial Times* 2004) (the programme is reciprocal). Similar arrangements involving the US, the Organization of American States, and other countries together with the private sector were initiated in the 1990s to counter drug smuggling (Flynn 2000).[7]

While the above trends relate to a more traditional form of delegated authority, there are many examples of new forms of high-tech surveillance and control that display a more complex form of disaggregation, especially the use of biometrics. Biometrics refers to the use of physical characteristics of the human body to identify individuals. The most developed use of biometrics is fingerprinting, Police forces have been using huge fingerprint databases for years. Faces, irises, and hand shapes have all also been converted into sets of unique mathematical measurements that can be stored on searchable databases. Video cameras have been used by police in an attempt to identify faces in passing crowds, although their current technical ability to do so effectively is disputed.[8]

The use of biometrics at border crossings and in airport security is increasing rapidly. The iris scanning programme at Amsterdam's Schiphol Airport, which allows participants to bypass long lines for conventional screening, has attracted positive press coverage and is spreading to other airports (Perri 2003).[9] The US VISIT programme mentioned above is based on the collection of biometric data and the US has demanded that countries whose citizens do not need visas must include biometric data consistent with International Civil Aviation Organization (ICAO) standards on passports by a particular date.[10] The European Union's Schengen Information System II, scheduled to become operational by 2007, will also include biometric data. In the future new technologies for control at a distance may be deployed, including the use of biometrics to verify that an authorized pilot is in control of the plane, and a system for ground control to take over the piloting functions if this is not verified (Dell and Bunney 2001).

Reliance on biometrics greatly increases government reliance on the private firms that produce this technology (OECD 2004). The International Biometric Group estimates that worldwide biometric sales will grow from US$ 600 million in 2002 to over US$ 4 billion in 2007 (Perri 2003). Automatic Fingerprint Identification Systems, a more bounded technology, are primarily provided by NEC (Japan), Printrack, owned by Motorola (US), SAGEM (France), and Cogent (US). More complex biometric systems, such as those used for ID cards, passports, and visas, are usually developed by consortia led by integrators (such as TRW, Unisys, Siemens, SAGEM, and IBM) and involving other large firms such as NEC and Polaroid. This is a worldwide market worth $50–100 million per year, roughly half the size of the fingerprint systems market, including for instance, ID cards in North America, Europe, Asia, and Africa.[11] Biometrics for industrial and commercial use includes other firms, such as Iridian for iris scanning and Cognitec for face recognition. SAGEM is a market leader in all types of biometric systems. The entanglement of public and private in these technologies is highlighted by the Schiphol program, which is 98 per cent owned by the Dutch government and the City of Amsterdam, relies on private-sector technology, and seeks to make money by franchising its programme to other airports (Perri 2003). The integration of public authority and private authority is evident not just in the involvement of firms in surveillance technologies, but in the government's concern with 'interoperability' that might otherwise be hindered by proprietary technologies (Bechtel and Svacek 2003: 132; Bodenheimer 2003).

Reliance on biometrics also greatly increases the role of technical authority. Where previously identification relied on the individual judgment of the border guard, biometrics transfers this assessment to highly technical computer programmes and mathematical algorithms.[12] Governments can exercise a great deal of control over this technology through performance specifications in contracts, but technical authority also retains some autonomy, for instance, in making the judgment about error rates, which have a major impact on policy judgments about the effectiveness of the systems and their impact on the people to whom they are applied.[13] Technical considerations limit the distance over which control can be exercised. For instance 'at 2.5 Gb/s (OC-48 rates) off-the-shelf-lasers [for transmitting video images through fibre optic networks] are available for up to 170 km dispersion limited spacing with direct modulation, and 600 km dispersion limited spacing with electro-absorption modulation' (Bechtel and Svacek 2003: 135).

Popular authority has played a larger role in this case than one would expect given the case's centrality to functions that the state has traditionally guarded in a most tightly controlled and secretive manner. US plans through its relatively secretive CAPPS and CAPPS II programme to make a colour-coded green, red, or yellow risk assessment of airline passengers based on a comparison of personal data with a vast database search (including for instance car ownership and magazine subscriptions) have run into resistance after protests about its implications for personal freedom and privacy (Rhodes 2004). Biometric technologies have stimulated a vigorous political and legal debate that draw on competing discourses of popular authority. These debates enable and constrain the use of biometrics in crucial ways. The supporters of biometrics formulate claims about the desire of citizens to enhance their personal security through an expanded use of these technologies. For instance, citizen opposition to face recognition surveillance on the streets of London turned to acceptance when officials claimed it had produced a 34 per cent drop in crime (McCormack 2003: 132). Sceptics draw on claims about the importance for freedom and individual privacy of limiting government use of these technologies. In California the latter set of arguments has resulted in laws that require face recognition technologies to immediately discard data on individuals that systems do not match to suspected criminals, significantly limiting their scope (McCormack 2003: 144). Technical authority is also in tension with popular authority: 'human beings have an almost blind faith in all things scientific, and biometric data is cloaked in the mantle of scientific truth. Thus, if a computer tells a government agent that a person's retinal scan matches that of a notorious criminal or someone who should be denied access to a building or a plane, or a country, it will be very difficult for the person to argue that the computer is mistaken' (Feldman 2003: 665).

There are a number of ways that arguments involving private authority have interacted with those involving popular authority. The application of biometrics and other security technologies have also been constrained by an economic logic that calculates the impact on business of delays such as those at airports that discourage flying (Kauvar et al. 2002: 2). The US travel trade surplus dropped from US$26 billion in 1996 to US$ 4 billion in 2003 (Travel Business Roundtable 2004). These arguments could be seen as drawing on a form of private authority. The creation of privileged groups of travellers that have the types of jobs, backgrounds, and incomes that allow them to pay for the type of biometric passes issued by Schiphol airport and avoid the inconveniences caused by screening, is also an expression of a market logic consistent with private authority that is in some tension with arguments based on the wellbeing of all citizens that are consistent with popular authority.[14] The interest of the firm most involved in face-recognition technology in self-regulation with regard to privacy issues, in part to forestall public regulation (McCormack 2003: 146), is another example. Arguments for the constitutionality of face recognition technology in the US have revolved around a distinction between public and private in which privacy rights are seen as not applying to someone who chooses to be in a public place, or when technologies are used that are available to the general public. On the other hand, 'biometric technology will be used in private commercial settings, in which individuals as a general matter do not enjoy the same types of process rights as they would in relation to government action, short of specific consumer legislation' (Feldman 2003: 666). Since biometrics are a representation of physical characteristics rather than thoughts, US courts have seen the Fifth Amendment's right against self-incrimination as not applicable (McCormack 2003: 137–41).

Looking at the case as a whole, then, it is clear that there has been a significant degree of disaggregation of authority, despite the counter-trend represented by the federalization of airline security in the US. To some degree this involves a more traditional delegation of authority from central government agencies to far-flung embassies, private firms, and technical experts. However it has also involved a more profound mediated dissemination of authority and mechanisms of control through the types of hybrid human/non-human networks and discursive systems identified by actor-network theory and the literature on governmentality. The firms and experts involved in biometrics are not autonomous, and do not signify a fragmentation of government authority. Rather their authority and that of governments is interdependent and mutually reinforcing. At the same time, it is challenged by new forms of popular authority that play out in and around these hybrid networks and discursive systems, modifying their operations, a form of resistance that can be missed if one only focusses on more traditional forms of democratic engagement centred on, for instance, voting or street protests.

Two other cases: Finance and the downloading of songs

Although it is not possible in the context of a single chapter to thoroughly examine other cases, it is useful to briefly look at two in order to carry out some comparisons that are relevant to assessing the merits of the propositions set out earlier. I look at the cases of finance and songs in turn.

In looking at finance over the last century it is apparent that central-ization reached a zenith in the middle of the twentieth century and has declined ever since.[15] Public sector centralization was evident in the widespread tendencies of states to restrict the flow of finance across borders, and to finance growth through state spending. This was especially evident in socialist systems, but the tendency was strong in market economies as well. Private-sector financial centralization was evident in the tendency of the largest corporations, which were based in the US, to finance most of their activities internally, through their own revenue generation, and to use financial techniques as a way for senior managers to control large centralized divisions within the firm. In other countries large corporations relied more heavily on bank or state finance, but the overall effect was similarly centralizing.

The subsequent disaggregation of finance is evident in the shift away from state control to market arrangements, and in the shift within the private sector from a hierarchical internal structure towards a more network structure of finance. The first of these can be seen in the wave of privatizations, in which state control of existing enterprises was replaced by the issuing of shares traded in stock markets. It is evident as well in the tendency for the state to assign the implementation of new projects, including the raising of finance for them, to market actors or public-private partnerships. These policies were systematically promoted across the world by international organizations such as the OECD or the World Bank. Within the private sector there was a major shift towards greater reliance on competitive capital markets for financing. The shift from a more hierarchical and centralized reliance on internal bank struc-tures for the governing of financial flows to these decentralized markets is a process known in the financial world as *disintermediation*.

Like airport and border security, there are many examples of hybridity in these processes of disaggregation. On the public sector side there has been a sustained effort over the past quarter century to create global level collaborative arrangements among regulators, mostly centred around a set of committees located at the Bank for International Settlements in Basel, Switzerland, such as the Basel Committee on Banking Supervision or the Financial Stability Forum. Initially this could be characterized as a disaggregation of authority from the nation-state to supranational public sector networks and groupings. However the entanglement of public, private, and technical authority is apparent as well. For instance in 1982 the Basel Committee sought to strengthen the control of its member regulators by requiring banks to report to their home regulator on their world-wide operations, called 'consolidated supervision'. This financial reporting was primarily carried out by the large multinational private-sector accounting firms (Arnold and Sikka 2001). Similarly, in a major initiative to improve its bank regulation standards in 2004, the Basel Committee shifted to a much greater reliance on highly technical proprietary risk modelling technologies managed internally by the big private-sector banks they were regulating. In general this public-sector standard setting relies to a great extent on financial markets to punish non-compliance, such as when investors are reluctant to buy shares of a bank$ that fails to meet the standards.

On the private-sector side, experts and electronic networks have played an ever growing role in governance. Associations of licenced professionals, governed by specific codes of conduct and defined practices, such as Certified Financial Planners or Chartered Financial Analysts, have become larger and more globalized. Electronic networks build rules into machine-systems, such as with the Clearing House Interbank Payment System in New York which handles 95 per cent of worldwide dollar transactions between banks, and which has a real-time process in which banks not complying with financial exposure standards are automatically excluded from further transactions.

The downloading of songs, while very different than finance, also displays parallel trends. Before the advent of the Internet the highly concentrated music industry controlled the production and dissemination of recorded music through a combination of their own oligopolistic industry structure[16] and national copyright laws. Tape recordings were a relatively minor challenge since the quality was poor, but with digital recording the threat to the industry of unauthorized copying grew dramatically, through the burning of compact disks and file sharing through the Internet. While there is some evidence that file sharing increases the sales of the music industry, the International Federation of the Phonographic Industry (IFPI) has characterized file sharing as piracy and argued that one in three disks sold worldwide are illegal, that the value of the illegal market is US$ 4.6 billion, and that this activity is a criminal threat to its existence (IFPI 2005).

The industry, organized especially through the IFPI and the Recording Industry Association of America, has pursued a multi-pronged campaign against unauthorized copying (Johnstone 2001), and the evolution of this campaign displays signs of processes of a disaggregation of authority. An initial emphasis was on revising copyright law to cover the unauthorized copying of songs[17] and to extend this to countries seen as havens for piracy through international agreements covering intellectual property more broadly, such as the Trade Related Intellectual Property provisions associated with the World Trade Organization, or the intellectual property provisions of the numerous bilateral investment treaties concluded between the home states of the multinational firms that dominate the music industry and other countries (LoVoi 1999). The industry tried to enlist the full weight of these states, especially the US, for instance, by making access to US capital or markets conditional on a vigorous enforcement of intellectual property rights.

While the industry claimed some temporary victories from this strategy it also failed to halt the explosive growth of unauthorized copying. A key part of the problem for the industry was the disaggregated character of the copying. Napster, a leading file sharing site, was shut down by legal action. But the industry's legal case rested in part on demonstrating that Napster had actively encouraged illegal sharing. Subsequently new peer-to-peer file sharing arrangements, not as dependent on deliberate coordination through a central location, made both the legal arguments and legal enforcement more difficult (David and Kirkhope 2004). The industry also had problems targeting users because the activity they wished to restrict was bound up with legitimate activity that lawmakers refused to restrict, such as the operations of internet services providers, or the multiple users of computer hard drives (Hoffman 2000).

In response to this disaggregated threat, the music industry began to search for disaggregated solutions. It invested heavily in various copying-restricting technologies such as 'watermarks' used to trace pirated music, to more sophisticated systems allowing limited copying.[18] New firms specializing in such technologies sprung up, such as MediaDefender's 'spoofer' programme which aimed to sell software that would flood file sharing networks with phony files containing anti-piracy messages (*Wall Street Journal* 2000). These strategies carried serious risks, such as investing in a technology that would quickly become obsolete, or that hardware producers would refuse to support, or that would be seen as punitive to the customers who had actually paid for the disks. These risks were dramatically highlighted in 2005 when Sony, faced with class action suits and a public relations disaster, had to take measures to compensate customers who purchased CDs with digital rights management technology that had secret features exposing purchasers' computers to hostile hackers.

Conclusion: The extent and variation of disaggregated authority

All three cases provide evidence in support of the contention that the disaggregation of authority is a concept worth considering in analysing governance and authority. In each case there are techniques that seek to exercise control at a distance in the manner highlighted by the governmentality literature, and to do so in a way that involves hybrid mixes of public authority, private authority, technical authority, and non-human objects such as machine systems, as highlighted by actor network theory. In the area of airline and border security this involves a shift towards greater reliance on highly technical biometric systems managed by private firms, and the conferring of particular types of special authority on private actors, such as the elite travelers with special identity cards who are authorized to bypass security checks, or the exporters authorized to vouch for the security of their shipments in exchange for speedy processing of their shipments at the border. In finance this involves a shift towards the use of internal proprietary risk management systems of banks by regulators in regulating banks, and towards reliance on professional practices and electronic networks to enact and reproduce rules. In the music industry this involves a shift away from simply relying on centrally enforced copyright law, to new technologies embedded on CDs that try to enforce rights automatically every time a user puts the CD in a computer in the privacy of his or her home. It would be impossible to understand the changes in governance occurring in these issue areas without taking this disaggregation of authority into account.

How useful are the propositions set out above in understanding variations in the pace and extent of disaggregation across these three issue areas? Although it is not possible to precisely measure disaggregation, there are some differences across the cases that would be good to understand.

The first proposition suggested that disaggregation would be more pronounced in areas more distant from the traditional responsibilities of the state. A comparison of the issue area most central to state security, airport and border security, to the area least central, song downloading, provides some evidence in support of this proposition. It is more likely that a known terrorist will be halted at the US border or at the boarding gate of an airline than that someone illegally copying a song will feel the force of the law. However this proposition, which is consistent with the views of those, such as realist international relations theorists, who see the disaggregation of authority as relatively insignificant, is clearly insufficient on its own. If we expand the range of people in the first case that authorities seek to control to include potential terrorists and their weapons then it is not at all clear that biometric-enhanced border and airline security will be more effective than digital-rights-management-enhanced CDs at accomplishing their intended goals. Indeed digital rights technology, while ostensibly about technical standards, is closer to traditional legal rules than standards in its degree of specificity and enforceability (Benoliel 2004). Thus an analysis of the source of the system of control (states as compared to firms) or the issue area (involving state security as compared to the profitability of an industry) is insufficient, and we should consider as well the relationships highlighted by the other two propositions.

The second proposition suggested that disaggregation of public authority will be more pronounced when it involves activities that lend themselves to mediation through networks, such as activities that have low sensory complexity and low externalities. This especially stresses the interaction between human and non-human actants, a relationship that is entirely ignored by many scholars, including those who would dismiss the relevance of disaggregated authority. The three cases strongly support the relevance of this proposition. Even a casual reading of the literatures on biometrics and digital rights management will reveal that the effectiveness of governance is heavily dependent on the potentials and limitations of existing technology. In the case of biometrics there are limits to the ability of existing devices to accurately recognize faces. In the case of finance the debate centres less on the physical aspects of technologies and their capacity to deal with sensory complexity, and more on intangible risk-management technologies and their inability to manage externalities, but all three are crucially about the degree to which human activity can be monitored and controlled by systems whose routine operations are managed by non-human actants. There is a strong similarity between the efforts to discriminate between acceptable and non-acceptable activities, whether these involve terrorism, piracy, or dangerous financial risks. There is identifiable variation in the pace of disaggregation that is related to this, even though all three cases display a hybridity in which traditional forms of public authority persist and reinforce new forms of authority. For instance face recognition technology has stalled because of technical problems and the demand that passports require biometrics has been postponed for the same reason, while reliance on proprietary risk management technologies in finance will be feasible only for the largest banks, and there will be a heavier reliance on more traditional procedures for governing the activities of smaller firms.

The third proposition suggested that the disaggregation of public authority will be more advanced in issue areas in which the factors that explain successful cases of citizen activism, such as easy strategic framing, citizens' organizational capacity, and elite support, are present, or in especially concentrated industries. This proposition highlights the politics of disaggregated authority, and questions of legitimacy and democracy. The three cases provide support for the relevance of this proposition. In the case of airline and border security, the legal actions resulting from citizens concerned about the negative implications for freedom of biometrics and the databases associated with them have been as important in restricting their use as have technical constraints. In the case of songs the conflict is between the oligopolistic industry that has tried to use its influence with states to impose legal restrictions on unauthorized file sharers, or that has tried to use its technical capacity to implement digital rights management in CDs, against its potential customers, who tend to see music as a form of personal expression that can be counter to the commercial values of big business and the heavy hand of the law. This feeling of customers is reinforced by the free-wheeling values that have been associated with the internet since its creation (Fox 2005). Charged words such as 'piracy' and 'digital rights management' are part of the industry's strategy to delegitimize unauthorized copying. The ability of the industry to achieve its goals will be very dependent on the degree to which it can prevail in this political struggle. In the case of finance the debate revolves around the dangers of regulatory burdens for the profitability and viability of regulated firms, but in this case it is a debate that is relatively restricted to elites and experts, and popular authority plays little role, a difference that is likely related in part to the differences with regard to the potential for strategic framing of pricing models for derivatives as compared to a hot new hip-hop artist.

Changes in the way that disaggregated authority is legitimized and challenged as compared to conventional public authority associated with more centralized states are especially important. The history of the legitimization of state authority has involved a shift from reliance by the sovereign on authority conferred by God, to an increasing reliance on the degree to which the rules associated with this authority are responsive to the preferences of citizens, especially as expressed through elections. Disaggregated authority can undermine this type of democratic legitimation of public authority, because some disaggregated processes can be harder for citizens to monitor and hold accountable, and because private and technical forms of authority are not necessarily aligned with the interests of citizens. On the other hand, disaggregation can provide new entry points and ways for citizens to intervene in policy processes, a point that is reinforced by the concept of popular authority as used in this chapter, which is broader than notions of democracy that focus on elections and voting. The case of airport and border security, a policy area that traditionally would not have allowed much specific input from citizens, is notable for the number of ways that challenges that could be characterized as expressions of popular authority have had a significant impact. In other areas where disaggregated processes are more open to or dependent on the influence of popular authority, such as the swapping of music files, the potential for citizens to influence disaggregated processes is even greater. In all cases *understanding* the disaggregated and intermediated character of contemporary authority is a crucial first step in influencing or challenging it.

Considering the three cases together, it is apparent that the concept of disaggregated authority is an important one, that the pace of disaggregation varies, and that the three propositions provide some insight into this variation. However in each case the way in which authority is being disaggregated is sufficiently complex and contingent that generalizations must be handled with caution. There is much valuable work to be done in understanding the disaggregation of authority, but this will always need to consider the particular paths taken by human and non-human actants as they engage one another in the far-flung networks that are such an important part of contemporary global governance.

Notes

The research assistance of Kaitlin Short is gratefully acknowledged as are comments by the editors on an earlier draft. This research has been funded by the Social Sciences and Humanities Research Council of Canada.

1. Such proof is problematic not just because it goes beyond the scope of this chapter, but also for methodological and epistemological reasons: sceptics can always make unfalsifiable claims that any instance of compliance can ultimately be reduced to interests and power.
2. An increasingly popular rational choice model relevant to disaggregation is principle-agent theory. While this theory provides some interesting insights, it fails to adequately theorize the larger changing context within which any particular case of delegation occurs. See Porter (2005b).
3. Even without the distinctive issues displayed by 9/11, border and airline security challenges are serious for the US government. An estimated 500 million people cross its borders each year, and more than 7.6 million containers

enter its ports (Bodenheimer 2003) and at any one moment 300,000 passengers are in flight above the US, equivalent to the population of some cities (Urry 2003: 61).

4. The US Office of Domestic Preparedness which has the responsibility of working with State, local, tribal, parish, and private-sector emergency response providers on terrorism-related matters has also been criticized by the US Congress for being overly bureaucratic and centralized (Bodenheimer 2003).

5. This was a part of a much larger US reliance on private security firms. See *Washington Times* (2003).

6. FAST is part of a US-Canada Smart Border initiative that includes biometrics-based NEXUS and CANPASS systems for individuals. There is also a similar US-Mexico Smart Border initiative.

7. US demands for information on airline passengers have triggered a dispute about privacy rights with the EU that has been referred to the European Court of Justice (*Financial Times* 2005). The EU rejected similar Canadian requests (*Aviation Daily* 2005).

8. The FaceIt system produced by Identix can scan 70 million images per minute on a standard personal computer with an error rate under favourable conditions of less than one per cent. On the other hand, a controversial application of the technology in the streets of Tampa was abandoned after six months when it failed to identify a single criminal (McCormack 2003: 131, 134). *Business Week* (2004) has said that the technology 'in several airports produced so many false positives ... that the technology is no longer considered useful'. See also Feldman (2003: 663).

9. Australia runs a similar programme called 'Smartgate'. In the US the first programme to be run by an airport and its private-sector partners was the Orlando 'Clear' pass, initiated in July 2005 (*Business Traveler News*: 2005).

10. The US Enhanced Border Security and Visa Entry Reform Act of 2002 required countries with visa waivers to have passports with biometric identifiers by 2004. However after it was clear that this deadline was unrealistic steps were initiated to extend it (Travel Business Roundtable 2004). In 2003 the ICAO agreed on a plan for the inclusion in passports of biometric data primarily based on face recognition and secondarily on fingerprint and iris recognition.

11. The size of the larger market for defence against terrorism is far larger. For instance the market size of the homeland security business in 2000 was estimated at $4 billion (*Engineering News-Record*: 2004). As one headline put it, 'The Winner of the War on Terrorism is ... US Industry' (Koerner 2002). The article notes that some businesses, such as financial services companies, used the pretext of the war on terror to lobby for legal changes that would allow them to sell personal data more easily. Other companies, such as Sun Microsystems, have pressed for a national ID card that they could be involved in supplying.

12. As Feldman (2003: 657) notes 'biometric systems generally are based on algorithms that analyse abstracted pattern representations of human characteristics'.

13. Poole (2005b: 2) provides an example of technical authority reinforcing the public authority of the Transport Safety Administration at the expense of

private airport authorities: 'once a year, it reallocates the screening work-force, to take into account changes in airline activity, using a confidential algorithm. These allocations may be tweaked occasionally during the course of a year, but airport directors have no idea how the algorithm works and little ability to influence the allocations.'

14. In the US a similar 'Registered Traveler' programme is being developed (Poole 2005a).
15. More about the points made in this chapter about finance can be found in Porter (2005a).
16. The big five (BMG Entertainment, Sony, AOL Time Warner, EMI, and Vivendi Universal Music Group) sell over 80 per cent of popular music (Fox 2005, citing W.S Coats et al. (2000))
17. Two key pieces of legislation are the US Digital Millennium Copyright Act and the European Copyright Directive. See Williams (2001).
18. For instance, in 1998 over 120 organizations and firms from the music and electronics industries formed a consortium to work on the Secure Digital Music Initiative. See Johnstone (2001: 141).

References

Accenture (2005) 'US Department of Homeland Security to Develop and Implement US-VISIT Program at Air, Land and Sea Ports of Entry', *Accenture Digital Forum*, online at: digitalforum.accenture.com, accessed 20 January 2006.

Airport Security Report (2005) 'Airports Seek More Control of Checkpoint Security', *Airport Security Report*, 12(16). Available through LexisNexis.

Airport Security Report (2004) 'Canada Awards Screening Contracts to Private Security Firms', *Airport Security Report*, 11(5) (10 March). Available through LexisNexis.

Arnold, P. J. and P. Sikka (2001) 'Globalization and the State-Profession Relationship: The Case [of] the Bank of Credit and Commerce International', *Accounting, Organizations, and Society*, 26(6) (August): 475–99.

Aviation Daily (2005) 'European Parliament Rejects EU-Canada Passenger Info Deal', *Aviation Daily*, (11 July): 2 [Reporter: Tardy, M.].

Bechtel, J. H. and J. F. Svacek (2003) 'Metro Optical Networks for Homeland Security', *Fiber and Integrated Optics*, 22(2) (March/April): 131–9.

Benoliel, D. (2004) 'Technological Standards, Inc: Rethinking Cyberspace Regulatory Epistemology', *California Law Review*, 92 (July): 1069–1116.

Bodenheimer, D. Z. (2003) 'Technology for Border Protection', *Journal of Homeland Security*, August, online at: www.homelandsecurity.org, accessed 20 January 2006.

Business Traveler News (2005) 'Orlando Privatizes Reg. Traveler', *Business Traveler News*, 22(11) (20 June): 1.

Business Week (2004) 'Welcome to Security Nation: Nearly Three Years after September 11, the feds are massively funding new anti-terror tools under development by America's technology wizards', *Business Week*, [Reporters: Magnusson, P., M. McNamee, M. Arndt, A. Aston, C. Palmeri, and O. Harif], (14 June): 32.

Coats, W. S., V. L. Freeman, J. G. Given and H. D. Rafter (2000) 'Streaming into the Future: Music and Video Online,' *Loyola of Los Angeles Entertainment Law Journal*, 20: 285–307.

David, M. and J. Kirkhope (2004) 'New Digital Technologies: Privacy/Property, Globalization and Law', *Perspectives on Global Development and Technology*, 3(4): 437–49.

Dell, M. and C. Bunney (2001) 'Biometrics and Aviation Security', *Biometric Technology Today*, 9(10) (30 November): 7–8.

Engineering News-Record (2004) 'Homeland Protection Industry Foresees Numbers in Safety', *Engineering News-Record*, 252(24) (14 June): 13.

Feldman, R. (2003) 'Considerations on the Emerging Implementation of Biometric Technology', *Hastings Communications and Entertainment Law Journal*, 25 (Spring/Summer): 653–81.

Financial Times (2004) 'Experimenting in the World's New Security Laboratory', *Financial Times*, [Reporter: Bowe, C.] (1 October): 2.

Financial Times (2005) 'Brussels Seeks Help on Transatlantic Security for 'Trusted' Companies', *Financial Times*, [Reporter: Minder, R.] (19 May): 12.

Flynn, S. E. (2000) *Globalization and the Future of Border Control*. New York: Council on Foreign Relations, online at: www.cfr.org, accessed 20 January 2006.

Fox, M. (2005) 'Technological and Social Drivers of Change in the Online Music Industry', *First Monday*, [Internet journal, special issue 'Music and the Internet'] (July), online at: www.firstmonday.org/issues/issue7_2/fox/, accessed 18 January, 2006.

Foucault, M., G. Burchell, C. Gordon and P. Miller (1991) The Foucault Effect: Studies in Governmentality: With Two Lectures by and an Interview with Michel Foucault. *Chicago: University of Chicago Press*.

Hoffman, K. J. (2000) 'Fair Use or Fair Game? The Internet, MP3 and Copyright Law', *Albany Law Journal of Science and Technology*, 11:153–79.

IFPI (2005) 'One in Three Music Discs is Illegal but Fight Back Starts to Show Results', Press release, online at: www.ifpi.com/site-content/antipiracy/ piracy report-current.html, (23 June), accessed 15 January 2006.

Johnstone, D. R. (2001) 'The Pirates are Always with Us: What Can and Cannot be Done about Unauthorized Use of MP3 Files on the Internet', *Buffalo Intellectual Property Law Journal*, 1 (Summer): 122–45.

Kauvar, G., B. Rosker, and R. Shaver (2002) *Safer Skies: Baggage Screening and Beyond*. Santa Monica: RAND Corporation.

Keck, M. and K. Sikkink (1998) *Activists Beyond Borders*. Ithaca: Cornell University Press.

Koerner, B. (2002) 'The Winner of the War on Terrorism is ... US Industry', *The Business* (1 September).

Koslowski, R. (2005) 'Real Challenges for Virtual Borders: The Implementation of US-VISIT' *Migration Policy Institute*, June, online at: http://www.migrationpolicy. org/pubs/Koslowski_Report.pdf, accessed on 7 May 2007.

Kunreuther, H., G. Heal and P. R. Orszag (2002) *Interdependent Security: Implications for Homeland Security Policy and Other Areas*, Policy Brief #108, Brookings Institution, available at www.brook.edu.

Latour, B., (1991) 'Technology is Society Made Durable', in J. Law, (ed.), *A Sociology of Monsters: Essays on Power, Technology, and Domination*. London: Routledge, 103–131.

LoVoi, J. (1999) 'Competing Interests: Anti-Piracy Efforts Triumph Under TRIPS, but New Copying Technology Undermines the Success', *Brooklyn Journal of International Law*, 25: 445–82.

McCormack, D. (2003) 'Can Corporate America Secure our Nation? An Analysis of the Identix Framework for the Regulation and Use of Facial Recognition Technology', *Boston University Journal of Science and Technology Law*, 9 (Winter): 128–155.

Marres, N. (2004) 'Tracing the trajectories of issues, and their democratic deficits, on the Web: The case of the Development Gateway and its Doubles', *Information Technology & People*, 17(2): 124–49.

Organization for Economic Cooperation and Development (2004) *The Security Economy*. Paris: OECD.

Perri, C. (2003) 'The eyes have it: Iris scanners a hit', *Miami Herald*, 9 January. Online at: http://www.biometricgroup.com/in_the_news/miami_herald.html, accessed on 7 May 2007.

Poole, R. W. (2005a) 'Registered Traveler Progress, Despite Carping', *Aviation Security Newsletter*, 15 (July), online at: www.reason.org, accessed 15 January 2006.

Poole, R. W. (2005b) *'Improving Management of the Aviation Security Workforce'*, Testimony before the House Committee on Homeland Security, 28 July. Los Angeles: Reason Foundation.

Porter, T. (2005a) *Globalization and Finance*. Cambridge: Polity.

Porter, T. (2005b) 'Private Authority, Technical Authority, and the Globalization of Accounting Standards', *Business and Politics*, 7(3), Article 2, online at: http://www.bepress.com/bap/vol7/iss3/art2, accessed 20 March 2006.

Rhodes, J. D. (2004) 'CAPPS II: Red Light, Green Light, or "Mother May I?"', *Journal of Homeland Security* (March), online at: www.homelandsecurity.org, accessed 5 July 2006.

Saldanha, A. (2003) 'Actor-Network Theory and Critical Sociology', *Critical Sociology*, 29(3): 419–32.

Travel Business Roundtable (2004) 'Statement Submitted for the Record to the Subcommittee on Commerce, Trade and Consumer Protection', Hearing on the Effects of Homeland Security Regulations on the Travel and Tourism Industry. June 23.

Urry, J. (2003) *Global Complexity*. Cambridge: Polity.

United States Government Accountability Office (2005) *Aviation Security*. Report to the Subcommittee on Aviation. (May), Washington: US Government Printing Office.

Wall Street Journal (2000) 'Firm Touts Technology to Beat Hackers', *Wall Street Journal*, 13 November: 1 [Reporter: Latour, A.].

Wall Street Journal (2005) 'Effort to Speed Airport Security is Going Private', *Wall Street Journal*, 12 January: D1 [Reporter: Schatz, A.].

Washington Times (2003) 'Use of Private Security Firms in Iraq Draws Concerns', *Washington Times*, 6 October [Reporter: Daragahi, B.].

Williams, S. (2001) 'The Digital Millennium Copyright Act and the European Copyright Directive' Legislative Attempts to Control Digital Music Distribution', *Loyola Intellectual Property and High Technology Journal*, 3 (Summer): 35–50.

Zald, M. N. (1996) 'Culture, Ideology and Strategic Framing' in D. McAdam, J. D. McCarthy and M. N. Zald (eds) *Comparative Perspectives on Social Movements: Political Opportunities, Mobilizing Structures, and Cultural Framings*. New York: Cambridge University Press, 261–74.

3
Governing Regulative Networks Beyond the State

Hans Peter Olsen

According to the much-cited maritime metaphor by Osborne and Gaebler (1992), states in the age of New Public Management are 'steering' (regulating), whereas 'rowing' (production and service provision) is delegated to non-state actors (Jordana and Levi-Faur 2004: 11). Although this imagery may be useful in depicting trajectories of privatization and contracting-out in many countries, it is in need of qualification, given the increased impetus of transnational regulation (Djelic and Sahlin-Andersson 2006). Studies have recognized how transnational regulatory networks govern areas as varied as banking (Marcussen 2007), information technology (Mattli 2003) and employment policy (Jacobsson 2004). Since the conduct of states to an increasing extent seems influenced by transnational networks, elements of 'steering' can be said to be installed beyond the realm of states. These observations challenge the image of the state as Weberian organized and unitary actors (Drori et al. 2006; Hall and Biersteker 2002). Transnational networks of organizations that issue and promote regulation – often in the form of voluntary standards – may, thus, be a crucial driver of what has been recognized as the disaggregation of state authority (Porter this volume; Rosenau 2007).

How do regulatory networks set sail in the rough seas of transnational governance? The functioning of specific organizations that produce international standards has been explored at some length in a number of studies. However, there is a research gap with regard to how transnational networks foster standardization (Tamm Hallström 2004: 190). At present, we have only rudimentary knowledge of the social mechanisms behind the entanglement of different types of organizations in transnational regulatory networks. Furthermore, little is known about how authority is enacted within these networks. With the aim of contributing to this research agenda, this chapter analyses the emergence of a transnational network of organizations that issues professional standards as a mode of regulation in the field of government auditing.

For at least two reasons, the standardization of government auditing is a case particularly rich in insights that can shed light on the wider phenomena of entanglement and authority in transnational regulatory networks. First, government auditing has become an increasingly important regulatory mechanism in many countries in recent decades, while waves of public sector reforms such as privatization, contracting out and new management styles have swept across the world (Hood 1995; Pollitt and Bouckaert 2004: 72–74; Power 1999: chapter 3). Second, as this chapter argues, the field of government auditing is undergoing a process of transnationalization in which various actors ranging from national supreme audit institutions (SAIs) to international financial institutions, accountants' associations and firms are becoming increasingly involved in standard-setting as a way of regulating the field. As such, it is a case of transnational governance that manifests itself through soft regulation in the form of voluntary standards produced by a network that spans both the public and private sectors and also beyond national boundaries.

Before proceeding, it is worth clarifying what is meant by the concept of a transnational regulatory network. Such entities have also been referred to as 'regulatory fields' (Djelic and Sahlin-Andersson 2006), 'regulatory spaces' (Hancher and Moran 1989), 'webs of governance' (Cerny 2000), 'regulatory webs' (Braithwaite and Drahos 2000), 'public–private networks and partnerships' (Risse forthcoming), 'global policy networks' (Kern 2004: 2–3) and 'mobile networks for regulation' (Tamm Hallström 2004). In this chapter, a transnational regulatory network is understood as 'a group of self-governing actors that interact within a more or less formalized institutional framework with a view to producing public policy' (Marcussen 2006: 181). The type of regulatory networks that this chapter investigates is those which produce rules in the form of standards that are voluntary for states to adopt. Such networks are particularly prevalent on a transnational scale and appear to be gaining importance globally (Kerwer 2005).

More specifically, this chapter examines the following three things. First, it outlines the antecedents of the current transnational development of the field of government auditing regulation. Second, drawing on theories of institutional change (Campbell 2004; Clemens and Cook 1999), it explores how public and private standard-setters have initiated close cooperation organized as a transnational regulatory network with a view to standardizing financial auditing internationally. Third, it considers empirical data on how the standardizing activities of the transnational regulatory network are carried out. The empirical underpinnings of the study are archival studies of documents from meetings in international government auditing fora cross-validated with interviews with central policymakers.

Pre-history of the post-regulatory state: The transnational course of government auditing

In a critique of state-centric accounts of regulation, Colin Scott (2004) introduces a 'post-regulatory state' perspective as a way of thinking about regulation as being dispersed among states and non-state actors. This chapter argues that rules of government auditing in many places are changing from being exclusively a matter of national public affairs to also being governed from beyond the state. As well as being a range of concrete analytical techniques aiming to strengthen financial accountability, government auditing also has a mentality or a mindset attached to it. The way government auditing is being conceived today is in many ways different compared to how it was thought of fifty years ago. Even though the practice of government auditing over recent decades has grown into becoming an indispensable part of the internal governance of most 'regulatory states' (Hood et al. 1999), the conception of government auditing is increasingly being developed outside the realm of individual states. Thus, Scott's (2004) claim finds empirical support in the transnational course of government auditing regulation.

To situate further analysis and to investigate the assertion of a growing transnationalization of government auditing regulation, this section traces the historical development of government auditing activities occurring between and beyond states. The section outlines how regulation of government auditing has moved from being distinctively state-specific (in independent sovereign states), to being mildly coordinated through inter-governmental cooperation, and finally into becoming influenced by a transnational standardizing network.

Figure 3.1 outlines the growth of internationally organized bodies of government auditing, such as international organizations, committees, and boards, from 1953 and onwards.

Since the founding of the International Organization of Supreme Audit Institutions (INTOSAI) in 1953, there has been a steady growth in the number of international 'clubs' for government auditing bodies. In order to identify distinct phases and possible turning points in the

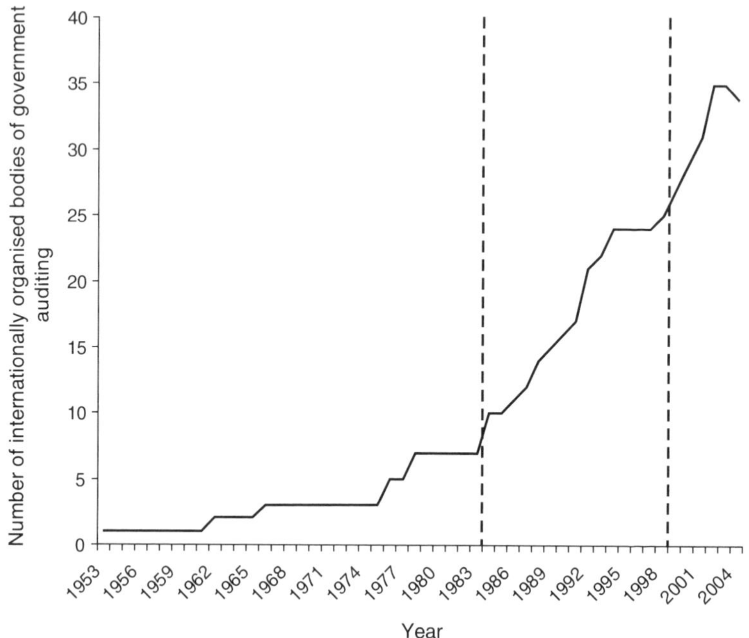

Figure 3.1 The growth of internationally organized bodies of government auditing

Sources: International Yearbook of International Organizations, INTOSAI (2004), INCOSAI proceedings (various years), INTOSAI committee websites. Sources are available at www.intosai.org and www.ifac.org.

transnationalization of government auditing, cluster analysis has been applied to the dataset.[1] The cluster analysis identifies three distinct phases: 1953–1983, 1984–1998, and 1999–2004. The three phases are marked by the dotted lines on Figure 1 and are described below.

1953–1983: The early internationalization of government auditing

The internationalization of SAIs has largely taken place within the auspices of INTOSAI. Following a meeting at the 1947 International Congress of Administrative Sciences in Bern, Switzerland, INTOSAI was founded in 1953 by officials from various SAIs, with the mission to facilitate the global spread of ideas and experiences on public finance control (INTOSAI 2004: 14; Rechnungshof der Republik Österreich 1962: 238). There has been a steady increase in the number of SAIs that have joined INTOSAI since the 1950s. To begin with, European and South and North American SAIs were primarily represented among INTOSAI members. Since the 1960s, membership has spread to nearly all other countries of the world. By 2004, 95 per cent of all sovereign states had established an SAI.

As the steady growth of the international SAI community unfolded, common activities among the organizations have taken pace. A cornerstone among the international activities of SAIs is the triennial International Congress of Supreme Audit Institutions (INCOSAI), where senior officials from SAIs meet and exchange ideas. Another basis for SAI internationalization is the Lima Declaration of Guidelines on Auditing Precepts, which was adopted at the 9th INCOSAI in 1977. This very general declaration of government auditing principles acts as a global point of reference for what SAIs are and what they do. Since the 1960s, the patterns of interaction between SAIs have been further strengthened by the creation of regional organizations for SAIs. Moreover, initiatives to form committees within the INTOSAI community to deal with specific government auditing issues, such as IT audit and environmental auditing, have propelled a generic identity of SAIs as public agents of financial accountability.

The international government auditing fora can be referred to as meta-organizations, i.e. organizations with other organizations rather than individuals as members. Meta-organizations generally share at least two features (Ahrne and Brunsson 2001, 2004). First, they are fairly easy to establish, since they can draw on organizational resources from their members. Second, meta organizations often use standards as a way of regulating their members. This has also been the case in the international community of SAIs.

1984–1998: Initiating international standardization of government auditing

To issue standards is a particularly attractive soft regulatory mechanism for meta-organizations because they often have a very mixed lot of members, hence making binding rules difficult both to decide upon and to enforce. This description certainly fits INTOSAI, where deep differences exist between those member SAIs organized according to an auditor general model, for example the British National Audit Office, and those SAIs that are functioning as court of audits as e.g. the French Cour des Comptes.

The expansion of standardization has also occurred within the international field of government auditing since 1984, when INTOSAI launched its standard-setting activities by establishing an Auditing Standards Committee, an Accounting Standards Committee, and an Internal Control Standards Committee. Between 1984 and 2005, these committees have been chaired by the SAIs of Australia, Belgium, Canada, Hungary, Saudi Arabia, Sweden, and the United States. Besides being intended to provide guidance on government auditing, international government auditing standards can also be viewed as benchmarks with which the performance of SAIs can be compared and, thus, as soft international rules.

The first provisional international government auditing standards were presented at the 13th INCOSAI in June 1989 in Berlin, Germany. Even though the standards were not eagerly accepted by all members of the SAI community (German Federal Court of Audit 1990: 48–53), the event marked a qualitative shift in the internationalization of government auditing as INTOSAI moved from being merely a club of SAIs into being an international policymaker in the field of public sector auditing. The major standards produced by INTOSAI are its 'Auditing Standards', 'Code of Ethics' and 'Implementation Guidelines for Performance Audit Standards', endorsed respectively at the INCOSAIs of 1992, 1998, and 2004.

Besides INTOSAI, another international standard-setter has entered the field of government auditing, namely, the International Federation of Accountants (IFAC). IFAC was formed in 1977 and has professional accountants' associations from numerous countries as its members (see also Loft and Humphrey 2006). The official aim of the organization is to develop and enhance the accountancy profession to enable it to provide quality services in the public interest. Since the late 1990s, IFAC's Public Sector Committee (now the International Public Sector Accounting Standards Board) has issued International Public Sector Accounting Standards (IPSASs). Between 1980 and 1991, IFAC's International Audit Practice Committee (IAPC) issued International Auditing Guidelines, and since 1991, International Standards on Auditing (ISAs). Originally, these standards were principally related to private firms, but over the years they have also been used by the Anglo-Saxon SAIs of Australia, Canada, South Africa, and the United Kingdom (INTOSAI Auditing Standards Committee 1995).

The differences between the standard-setting of INTOSAI and IFAC are evident when looking at the respective standards of the two organizations. INTOSAI's (1998) Code of Ethics and Auditing Standards comes in a booklet of about 75 pages, whereas IFAC's ISAs and related standards are published in a volume of about 1,000 pages (IAASB 2005a). The difference in quantity reflects the fact that INTOSAI's standards deals with principles of a general nature, whereas IFAC's standards offer more specific guidance on auditing.

By the 1990s, there was uncertainty in the international field of public sector auditing about whether the two international standard-setters would compete or cooperate. In the SAI community, there was a mixture of attitudes regarding IFAC. Some SAI officials believed that IFAC was disdainful of the sometimes rigid decision-making procedures of INTOSAI, others had great respect for the expertise and professionalism of IFAC, and yet others mistrusted IFAC for working mainly in the interests of a few big accountancy firms (author's interview with SAI senior officials). Correspondingly, divergence developed with regard to what standards SAIs were following: some used INTOSAI's standards, others used IFAC's, and yet others used their own national standards or a mixture of the repertoire of standards available to them (United States General Accounting Office, 2003a). An example of the multifarious usage of auditing standards is evident in the European Court of Auditors implementation guidelines for INTOSAI's Auditing Standards (European Court of Auditors 1998).[2] These guidelines based on INTOSAI's standards also made references to IFAC's ISAs and thereby signalled that ISAs were also applicable to government auditing.

1999–2004: Transnationalizing government auditing

In July 1999, INTOSAI's Committee on Accounting Standards under the leadership of the Comptroller General of the United States, David M. Walker, met with the Public Sector Committee of IFAC (International Journal of Government Auditing 1999: 17). At the time, IFAC feared that INTOSAI would produce their own accounting standards in direct competition with IFAC (author's interview with SAI senior official). At the meeting, however, IFAC was assured that this was not the case. Subsequently, in January 2000, INTOSAI's Committee on Accounting Standards was granted observer status at IFAC's Public Sector Committee (Board of Audit and Inspection of Korea 2002: 39). Since this event, a shift from separation and/or competition towards cooperation between INTOSAI and IFAC has occurred.

In March 2002, the Auditing Standards Committee of INTOSAI decided to 'initiate a very substantial cooperation with IFAC to contribute with the public sector perspective in the ongoing revision of old ISAs as well as the development of new ones' (Ahlenius 2003: 2). This event marked that a transnational and cross-sectional network of organizations was being formed with a view to regulating government auditing by issuing and disseminating International Standards on Auditing (ISAs) for both the private and the public sector.

ISAs are now formulated by the International Auditing and Assurance Standards Board (IAASB), which is comprised of members from national accountants' associations and the major international accountancy firms, national regulators and so-called public members from academia and the public sector.[3] The objective of the IAASB is to promote worldwide uniformity of auditing practice and related services (Hayes et al. 2005: 10). In view of this, the chairman of the IAASB has portrayed the formation of the transnational and boundary-spanning collaboration as, 'an important step towards the globalization of auditing standards' (IAASB 2003: 11). The standard-setting is conducted in consultation with international financial and regulatory organizations, such as the International Organization of Securities Commissions (IOSCO), the European Commission and the World Bank (IAASB 2005b: 19). Furthermore, SAI officials participate in the IAASB's standard-drafting task forces. The rationale for the SAI involvement is that the ISAs should be applicable to SAIs throughout the world, with the possible amendment of so-called practice notes on specific public sector issues (Ånerud 2004). Thus, in the case of special public sector circumstances, such practice notes would 'translate' an ISA into a standard that would offer appropriate guidance for public sector auditors.

Embarking a transnational standardizing network

Why and how could such a transnational arrangement as the regulatory network formed around IFAC and INTOSAI come about? If the arrangement is viewed as the creation of new rulemaking given the institutionalization of relations between standard-setting bodies, the growing body of theoretical literature on institutional emergence and change can help to explain the issue. A core argument drawn from this literature is that institutional change, in this case the creation of a transnational regulatory network, comes about as result of actors' choice given institutional constraints. Based on this postulate, I propose the following explanatory model:

1. A critical juncture in the form of a commonly perceived crisis destabilizes an existing institutional order within a particular field (Abbott 1997; Campbell 2004: 68–69; Clemens and Cook 1999). The destabilization is initiated by institutional entrepreneurs that influence the discourses that underpin the institutions within the given field (cf. Phillips et al. 2004: 648).

2. The crisis gives institutional entrepreneurs, particularly those working at the intersections of different fields, room for manoeuvre to purposefully build up and shape a transnational governance network (Christensen et al. 1997; DiMaggio 1988; Pierson 2004: 136–137). Given that critical junctures can be used as an opportunity or pretext by institutional entrepreneurs to advocate changes, it is the entrepreneurship internal to the field rather than merely the external shocks that brings about change. The interests, resources, and proximity to different environments of the entrepreneurs are expected to have an impact on the institutionalization of the regulatory network (cf. Campbell 2004: 173–183).

In the following, this model is applied to the case of a transnational regulatory network within the field of government auditing.

A critical juncture in global economic governance

The Asian financial crises in 1997 came as shock to the major international financial institutions (Islam and Chowdhury 2000). One response to the crisis from the World Bank and the IMF was to prioritize their attention on institutional reform. An area of particular interest was auditing and accounting systems in developing and newly industrialized countries where much of the economy had been functioning beyond the reach of auditing. Given that SAIs of developing countries audit large parts of the loans and aid received from the World Bank, the motive of the World Bank has been to induce more comprehensive and uniform standards for the auditing of how development aid and loans are spent (Wolfensohn 2004: 2). In this setting, the World Bank regarded INTOSAI's auditing standards as too vague and inadequate as a means of improving the economic governance of developing countries, whereas IFAC's standards were believed to have a greater impact (author's interview with World Bank senior official).

In a number of ways, the World Bank has been a particularly influential actor in shaping the transnational regulatory network on government auditing. One initiative was the joint programme of the IMF and the World Bank in creating or sponsoring more comprehensive international standards as part of a so-called new international financial architecture. The standard-setting initiative boosted the status of IFAC as a global regulator at the end of the 1990s, when it's auditing standards got official recognition from such prominent organizations as the IMF, the World Bank, the WTO, the Financial Stability Forum, and IOSCO (World Bank / IMF 2000: 8–9).

In July 2000 a senior World Bank executive sent a letter to the top officials from those SAIs that were leading INTOSAI's main committees as well as IFAC, regional development banks, the OECD, and the International Forum on Accountancy Development. The letter soon became famous in these circles as it provocatively described INTOSAI as a passive actor with regard to strengthening financial accountability internationally. The letter claimed that INTOSAI was an organization 'more spoken about than spoken to', and that the SAIs constituted a hole in the 'international financial architecture bucket' by having a 'non-compliance mindset' towards national and international rules on public sector accountability. The effect of this letter was a profound change in the way international organizations could articulate their expectations with regards to SAIs.

The assault on the previously undisputed glory of the international SAI community was, however, tiny in comparison to the shaming of the private sector accounting profession after the downfall of Enron in 2001. Following the US Sarbanes-Oxley Act of July 2002 and the establishment of the Public Company Accounting Oversight Board (PCAOB) charged to monitor the auditing of public companies in the US, the hitherto self-regulatory prerogative of the accounting profession was challenged (Ånerud 2004: 21).

Institutional entrepreneurship

The climate of external critique at the beginning of the 2000s of both INTOSAI and IFAC resulted in new conditions for how the two international bodies could continue their standards-setting activities and retain their authority. The two international standard-setters had by 2001–2002 reached a disequilibrium or a 'choice point' in their historical development as a result of new conditions and expectations in their environment. 'During this key choice point, or "critical juncture", a particular option [...] is selected from among two or more alternatives. The choice made [...] is consequential because it leads to the creation of institutional patterns that endure over time' (Mahoney 2001: 112).

The choice point of the two standard-setters was essentially a matter of how inclusive or exclusive their standards and standard-setting procedures should be. As a general observation, standard-setters can either produce standards all by themselves or depend on and patch up the standards of others. The US Government Auditing Standards is largely an example of the former (United States General Accounting Office 2003b), and the European Court of Auditors implementation guidelines for INTOSAI's Auditing Standards is an example of the latter (European Court of Auditors 1998). These two ideal-types of standard-setting outline a continuum of the extent to which few or many regulators should be enrolled into the standard-setting process.

At a meeting of INTOSAI's Auditing Standards Committee in Stockholm on 26 September 2002, the following options were debated: INTOSAI could either continue to produce financial auditing standards themselves (option 1) or use various existing standards as a basis for INTOSAI's standards (option 2). A third option, which was put forward by the Swedish chairman of the committee, was to initiate collaboration with IFAC and make use of the ISAs of the IAASB. This option (option 3) entailed some elements of the two other options as INTOSAI would have the opportunity to influence the ISAs as they are made and the standards formulated by IAASB could be amended with specific practice notes for public sector auditing.

The options were at the outset subject to disagreement within INTOSAI, but in October 2002, INTOSAI's Governing Board decided to go on with option 3. An explanation of that decision could be that option 1 was viewed as unfeasible given the demand for comprehensive standards by some SAIs and the World Bank, the resource intensive nature of formulating standards of a high quality and the rather inflexible nature of INTOSAI's decision-making procedures at the time. Option 2, on the other hand, could be viewed as undesirable because it would leave the core standard-setting business to other actors than INTOSAI.

IFAC was facing a somewhat similar choice between continuing its hitherto standard-setting activities but thereby risking losing authority to other regulators, or stretching its collaboration and consultation with other parties. IFAC chose the latter, presumably to maintain its authority as a global standard-setter and with the declared goals of remedying the legitimacy-crisis of the accounting profession and rebuilding public confidence in accounting (IFAC 2003). A major move in this direction was the creation of the IAASB under the slogan of producing auditing standards 'protecting the public interest' (IAASB 2004). A central feature of the new institutional setup of the IAASB was an increased number of members compared to the former IAPC (from 14 to 18). Furthermore, the new entity signalled more interaction and consultation with other actors, and greater transparency and openness towards the greater public. In this setting, IFAC became interested in linking up with SAIs, which was broadly acknowledged as important elements of modern states: as agents of transparency or 'pillars of integrity' (Dye and Stapenhurst 1998). An additional motivation for IFAC to engage with

INTOSAI was that harmonization of public and private auditing standards could give private accountancy firms better access to the market of public sector auditing (author's interview with IFAC official).

Essentially, the transnational governance network appears to have been formed in order for the two international standard-setters to exchange different kinds of benefits, such as the image of decision-making capacity (IFAC -> INTOSAI), public legitimacy (INTOSAI -> IFAC), and information (both ways). Furthermore, the new mode of collaboration could function as a shield against threats to INTOSAI and IFAC or even as a means to acquire resources from their respective environments.

However, the creation of the transnational regulatory network arose from more than a trade-off between what INTOSAI and IFAC perceived as preferred and possible at the time. It is plausible that the external shocks that had shaken both standard-setting communities were a prerequisite for the venture, since such cooperation by most people had been seen as unlikely in the 1980s and the 1990s. In this way it is fair to say that a particular 'opportunity window' had paved the way for the transnational network (author's correspondence with former senior SAI official). In addition, the globalization of accounting standards organized around the International Accounting Standards Board provided a template for a multi-stakeholder regulatory network in the area of auditing.

Nevertheless, the new institutional arrangement did not come about automatically or unchallenged, because some groups within INTOSAI and IFAC feared that it would jeopardize their authority. Some SAIs – in particular Continental-European – were sceptical about what they feared was a Faustian deal with Big Business. Likewise, there was uneasiness on IFAC's Board as to whether the new arrangement would slow down IFAC's standard-setting activities given the increased board size of the IAASB (author's interview with IFAC official). There was also scepticism as to whether an increase in the number of non-auditors on the board and increased consultation with the Consultative Advisory Group (CAG) would threaten the interests of the accounting profession.

Why then was the network formed despite these signs of disagreement within INTOSAI and IFAC? Evidence suggests that a small group of skilful institutional entrepreneurs played a crucial role here. These entrepreneurs had central positions within INTOSAI, IFAC, and the World Bank, and many of them had varied working experience from both the public and private sector as well as from international cooperation. Given the professional biographies of these actors, it is appropriate to call them entrepreneurs 'located at the interstices of several social networks, organizations, and institutions' (Campbell 2004: 178, italics removed).

The entrepreneur's familiarity with existing arrangements of public-private cooperation made it possible to present operational models of such arrangements to the decision-makers within INTOSAI and IFAC. This made the idea of a transnational regulatory network more appealing. An IFAC official had extensive experience with joint public and private standard-setting on auditing in Canada. Similarly, a member of INTOSAI's Auditing Standards Committee had experience with the UK system, where the National Audit Office makes use of auditing standards formulated by the non-governmental Auditing Practices Board. The British system of amending so called 'practice notes' to the auditing standards issued by a private standard-setter was to become a template for the cooperation between INTOSAI and IFAC.

The combined experiences of the institutional entrepreneurs from the different corners of the world of auditing are likely to have stimulated the new idea of creating a transnational regulatory network. Thus, it was initially an official from the World Bank who had previously worked in the US Government Accountability Office who conceived the idea of cooperation between INTOSAI and IFAC and who facilitated the initial contacts between both organizations (Holmerin 2002: 8).

In addition to working as an intermediary or a broker in the design of the network, the World Bank also commanded financial resources, which were used to support the formation of the network. In addition, a report made on the World Bank's initiative that compared IFAC and INTOSAI's auditing standards was issued in September 2002. The report was an updated version of a previous study made by IFAC's Public Sector Committee, and it concluded that IFAC and INTOSAI's auditing standards were generally compatible. Hence, the report suggested that there were no decisive barriers to collaboration on standard-setting between INTOSAI and IFAC.

The role of the different institutional entrepreneurs is considered further in the conclusion. Before doing so, the standards-setting procedure of the transnational regulatory network is briefly reviewed.

Manoeuvring a standardizing network

Formulating International Standards on Auditing (ISAs) that – according to IFAC – are supposed to be sector-neutral (i.e. equally applicable to the private, public, and voluntary sectors) is a complicated and delicate enterprise. The cycle of developing an ISA from project proposal to finalized standard often takes between eighteen months and two years and involves draft proposals formulated by a working group of experts, debates at IAASB meetings, and wider consultation through exposure drafts that are subject to external comments. Since the partnership between INTOSAI and IFAC has only been in full operation since 2004, there is, so far, only preliminary empirical evidence available on how the standard-setting is functioning, which actors gets their ideas into the final standards, and how they do so.

The first ISA revision that INTOSAI has taken part in developing all the way from the outset of the standard-setting process is ISA 230 on audit documentation. The comments on the ISA 230 exposure draft received by the IAASB were on the agenda at its meeting in Rome in June 2005. Figure 3.2 displays the distribution of different actors' change proposals that were received by the ISA 230 Working Group and those proposals that were successful in causing changes to a redrafted version of the standard.

Figure 3.2 shows that professional associations of accountants, which are grouped as either 'IFAC members bodies' or 'other organizations', produce the majority of comments filed to the ISA working group. The

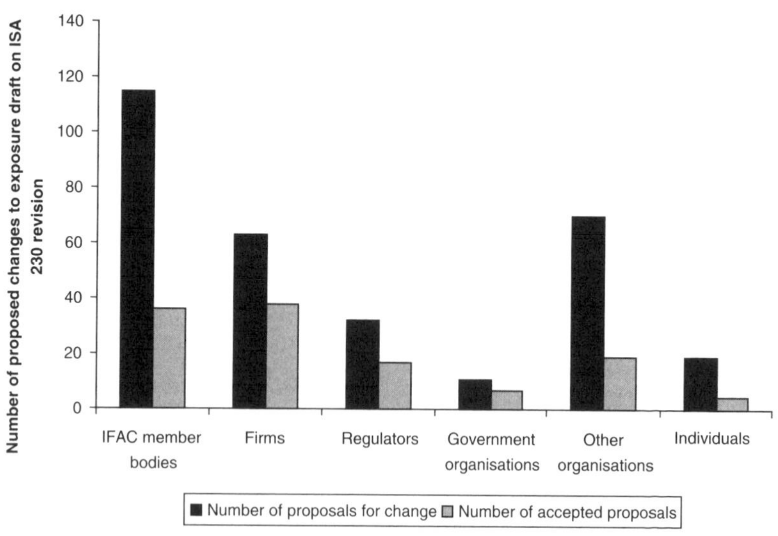

Figure 3.2:   Number of proposed changes to exposure draft on ISA 230 revision

Source: Author's creation based on information from background papers from the IAASB meeting in Rome in June 2005.

label 'firms' predominantly stands for the 'Big 4' accountancy firms and 'regulators' represents, among others, the Basel Committee on Banking Supervision, the European Commission, and the International Organization of Securities Commissions (IOSCO). It also appears from figure 2 that government organizations, such as SAIs and associations of public sector accountants, have been less keen on commenting on the ISA exposure draft. One reason for this could be that the idea of the new transnational regulatory setup has yet to become salient in the international SAI community. Another reason could be that some SAIs view the ISAs as having a distinctively Anglo-Saxon and private sector flavour that makes the standards less appealing. A third reason could be that the formulation of ISAs is a specialized undertaking with which only a limited amount of professionals possessing expertise and organizational resources engage (author's interview with SAI official).

Figure 3.2 also suggests that there are differences in how successful different types of organizations are in getting their ideas into the auditing standards. An interpretation of the figure may be that some organizations are listened to more than others when the standards are made. Whereas firms and regulators get their way with almost 60 per cent of their suggestions for changes to the standards, the remaining actors are only successful one third of the time. Comparisons of means tests of the data, however, show no significant differences between the groups with regard to whether their proposals are accepted or not. Thus, as of yet, there is no conclusive statistical evidence that some organizations are listened to more than others in IAASB's standard-setting procedure.

The group of government organizations stands out in the dataset on which the figure is based because of a high standard deviation, implying major differences on how successful different public sector organizations are with their comments. The US Government Accountability Office got approval of 70 per cent of its change proposals, making it one of the most successful organizations among all of those that commented on the ISA exposure draft. Accordingly, there are no clear signs that the public sector is kept away from influencing the standards produced.

As different types of organizations are likely to be ascribed different kinds of authority (Porter this volume), there is more to the matter of how the different organizations influence the standardization process. The formal procedure of commenting on exposure drafts to new standards is, thus, likely to be only the top of the iceberg. It is possible to distinguish between 'front-door influence', meaning commenting on exposure drafts, and 'back-door influence', in the sense of getting certain issues into new standard proposals through IAASB's Consultative

Advisory Group, seeking to influence who gets on the specific ISA working groups or through informal communication with the working group. Seeking this kind of 'back door' influence as early as possible in the standard-setting process may be much more effective than trying to influence the standards 'through the front door'. This is so because it is difficult to add new ideas to the standards once the general principles have been settled (author's interview with SAI official; author's interview with IFAC official). Because the standard-setting takes place between numerous actors with various positions on how the standards should be, the timing and utilization of different strategies, both 'back-door' and 'front-door' may be important for the relative success of the actors working in the transnational regulatory network. For those other organizations than the rich (firms) and powerful (regulators), 'back door' strategies may be particularly attractive

Conclusion: Rowing, steering, piloting, and mapmaking in the new age of regulatory capitalism

The chapter has shown how a transnational network for the governance of government auditing has emerged around the initiated collaboration between the two international standard-setters, INTOSAI and IFAC. The case of this network's creation fits well with an agency-oriented neo-institutional explanatory model. Thus, empirical evidence suggests that critical junctures in the development of INTOSAI and IFAC's respective standard-setting activities – spurred by the global financial crisis and major accountancy firm scandals – paved the way for institutional entrepreneurship. A group of skilful entrepreneurs, with experiences from both the public and private sector at both a national and international level, managed to convince the decision-making bodies of INTOSAI and IFAC to set up a transnational regulatory network. The evidence presented also indicates that there may be considerable differences as to who gets their will in the process of formulating standards in a transnational network.

Returning to the seafaring metaphor introduced in the beginning of the chapter, the case of transnational regulation of government financial auditing offers some material for amendment. The transnational regulation of government auditing does indeed take place in uneasy waters as the relative authority of various organizations is dispersed and in motion. Government auditing itself can be depicted as 'steering' given its role as internal regulation in states. However, some of the tasks of financial auditing in the public sector can also be viewed as 'rowing' – a task which some states prefer to do themselves and others have contracted out to private firms (Johnsen et al. 2004).

Going further with the maritime use of metaphors, the standards that guides government auditing can be portrayed as 'maps' that are crucial for which course is set (cf. Brunsson and Jacobsson 2000: 14–15). The partial delegation of 'map-making' or standard-setting authority from INTOSAI to the IAASB may imply that states get more comprehensive maps. However, it also means that most maps are produced by non-state actors such as private accountancy firms rather than SAIs.

The case described here also tells how the major international financial institutions saw it as their task to 'pilot' states through troubled waters in the wake of external shocks such as the Asian Financial crisis, by inducing states to follow ISAs, which the World Bank and the IMF considered as better and more comprehensive 'maps'. In this sense the World Bank has attempted to make SAIs more governable for the international financial institutions through the expansion of global auditing standards.

The instances of 'map-making' and 'piloting' can be referred to as governance at a distance (Rose and Miller 1992) or meta-governance (Kooiman 2000: 159–161), i.e. shaping the conditions for the governing activities of other actors – in this instance the standard-setting activities of the IAASB:

> Metagovernance involves managing the complexity, plurality, and tangled hierarchies found in prevailing modes of co-ordination. It is the organization of the conditions for governance and involves the judicious mixing of market, hierarchy, and networks to achieve the best possible outcomes from the viewpoint of those engaged in metagovernance. In this sense it also means the organization of the conditions of governance in terms of their structurally inscribed strategic selectivity, i.e., in terms of their asymmetrical privileging of some outcomes over others (Jessop 2003: 6).

As this chapter has shown, metagovernance is on the rise within the field of government auditing. For public and private sector organizations alike, the costs of being influential through the transnational regulatory network is likely to be that they, in turn, are being influenced by the other organizations in the network.

Notes

The author is very grateful to Rolf Elm-Larsen, Martin Marcussen, Tony Porter, Kerstin Sahlin-Andersson and the editors of this volume for guidance and advice.

1. Cluster analysis was introduced to studies of time series data by Campbell and Allen (2001) in an analysis of the development of taxation in the United States. The purpose of cluster analysis is to find simple patterns by calculating correlations in a data matrix. There are no given criteria for how many clusters the data should be divided into, but it is often useful to apply as few clusters as possible. In this case, a k-means cluster analysis was conducted using the greatest squared Euclidian distance between the clusters. Explorative analysis suggests a reasonable categorization of three clusters.
2. The EU has been a driving force in the international harmonization of auditing standards since large parts of the EU budget is also governed by its member states. Thus, the EU has an interest in common auditing standards.
3. Following an IFAC task force report issued on 2 November 2001, the IAPC was restructured and renamed the IAASB in 2002.

References

Abbott, A. (1997) 'On the Concept of the Turning Point', *Comparative Social Research*, 16: 85–105.

Ahlenius, I.-B. (2003) *Auditing Standards and Ethics – an INTOSAI Perspective.* Address at the XVII Annual Conference on New Developments in Government Financial Management for Government Financial Managers in Miami, April 2003. Stockholm: The Swedish National Audit Office.

Ahrne, G. and N. Brunsson (2001) *Metaorganisationer – identitet och auktoritet.* Score Rapportserie 2001:6. Stockholm: Stockholm Centre for Organizational Research.

Ahrne, G. and N. Brunsson (2004) 'Soft Regulation from an Organizational Perspective', in U. Möth (ed), *Soft Law in Governance and Regulation. An Interdisciplinary Analysis.* Cheltenham: Edward Elgar, 171–190.

Board of Audit and Inspection of Korea (2002) *Proceedings Seventeenth International Congress of Supreme Audit Institutions, Seoul, Korea, October 2001.* Seoul: Board of Audit and Inspection of Korea.

Braithwaite, J. and P. Drahos (2000) *Global Business Regulation.* Cambridge: Cambridge University Press.

Brunsson, N. and B. Jacobsson (2000) 'The Contemporary Expansion of Standardization', in N. Brunsson and B. Jacobsson (eds), *A World of Standards.* Oxford: Oxford University Press, 1–20.

Campbell, J. L. (2004) *Institutional Change and Globalization.* Princeton: Princeton University Press.

Campbell, J. L. and M. P. Allen (2001) 'Identifying Shifts in Policy Regimes. Cluster and Interrupted Time-series Analysis of U.S. Income Taxes', *Social Science History*, 25 (2): 187–216.

Cerny, P. G. (2000) 'Embedding global financial markets: securitization and the emerging web of governance', in K. Ronit and V. Schneider (eds), *Private Organizations in global Politics.* London: Routledge, 59–82.

Christensen, S., P. Karnøe, J. Strandgaard Pedersen and F. Dobbin (1997), 'Actors and Institutions: Editors' Introduction', *American Behavioral Scientist*, 40 (4): 392–396.

Clemens, E. S. and J. M. Cook (1999) 'Politics and institutionalism: Explaining durability and change', *Annual Review of Sociology*, 25: 441–66.

DiMaggio, P. (1988) 'Interest and Agency in Institutional Theory', in L. G. Zucker (ed), *Institutional Patterns and Organizations. Culture and Environment*. Cambridge: Ballinger, 3–22.

Djelic, M-L. and K. Sahlin-Andersson (eds) (2006) *Transnational Governance: Institutional Dynamics of Regulation*. Cambridge: Cambridge University Press.

Drori, G. S., J. W. Meyer and H. Hwang (2006) *Globalization and Organization: World Society and Organizational Change*. Oxford: Oxford University Press.

Dye, K. M. and R. Stapenhurst (1998) *Pillars of Integrity: The Importance of Supreme Audit Institutions in Curbing Corruption*. EDI Working Papers. Washington DC: Economic Development Institute of the World Bank.

European Court of Auditors (1998) *European Implementing Guidelines for the Intosai Auditing Standards*. Luxembourg: European Court of Auditors.

German Federal Court of Audit (1990) *13th INCOSAI 89 Conference Proceedings*. Frankfurt am Main: Federal Court of Audit.

Hall, R. B. and T. J. Biersteker (2002) 'The emergence of private authority in the international system', in R. B. Hall and T. J. Biersteker (eds), *The Emergence of Private Authority in Global Governance*. Cambridge: Cambridge University Press, 3–22.

Hancher, L. and M. Moran (1989) 'Organizing Regulatory Space', in L. Hancher and M. Moran (eds) *Capitalism, Culture, and Economic Regulation*. Oxford: Clarendon Press, 271–300.

Hayes, R., R. Dassen, A. Schilder and P. Wallage (2005) *Principles of Auditing. An Introduction to International Standards on Auditing*. Harlow: Prentice Hall.

Holmerin, K. (2002) *Restructuring and Expanding Government Auditing Standards – INTOSAI Perspective*. Address at the XVI Annual Conference on New Developments in Government Financial Management for Government Financial Managers in Miami, April 2002. Stockholm: The Swedish National Audit Office.

Hood, C. (1995) 'The "New Public Management" in the 1980s: Variations on a Theme', *Accounting, Organizations and Society*, 20 (2/3): 93–109.

Hood, C., C. Scott, O. James, G. Jones and T. Travers (1999) *Regulation Inside Government. Waste-Watchers, Quality Police, and Sleaze-Busters*. Oxford: Oxford University Press.

IAASB (2003) *Annual Report 2002*. New York: International Auditing and Assurance Standards Board.

IAASB (2004) *Annual Report 2003*. New York: International Auditing and Assurance Standards Board.

IAASB (2005a) *Handbook of International Auditing, Assurance, and Ethics Pronouncements. 2005 Edition*. New York: International Auditing and Assurance Standards Board.

IAASB (2005b) *Annual Report 2004*. New York: International Auditing and Assurance Standards Board.

IFAC (2003) *Rebuilding Public Confidence in Financial Reporting. An International Perspective*. New York: The International Federation of Accountants.

The International Federation of Accountants, www.ifac.org, accessed 1 November 2006.

International Journal of Government Auditing (1999) 'Inside INTOSAI', in *International Journal of Government Auditing*, 26 (4): 17.

International Organization of Supreme Audit Institutions, www.intosai.org, accessed 1 November 2006.

INTOSAI (1998) *Code of Ethics and Auditing Standards*. Vienna: International Organization of Supreme Audit Institutions.

INTOSAI (2004) *INTOSAI, 1953–2003*. Vienna: International Organization of Supreme Audit Institutions.

INTOSAI Auditing Standards Committee (1995) *Report on the Auditing Standards Committee Activities, Prepared for the XV INCOSAI, 25 September – 2 October2*. Canberra: Australian National Audit Office.

Islam, I. and A. Chowdhury (2000) *The Political Economy of East Asia. Post-crisis Debates*. Oxford: Oxford University Press.

Jacobsson, K. (2004) 'Between Deliberation and Discipline: Soft Governance in EU Employment Policy', in: U. Möth (ed.), *Soft Law in Governance and Regulation. An Interdisciplinary Analysis*. Cheltenham: Edward Elgar, 81–102.

Jessop, B. (2003) *Governance and Metagovernance: On Reflexivity, Requisite Variety, and Requisite Irony*, Department of Sociology, Lancaster University, Lancaster. Online at http://www.comp.lancs.ac.uk/sociology/papers/Jessop-Governance-and-Metagovernance.pdf, accessed on 24 February 2005.

Johnsen, Å., P. Meklin, L. Oulasvirta and J. Vakkuri (2004) 'Governance Structures and Contracting Out Municipal Auditing in Finland and Norway', *Financial Accountability & Management*, 20 (4): 445–477.

Jordana, J. and D. Levi-Faur (2004) 'The politics of regulation in the age of governance', in J. Jordana and D. Levy-Faur (eds) *The Politics of Regulation. Institutions and Regulatory Reforms for the Age of Governance*. Cheltenham: Edward Elgar, 1–28.

Kern, K. (2004) *Global Governance Through Transnational Network Organizations – The Scope and Limitations of Civil Society Self-Organization*. Discussion Paper SP IV 2004-102. Berlin: Wissenschaftszentrum Berlin für Sozialforschung.

Kerwer, D. (2005) 'Rules that Many Use: Standards and Global Regulation', *Governance*, 18 (4): 611–632.

Kooiman, J. (2000) 'Societal Governance: Levels, models, and Orders of Social-Political Interaction', in J. Pierre (ed), *Debating Governance. Authority, Steering, and Democracy*. Oxford: Oxford University Press, 138–164.

Loft, A. and C. Humphrey (2006) 'IFAC.ORG: Organizing the world of auditing with the help of a website', in H. K. Hansen and J. Hoff (eds) *Digital Governance://Networked Societies. Creating Authority, Community and Identity in a Globalizing World*. Copenhagen: NORDICOM/Samfundslitteratur Press.

Mahoney, J. (2001) 'Path-Dependent Explanations of Regime Change: Central America in Comparative Perspective', *Studies in Comparative International Development*, 36 (1): 111–141.

Marcussen, M. (2006) 'The Transnational Governance Network of Central Bankers', in M-L. Djelic and K. Sahlin-Andersson (eds) *Transnational Governance: Institutional Dynamics of Regulation*. Cambridge: Cambridge University Press, 180–204.

Marcussen, M. (2007) 'The Basel Committee as a Transnational Governance Network', in M. Marcussen and J. Torfing (eds) *Democratic Network Governance in Europe*. London: Palgrave-MacMillan, 214–231.

Mattli, W. (2003) 'Public and Private Governance in Setting International Standards', in M. Kahler and D. A. Lake (eds) *Governance in a Global Economy. Political Authority in Transition*. Princeton: Princeton University Press, 199–225.

Osborne, D. and T. Gaebler (1992) *Reinventing Government*. Reading: Addison-Wesley.

Philips, N., T. B. Lawrence and C. Hardy (2004) 'Discourse and Institutions', *Academy of Management Review*, 28 (4): 635–652.

Pierson, P. (2004) *Politics in Time. History, Institutions, and Social Analysis.* Princeton: Princeton University Press.

Pollitt, C. and G. Bouckaert (2004) *Public Management Reform: A Comparative Analysis. Second Edition.* Oxford: Oxford University Press.

Power, M. (1999) *The Audit Society: Rituals of Verification. Paperback edition.* Oxford: Oxford University Press.

Rechnungshof der Republik Österreich (1962) *IV. Internationaler Kongres der Obersten Rechnunskontrollbehörden 18. bis 26. Mai 1962.* Wien: Rechnungshof der Republik Österreich.

Risse, T. (forthcoming) 'Transnational Governance and Legitimacy', in A. Benz and I. Papadopoulos (eds), *Transnational Governance*. London: Routledge.

Rose, N. and P. Miller (1992) 'Political Power beyond the State: Problematics of Government', *British Journal of Sociology*, 43 (2): 173–205.

Rosenau, J. N. (2007) 'Governing the Ungovernable: The Challenge of a Global Disaggregation of Authority', *Regulation & Governance*, 1 (1).

Scott, C. (2004) 'The Politics of Regulation. Institutions and Regulatory Reforms for the Age of governance', in J. Jordana and D. Levy-Faur (eds) *The Politics of Regulation. Institutions and Regulatory Reforms for the Age of Governance.* Cheltenham: Edward Elgar, 145–174.

Tamm Hallström, K. (2004) *Organizing International Standardization. ISO and the IASC in Quest of Authority.* Cheltenham: Edward Elgar.

United States General Accounting Office (2003a) *Survey of Supreme Audit Institutions (SAIs).* Report delivered at the INTOSAI Auditing Standard Committee meeting in Bratislava, Slovakia, in September 2003. Online at: http://asc.rigsrevisionen.dk/composite-41.htm, accessed on 22 August 2005.

United States General Accounting Office (2003b) *Government Auditing Standards 2003 Revision.* June 2003. Washington DC: United States General Accounting Office.

Wolfensohn, J. D. (2004) 'Accountability Begins at Home', *International Journal of Government Auditing*, 31(1): 1–3.

World Bank / IMF (2000) *International Financial Architecture. An Update of Bank Activities.* DC/2000-20. Washington DC: Development Committee. Joint Ministerial Committee of the Boards of Governors of the Bank and the Fund on the Transfer of Real Resources to Developing Countries.

Ånerud, K. (2004) 'Developing International Auditing Standards: Cooperation between INTOSAI and the International Federation of Accountants', *International Journal of Government Auditing*, 31(4): 20–24.

4
Internet Regulation – Multi-Stakeholder Participation and Authority

Mikkel Flyverbom and Sven Bislev

The Internet is often described as a domain where privatized self-regulation has taken root, to the extent that other authoritative actors – states in particular – have refrained from getting involved in a coordinated manner. In arguing for the difficulty that states have in governing the Internet, Spar writes, 'The only way for governments to rule cyberspace is through coordinated international agreement – an ambitious and highly unlikely prospect' (Spar 1999: 32). From her perspective, governments are backing away from the regulation of cyberspace and the private sector is moving in. The explanations for the position of Internet regulation at the frontiers of 'private authority' are often related to technical features and their globalizing and decentralizing implications. In these accounts, 'cyberspace, unlike governments, slip seamlessly and nearly unavoidably across national boundaries' (Spar 1999: 32). Furthermore, '[t]here are literally hundreds of thousands of networks that make up the global Internet', which suggests that this 'vast collaboration of many components' is required to operate on the basis of cooperation, and cannot be centrally controlled (Cerf 2003). Finally, from a legal point of view, the Internet is often seen as difficult to regulate: it challenges the basic building blocks of regulatory systems such as a defined space to regulate, a national jurisdiction, and the possibility of assigning personal, legal responsibility to identifiable citizens (Lessig 1999).

It is wrong, however, to infer that no regulation takes place, and it is our contention that this is a model case of the development of an entangled (Porter this volume) plurality of public and private authority.

Myriad technical and private sector bodies take decisions with far-reaching consequences for the shape and development of the Internet. Codes (Lessig 1999) and protocols (Galloway 2004) set out to regulate what can and cannot be done. National governments often try to exert a degree of national, direct control over content, such as the unsuccessful attempts at establishing the US Communications Decency Act, which was passed in 1995, and then withdrawn in 1997 on the grounds that it violated the First Amendment's guarantee of freedom of speech. For the US, implementation of such laws proved difficult in a privatized telecommunications universe. Other governments retain the old monopolies and can do more. The Chinese government regularly closes down access to particular sites that are deemed unhealthy for Chinese nationals (Deibert 2003; Mengin 2004). Dictators like the Nepalese king in 2004 likewise clamp down on communications, sometimes effectively strangling the Internet in their territory. In the realm of Internet content, a number of states have pushed the content-providing industry to develop codes of conduct, standards, and other self-regulatory tools (Price and Verhulst 2000). But these attempts at national regulation have been sporadic and *ad hoc*.

In this chapter we set out to investigate the emergence of Internet regulation as a global, political issue area in the context of the United Nations. Since the late 1990s, governments have come to realize that despite its challenges for regulation, the Internet is too important to be left to privatized self-regulation. Recently, governments, as well as a number of non-state actors, have taken up the issue of Internet regulation and sought to develop an international agreement. The most significant initiative, and the one we are following here, took place in the context of the United Nations and revolved around the two-phased World Summit on the Information Society (WSIS). Our empirical data consist of participant observations, interviews, mailing lists, and documentary research, collected systematically during the more than three-year-long period where the UN has actively convened discussions about Internet regulation.

Although the process did not lead to a new regulatory framework, we argue that it made Internet regulation into an object of global governance, and allowed a new configuration of state and non-state actors to emerge. The chapter sheds light on how the disaggregation of authority plays out in the area of the global governance of the Internet. In particular, it shows how the process has both spurred a reconfiguration of the involvement of different actors and led to a clash between different modes of governance, in particular intergovernmentalism and self-regulation.

Finally, the chapter shows how multi-stakeholder participation was introduced and accepted as a key governmental technology which invited a number of participants to become entangled in a web of inter-relations. By representing governments, international organizations, the private sector, and civil society groups as 'stakeholders', this governmental technology was able to operate through strategies of cooperation and consensus. In this web, communicative interactions among the participants were made possible, and otherwise incompatible positions of governance were bracketed – at least for a while.

Below, we briefly introduce the analytical framework that we use in the investigation. We then flesh out, first, how the UN-initiated discussion about Internet regulation came about; second, we throw some light on the processes through which the different actors were constructed and engaged as 'stakeholders' in relation to Internet regulation and the modes of coordination came about; and, third, discuss the way in which this issue area has been institutionalized as a field of multi-stakeholder participation and its ramifications for governance in terms of the emergence of entangled public and private authority.

A governmentality approach

Inspired by the work of the late Foucault, a wealth of theoretical and empirical contributions have developed *governmentality* as an analytical approach capable of grasping and conceptualizing new forms of governance and new configurations of authority beyond the classical institutional dichotomy of public and private (see Hansen; Larner, this volume). In the case of Internet regulation, a governmentality perspective sheds light on how different actors are enlisted as 'stakeholders' in forms of rule which revolve around empowerment, cross-sectoral cooperation, and consensus. This focus on the advanced liberal forms of governing is shared by many recent contributions to governmentality studies (Dean 1999; Larner and Waters 2004; Abrahamsen 2004). The governmentality literature is broadly concerned with the role of power and knowledge in regulation, and in particular with the 'technologies' and 'political rationalities' that structure governmental activities (Dean 1999; Miller and Rose 1990; Rose and Miller 1992). An analytics of governmentality allows for a focus on relations more than on actors and structures, and invites us to single out the mundane practices involved in governance as units of analysis (Bevir 2003; Flyverbom 2006; Hoff 2003).

Our analytical framework consists of three concepts taken from the governmentality literature – *problematization, governmental technology,* and *political rationality* – which are put to use in the analysis of the interactions taking place among the involved groups of stakeholders. To use a governmentality approach implies that we focus on how the involved stakeholders construct Internet regulation as an object of governance, as well as how these interactions are organized around particular technologies and rationalities. We use the term *problematization* to capture the complex of concerns which has given rise to the recent debates over Internet regulation in the context of the UN. Foucault described his entire work as concerned with problematizations, i.e. 'how and why were very different things in the world [such as madness, crime, and sexuality] gathered together, characterized, analyzed, and treated' as a problem (Foucault 1985: 65–66). Dean, in line with other governmentality theorists, argues that 'an analysis of government directs us to examine the different and particular contexts in which governing is called into question, in which actors and agents of all sorts must pose the question of how to govern' (Dean 1999: 27). In our analysis, we use the term *problematization* to characterize the particular processes, moment, and context in and through which a number of concerns, ideas, and groups facilitated the emergence of the Internet as a 'target of social regulation' (Foucault 1985: 65–66).

As noted, the governmentality perspective suggests practices as the objects of analysis. Practices are carried out via *governmental technologies*, that is, the 'humble and mundane mechanisms, which appear to make it possible to govern' (Miller and Rose 1990: 8). These, in turn, fuel and are fuelled by *political rationalities*, i.e. 'the changing discursive fields within which the exercise of power is conceptualized, the moral justifications for particular ways of exercising power by diverse authorities, notions of the appropriate forms, objects and limits of politics, and conceptions of the proper distribution of such tasks among secular, spiritual, military and familial sectors' (Rose and Miller 1992: 175).

It is on the backdrop of these analyses that we conceptualize the *governmentality* of Internet regulation. In our case, we note that the public authority forming the backbone of modern state governance is being challenged, changed, and complemented by other forms of authority, and that the emerging governmentality in this case is one that operates in a very different way from classical regulation.

The Internet as an object of global governance

Technically, the Internet can be distinguished from other information and communication technologies (ICT) by its reliance on a particular technical platform, and thus be defined as 'the global data communication system formed by the interconnection of public and private telecommunication networks' using the Internet protocols, such as IP, TCP, and DNS (Mathiason et al. 2004: 6). Internet regulation is part of the larger policy complex of ICT policies (Braithwaite and Drahos 2000; Siochrú and Girard 2002). Parts of our discussion will inevitably relate to that broader context, but we focus on the regulation of the Internet. Older ICTs are coordinated by the International Telecommunication Union (ITU), but the Internet is subject to a multiplicity of dispersed activities. In the context of the UN-sponsored World Summit on the Information Society (WSIS), however, the discussion about the proper place for Internet regulation to be discussed and carried out re-emerged – to the degree that it became the main issue on the agenda during the final negotiations and made it to the headlines of the world's major newspapers.[1]

Historically, the Internet has had a fascinating trajectory. The short and rapidly developing history of the Internet began in the research community, where the US Defense Department initiated the first attempts at connecting computers and sending data packages. In the first stages of the Internet, when it was still run by researchers and technicians, it only existed inside the US research system. Most decisions were made by the architects and technicians behind the key technologies that made its emergence possible. Technical groups and private bodies simply developed and coordinated all the needed functions without interference, and continue to do so today. One such body, the Internet Engineering Task Force (IETF), single-handedly developed the used standards, and until the mid-nineties, the allocation of names and addresses, such as .com and .edu, was carried out by a single man, Jon Postel, who ran another key administrative body, the Internet Assigned Numbers Authority (IANA) (Abbate 1999; Hofmann 2005). Technical standards have historically been produced through a decision-making process, where participants are neither elected or representative, nor authorized by a sovereign state. They operate according to expectations of openness, transparency and professionalism (Frankel 2004: 93). So, while the Internet was initiated by the US government, its development was left in the hands of the users and producers – thus becoming an area where private regulation plays a central role. For many years, European governments showed only very little interest in the Internet, and the US kept its hands off, and therefore the Internet flourished more or less without any sort of governmental intervention.

In the mid-nineties, there were attempts at building an ITU-based multilateral governance system, but the US government opted for self-regulation, carried out by the technical community and the private sector. The most visible body created to manage the core resources of the Internet is the Internet Corporation for Assigned Names and Numbers (ICANN), which operates on the basis of a memorandum of understanding with the US Department of Commerce. This body manages the domain name system of the Internet and the root servers. The widespread discussions about the legitimacy of ICANN – as a private organization under contract to the US government – has not only brought public and political attention to the issue, but may also be the spark that ignited growing concerns about the importance of the Internet, and made the UN and the ITU convene the World Summit on the Information Society (WSIS) (Klein 2003).

The WSIS and related activities around the UN – the creation of the UN ICT Task Force (UNICTTF) and the Working Group on Internet Governance (WGIG) – have focussed the interest on how to govern the global information society. It has become clear that with close to one billion Internet users, this is an emergent transnational issue area which must be addressed politically. The WSIS process provides a fascinating laboratory in which phenomena such as the creation of an object of governance, governance principles and arrangements, as well as the constellation of authorities, can be investigated. This broad and intense interest in the politics of the Internet can be seen as constituting a problematization that questions the very activity and logic of governance in the area, the object to be governed as well as the roles and responsibilities of the organizations involved in, and relevant to, the regulation and running of the Internet.

Mechanisms for stakeholder interactions

The UN-initiated problematization of Internet regulation – that is the attempts at reconfiguring modes of governance as well as the constellation of authorities – was initiated at the beginning of the WSIS process, gained momentum in the UNICTTF and was placed centre stage with the creation of WGIG. These two bodies constitute significant experiments in bringing together not only member states, but also business, civil society groups, and international organizations in collaborative, dialogical forums. Like the more well-known UN Global Compact, these bodies revolve around learning, best practice, and other soft forms of governance. They do not deliver policies and binding agreements, but facilitate dialogues and attempts at reaching a rough consensus among groups with very different concerns. Both of these bodies have been created at the margins of the UN system to enable the participation of non-state actors on an equal footing with government representatives.

These two bodies have established multi-stakeholder participation as a key governmental technology in the area of Internet regulation. Their attempts at facilitating and stabilizing stakeholder interactions have revolved around such initiatives as dialogues and consultations. The interactions facilitated by these provide important insight into the concerns, proposals and aspirations of myriad stakeholders that have emerged as part of the problematization of Internet regulation. In the following, we investigate the ways in which multi-stakeholder participation positioned the different actors as stakeholders around a governmental field and invited them to interact and collectively construct the Internet as an object of global governance with socio-political relevance and potential.

The first group of actors, *governments*, has a natural claim to *public* authority and would seem the natural regulators and power holders in such an infrastructural area, fraught as it is with issues of economic, political, cultural, and security importance. The problematization of Internet regulation and the emergence of the governmental technology of multi-stakeholder participation were driven by a joint realization on the part of governments and the UN alike that this would allow both of them to play a role in Internet regulation. Governments have – by far – been the most visible group of stakeholders in all of the UN-initiated Internet regulation activities, and delivered both the majority of participants and interventions at meetings. Their expressed concerns included the 'digital divide' between rich and poor nations, the fear of being left out of what is becoming the most important global technological field, and a wish to secure the future national sovereignty over, access to, and stability of, the Internet. The initial push for intergovernmental regulation of the Internet came primarily from developing countries, such as India, China, Syria, and Brazil. Unhappy with what they saw as unilateral US control of the Internet, these countries called for Internet regulation to be placed within the ITU, where these countries have all the benefits of an intergovernmental organization: established procedures giving only national delegations the right to vote and a central location easily reached by the Geneva missions. But also issues relating to Internet content, such as spam, Internet crime, and immorality worried a number of nations. While very quiet at the outset, and seemingly in favour of maintaining status quo, the European Union finally presented a proposal for the creation of a global oversight body under the auspices of the UN, but not within the ITU. The US was, with a few exceptions, absent and silent on the issue of Internet regulation as it was discussed within the UN, and even declined the offer to become a member of WGIG (Executive Coordinator WGIG: 2005).

The second major group of actors, *business*, is the main proprietor of *private* authority. Businesses took part in the problematization and resulting attempts at reconfiguring Internet regulation in a number of ways, particularly through participating in the activities of UNICTTF, WGIG, and WSIS. The International Chamber of Commerce (ICC) has played a key role, coordinating business activities during the WSIS via the Coordinating Committee of Business Interlocutors (CCBI) and participating in the WGIG. The ICC sought to shape the work of the UN ICT Task Force by having its representatives function as vice-chairmen of the body, and by being a very active participant in all the important Internet regulation meetings held by the UN in 2003–2005. Other business groups and private, technical organizations such as the Internet Society and ICANN have taken part in these activities, although in a less consistent manner. But also individual businesses such as Hewlett-Packard and Cisco Systems have deemed the issue of Internet regulation and the broader WSIS issues so important that they took part in the relevant fora and meetings.

The immediate reason for business to take part has been the concerns over the future growth and stability of the Internet, which has become central to commerce and business operations (ICC interview 2005). Particularly ICC and Cisco, but also IBM and smaller ICT companies, argued against governmental interventions in the management of the Internet. Furthermore, business also tied in their concerns about the potential damage of a new Internet regulation framework with the broader global information society issues addressed during WSIS and in the two bodies. In particular, large ICT companies used their engagement in these discussions to highlight their Corporate Social Responsibility (CSR) activities (see Blasco and Zølner, this volume). To a certain extent, CSR is part of the naturalization of the idea of business as a political institution and arena (Deetz 2003: 175). It also constitutes an element in the blurring of distinctions between public and private and between industrial and societal regulation (see Hansen, this volume; Siochrú and Girard 2002: 5–10).

For business, the focus on CSR activities was a way to show governments and other stakeholders the benefits of letting self-regulation and market-driven approaches prevail (Hewlett-Packard representative in UNICTTF 2003). Business participants sought to downplay the importance of Internet regulation and called for attention to broader issues, such as infrastructure, access, and capacity-building. The discourse of the participating corporations and business organizations has been ambivalent – a mixture of social responsibility and liberal laissez-faire (see Bislev and Flyverbom 2007). Business was an important part of the activities surrounding Internet regulation, but their activities were more focussed on maintaining the status quo than on concrete, positive, inputs to the creation of a new global governance arrangement for the Internet.

The third group of actors to intervene in the context of multi-stakeholder processes within the UN, *civil society*, was made up of NGOs, UN advocacy groups, Internet activists, researchers, and technical and professional groups, most of which have a longstanding interest in Internet-related issues. These groups act on a basis of scientific and moral authority, and a number of them have been involved in ICANN and other existing Internet regulation arrangements. As these groups came together for the first time in this UN-sponsored governance process (Flyverbom 2006; Mueller et al. 2007), the prevalent concern was to make sure that neither business self-regulation – given its negative consequences for those parts of the world that do not offer business opportunities – nor intergovernmental regulation – given its bureaucratic and controlling tendencies – would be allowed to dominate the area of Internet regulation. As the second most important group in terms of developing the Internet, civil society saw itself as a key stakeholder, but had to establish its own position by means of commitment, enthusiasm, and time. The reliance on this resource, combined with references to the role of this sector as representatives of the global public interest and the high level of expertise held by many members of the group, forms the key strategies employed by civil society. More than anyone else, this group has advocated and sought to establish multi-stakeholder participation as the overarching principle of Internet regulation. And in this respect, the group has been very successful. Through persistent participation and precise interventions, this group functioned as the source and designer of many of the procedural features of WGIG and the shape of the activities taking place within this forum. One of the most important groupings was the Internet Governance Caucus, which – enabled by an email list and a core group of very active members – managed not only to gain almost all the civil society seats in WGIG, but also to play a central role in writing up the final report and delivering many of the final proposals.

For the fourth category of actors, *international organizations*, authority resides in their mixed nature. While most are strongly influenced by their state sponsors, international organizations are typically public, private, and specialist/scientific at the same time. For the specialized UN agencies (WIPO, ITU, ILO, UNESCO, and the World Bank), the governmentalization of the Internet provided an opportunity to treat this area as a global governance issue like so many others: different nations held incompatible views on how to govern in this area, and therefore there was a need for a broad discussion, involving also – in line with a general trend in the last decade – the participation of NGOs and businesses. But this is not to say that all international organizations sought to function as disinterested facilitators. As the agency leading the entire WSIS process, ITU attempted to steer the scope and direction of the work of WGIG towards only ICANN-related issues, but was met with strong resistance from many other participants. ITU was perceived by many to be bureaucratic, slow and dominated by developing country interests, which may be why most participants, except for developing countries, resisted a major role to be played by the ITU in Internet regulation. So rather than gain a role as the home for Internet regulation, ITU has – along with the UNICTTF Secretariat and the WGIG Secretariat – worked as a facilitator for the governance process, bringing the participants together, and arranging the different meetings and activities. The other UN agencies used their invitation as stakeholders to bring attention to their respective areas of concern as they intersected with Internet governance. Some of this work was defensive, as when the World Intellectual Property Organization (WIPO) sought to maintain its control over all issues related to intellectual property rights, strongly supported by both the private sector and the majority of governments. But others, like UNESCO and ILO, brought more general principles and concerns such as freedom of expression, workers' rights, and multilingualism to the table.

While these different groups entered the problematization of Internet regulation from very different angles and with very different concerns and aims, they ended up collectively constructing the Internet as an object of global governance with broad-based relevance and wide-reaching ramifications for development, human rights and other socio-political concerns. This process was made possible because of the reliance on multi-stakeholder participation as a governmental technology that was able to transform a myriad of groups into *stakeholders*. The significance of multi-stakeholder forms of governance thus lies in their ability to connect and reconstruct actors around particular technologies and rationalities. Most, if not all, participants came to see multi-stakeholder participation as a useful way of formulating and stabilizing the relationship between private and public, economic and political actors. While a number of other governmental technologies – such as subsidiarity, public-private partnerships, and state control – were proposed, what emerged as the key mode of governance was this. This governmental technology facilitated the move from a clash between those calling for a traditional intergovernmental agreement and those in favour of the continuation of self-regulation towards an acceptance of the need for hybrid forms of governance, where intergovernmental and self-regulatory approaches could co-exist. Likewise, there was a growing acceptance that a new division of labour among the different stakeholders was necessary and beneficial. For instance, the Indian delegation, which had previously insisted on an intergovernmental institution to be in charge of Internet regulation, ended up arguing that this 'is not to say' that governments and an intergovernmental organization 'should decide on every minor little detail' (Indian delegation 2005, WGIG consultations). Similarly, business, while never favouring the creation of a new body to address Internet regulation, moved from the image of 'plumbing' and unproblematic self-regulation by users and companies (IBM representative 2004), towards an acceptance of multi-stakeholder participation as the preferred governmental technology to be used when addressing the global governance of the Internet.

With the final WSIS decision to create a UN-based 'forum for multi-stakeholder policy dialogue' (Tunis Agenda 2005), namely the Internet Governance Forum, multi-stakeholder participation has been given new momentum and institutional anchorage in the UN.

Political rationalities and the configuration of authority

The reliance on multi-stakeholder participation, both as a discourse and a governmental technology, was strengthened during the problematization of Internet regulation. As such it not only provided a mode of governance that most participants could subscribe to, but also worked to set the principles and targets for this emerging transnational issue area. This section delves into the discussions about Internet regulation that multi-stakeholder participation facilitated. These discursive manifestations of the emergence of both an *object* – and a *mode* – of governance give important insights into the political rationalities at play.

One salient cluster of discussions revolved around the need for governance, the model of governance to apply, and the possible outcomes of such different models. For instance, it was discussed what kind of governance the Internet should be subjected to – i.e. (technical) *coordination*, (top-down, governmental) *regulation* or (soft, multi-stakeholder) *governance* were suggested. The ICC, for instance, demanded that a clear line should be drawn between technical coordination and public policy making, and that most of what was referred to as Internet governance in the context of the UN should rather be thought of as technical coordination and not politicized and subjected to governmental oversight or regulation. The most persistent discursive construction used by those in favour of status quo in Internet regulation was to argue 'if it ain't broke, don't fix it' (Chairman of the Board of ICANN 2004), in an attempt to depict Internet regulation as a misconception, to be replaced by technical coordination or 'plumbing'. The implicated consequence, namely that it should be taken off the political agenda in WSIS and elsewhere, was challenged consistently by developing countries, civil society organizations, and researchers (APC member of WGIG 2005; Mueller et al. 2004). And while calls for maintaining the status quo were heard all along, the process made it clear to most of those involved that Internet regulation could not be done away with, but needed to be addressed and taken seriously, also by ICANN (Chairman of ICANN 2005). The refusal of this attempt to do away with Internet regulation altogether was the very basis for the creation of WGIG. Rather than simple technical coordination or 'plumbing', most of what a body like ICANN does should be seen as having ramifications for the public, and therefore should be thought of as forms of governance. One of the main outcomes of the UN problematization of Internet regulation was that the area was established as political and as an object of global governance – as opposed to something that could not or should not be subjected to regulation at all (Jensen 2005).

As shown by Lessig (1999: 24 ff.), the construction of the Internet as outside the reach of regulation has been very common among its users and creators. An insistence on the uniqueness of the Internet was used as an argument used to argue against giving ITU the regulatory authority. The Internet, it was argued, is so different in terms of architecture (end-to-end, not broadcast, etc) that it cannot be compared to other telecommunications activities, not to mention economic or other activities (Pisanty 2005). The uniqueness argument was employed in particular by the groups involved in existing Internet regulation arrangements to construct its governance as outside the reach and mandate of ITU and other intergovernmental forms of regulation. In these discussions, a specific technical- governance discourse emerged, using technical features of the Internet as the model for the form of governance to be developed. It was argued that

- governance should be 'layered' like the Internet (Chairman of the Board of ICANN 2004);
- the governance of the network of networks making up the Internet should be a 'mechanism of mechanisms' (Kleinwächter 2005); and

- 'governance should be as flexible as the Internet itself' (de la Chapelle 2004);
- an 'Internet governance protocol' needs to be developed, that is, a governance system based on or modelled upon the suite of protocols[2], TCP/IP, that makes connectivity among different computers possible (Kleinwächter 2004).

Frequently, when a new ICT emerges, policymakers tend to accept blindly the '"revolutionary" rhetoric that often accompanies a new communications technology' (Napoli 2001: 2). The result is that new regulatory arrangements become 'technologically particularistic' because they are crafted on the basis of the characteristics of the individual technologies (ibid: 1). This was also the case in the UN discussions about Internet regulation, where technical arguments were used to justify political action, and regulation was constructed as a mirror of the technology it is supposed to affect (Napoli 2001). The discussions reflect what Barry (2001) terms the emergence of a technological society, where technology becomes the model for political action. The argument about essential difference or uniqueness is another well-known feature of the regulation of new technologies.

Other participants argued against, pointing out that the use of technology as a model for political action neglects many of the concerns that drive public regulations: the dangers of abuse, the emergence of new forms of power, the consequences for several areas of societal life. Developing countries argued against the uniqueness position. According to the representative of the Indian delegation, for instance, 'there is nothing uniquely different about the Internet that dictates a completely different oversight mechanism at the global level compared to various other fields of human activity' (Indian delegation 2005). These voices were, however, minor in comparison to the broadly accepted view of the Internet as unique.

In terms of the perceived outcomes, the discussions revolved around the potentials and problems of regulating the Internet. The business community saw the problems of Internet regulation as one of securing the transactions that made money for them – but also as one of allowing the freedom of technical development, a process that allows the hardware and software providers to push their products without barriers. The absence of government regulation was maintained as the key to the future growth of the Internet. Civil society organizations argued against what they saw as a 'controlling approach to Internet governance' (APC member of WGIG, 2005) and proposed instead to think of Internet governance as a form of *'protection'* (Kleinwächter 2005) and an 'enabling' of this communication technology (Doria 2005). It would be disastrous, they said, to force a 'hierarchical top-down model' unto the 'decentralized structure on which the Internet was so successfully built' (ISOC representative 2005). Conversely, developing countries in particular used the argument of unequal access to emphasize a need for national and intergovernmental control. Out of these discussions emerged a distinction between *control* and *protection* of the Internet. This opposition to 'control' must be distinguished from the early descriptions of the Internet as a space that cannot be regulated: it is more concerned with the question of how to design an appropriate and Internet-sensitive regulatory framework than with whether or not the Internet can or cannot be regulated.

The political rationalities that characterize the discussions about Internet regulation and tie in most directly with multi-stakeholder participation as a governmental technology revolve around three dimensions:

- the importance of facilitating collaboration and consensus among stakeholders, rather than only relying on existing intergovernmental mechanisms;
- an interest in the facilitation of governance, of establishing procedures without regulating substantial issues;
- a particular conception of sectorial boundaries and the roles and responsibilities of different types of actors, including the need to reconfigure these into a collaborative multi-stakeholder effort.

With regard to the first of these dimensions, the discussions about Internet regulation were initiated and convened by the UN in a soft-handed manner, where very few substantive proposals and procedural guidelines were given. In this way, the process followed a political rationality representing governance as first and foremost a matter of facilitation and brokerage. Rather than attempting to assume control of the Internet – a highly unlikely prospect anyway – the UN found a place for itself as the convener of the sort of 'institutionalized cooperation' (Cutler et al. 1999: 334) often found to be a distinguishing feature of private authority. Through the facilitation and institutionalization of interactions and cooperation among different, existing authoritative actors, the UN was able to position itself as an authority in the area of global Internet regulation. In this way the UN has developed its role from convening meetings between public, intergovernmental actors, all

coming with their own brand of authority, to connecting and institu-
tionalizing the entanglement of the four types of authority that Porter
refers to in this volume, namely scientific, moral, private, and public ones.

With regard to the issue of *sectors, roles, and responsibilities*, the process
constructed and revolved around a conception of four legitimate groups
of stakeholders: states, businesses, NGOs, and international organizations. Clearly, this breaks with the idea of representative democracy and
seeks to replace it with a participatory notion of democracy. But it also
gives insights into the political rationality and the distribution of roles
and responsibilities to which the process gave rise. Multi-stakeholder
participation worked not only, even primarily, to pool different kinds of
resources that would make the whole become greater than its parts.
Rather, it functioned as a way to make communication among adver-
saries possible. The kind of interaction made possible by constellations
of stakeholders able to agree on a governmental technology – multi-
stakeholder participation – was, however, fragile and relied on the
ability and willingness to find common ground. In this respect, we may
think of the process as enabling the entanglement of different political
rationalities and discourses. But what made this entanglement possible
was not a deep, negotiated consensus but a way of working that allowed
the key concepts to remain 'polysemic' (Barry 2001), i.e. vague and open
to multiple interpretations.

Conclusion

The WSIS negotiations on Internet regulation, which deadlocked
already during the first part in Geneva in 2003, ended with a US refusal
to relinquish control of the core resources. Also business and NGOs
spoke against the demands made by developing countries – like China
and India – that ITU should take over the control of the Internet. Thus,
the November 2005 WSIS meeting did not produce a new governance
arrangement, but an agreement was made to create a global forum
where all stakeholders can discuss Internet regulation, but not interfere
in existing regulatory activities. This Internet Governance Forum thus
will have no regulatory 'teeth', but ensure that the issue continues to be
addressed in a comprehensive, transparent and inclusive manner.

The main outcome of the problematization of Internet regulation was
the acceptance that all aspects of Internet regulation, even the management of technical features, may have political consequences and should
be addressed in an open, international, and inclusive forum. In this way,
the ICT domain has been transformed from an obscure, technical, and

dispersed set of activities to a highly visible socio-political, fairly integrated, and collectively addressed issue area. Thus, also Internet regulation has been constructed as a regulatory issue with far-reaching consequences for broad issues like development, gender, and human rights (Flyverbom 2006; Jørgensen 2006).

With regard to the mode of governance and entanglement of authority that the process gave rise to, it is a key finding that multi-stakeholder participation emerged and was institutionalized as the primary governmental technology in discussions about the global governance of the Internet. More than anything, this mechanism allowed for a diverse group of stakeholders to coalesce around a common concern, even if their proposed solutions differed radically. The Foucauldian concept of 'governmentality' points to the existence of a plurality of rationalities of governance. Each of them has its own logic, its own terminology, its own historicity and context (Miller and Rose 1990; Burchell 1991; Rose and Miller 1992; Barry 1996; Rose 1999). The elements of the governmentality pointed out here centre around a view of governance as brokerage and attempts at reconfiguring authority in Internet regulation. Multi-stakeholder participation is an important facet of this emergent governmentality, which, in the context of a late-liberal, post-welfare society, puts little emphasis on the public-private distinction, and whose notions of democracy are assuming new forms (Rose and Miller 1992; Dean 1999). Instead of viewing popular representation and democracy as the only or most legitimate form of authority, the UN-initiated problematization of Internet regulation allowed for entangled authority arrangements to emerge as the most legitimate way of dealing with this new object of global governance. Our investigation shows how Internet regulation has been recast along the lines of advanced liberal modes of governance, which work by engaging different actors as stakeholders in attempts to problematize and reconfigure issues of socio-political importance. The institutionalization of the governmental technology facilitating such cross-sectorial interactions and entanglements – in the Internet Governance Forum – shows that the problematization and governmentalization of the Internet have the power to lure governments and private actors into working together in new ways, as well as to challenge preconceived notions of regulation and democracy.

Notes

1. See, for instance, 'Compromise reached in Tunis on Internet Control', *International Herald Tribune*, 16 November 2005; 'A compromise of Sorts on

Internet Control, *The New York Times*, 16 November 2005 and; 'Tunis Talks find Internet Stalemate', *The Times UK*, 16 November 2005.
2. A computer protocol is 'a set of recommendations and rules that outline specific technical standards' (Galloway 2004: 6), such as those used on the World Wide Web, and 'has succeeded as a dominant principle for organization of distributed networks' (ibid: 120).

References

Abbate, J. (1999) *Inventing the Internet*. Cambridge, MA: MIT Press.

Abrahamsen, R. (2004) 'The Power of Partnerships in Global Governance', *Third World Quarterly*, 25(8): 1453–1467.

APC (2005) Personal interview with member of WGIG, representing the Association for Progressive Communications (APC). UNICTTF meeting, Dublin, 14 April.

Barry, A. et al. (eds) (1996) *Foucault and Political Reason: Liberalism, neo-liberalism, and rationalities of Government*. Chicago: University of Chicago Press.

Barry, A. (2001) *Political Machines: Governing a Technological Society*. London and New York: Athlone Press.

Bevir, M. (2003) 'Governance and Interpretation: What are the Implications of Postfoundationalism?', *Public Administration*, 82(3): 605–627.

Bislev, S. and M. Flyverbom (forthcoming 2007) 'Transnational Private Governance of the Internet – the Roles of Business', in J.C. Graz, and A. Nölke (eds), *Transnational Private Governance and its Limits*. London: Routledge.

Braithwaite, J. and P. Drahos (2000) *Global Business Regulation*. Cambridge University Press: Cambridge.

Burchell, G. et al. (eds) (1991) *The Foucault Effect: Studies in Governmental Rationality*. Hemel Hempstead: Harvester-Wheatsheaf.

Cerf, V. G. (2003) 'Foreword: Who Rules the Net?', in A. Thierer and C. W. Crew Jr., *Who Rules the Net? Internet Governance and Jurisdiction*. Washington DC: Cato Institute.

Chairman of the Board of ICANN (2004) Intervention at UNICTTF Global Forum on Internet Governance, UN, New York.

Chairman of ICANN (2005) Letter to the Chair of the Governmental Advisory Committee of ICANN, available online at http://www.icann.org/correspondence/cerf-tarmizi-08nov05.pdf, accessed on 11 May 2007.

Chapelle, B. de la (2004) Intervention made at UNICTTF Global Forum on Internet governance. UN, New York.

Cutler, C. A., V. Haufler and T. Porter (eds) (1999) *Private Authority and International Affairs*. Albany: State University of New York Press.

Dean, M. (1999) *Governmentality: Power and Rule in Modern Society*. London: Sage Publications.

Deetz, S. (2003) 'Disciplinary Power, Conflict Suppression and Human Resources Management', in Alvesson, M. and H. Willmott (eds), *Studying Management Critically*. London: Sage Publications, 23–45.

Deibert, R. (2003) 'Black Code: Censorship, surveillance and the Militarization of Cyberspace', paper for *International Studies Association Conference*. Portland, Oregon.

Doria, A. (2005) Intervention made at WGIG consultations, UN, Geneva.

Executive Coordinator, WGIG (2005) Personal interview, Geneva, 15 February.

Flyverbom, M. (2006) *Making the Global Information Society Governable: On the Governmentality of Multi-stakeholder Networks.* Copenhagen: Department of Intercultural Communication and Management, Copenhagen Business School.

Frankel, C. (2004) 'Europæisk Netværksstyring af IKT', in J. Hoff *Danmark som Informationssamfund.* Århus: Århus Universitetsforlag, 89–104.

Foucault, M. (1985) 'Concluding Remarks', in J. Pearson (ed) *Discourse and Truth: The Problematization of Parrhesia: six lectures given at the University of Berkeley, Oct–Nov 1983*, available online at http://foucault.info/documents/parrhesia/, accessed on 11 May 2007.

Galloway, A. R. (2004) *Protocol: How Control Exists After Decentralization.* Cambridge: MIT Press.

Hewlett Packard member, UNICTTF (2003), Personal Interview, WSIS Geneva, 12 December.

Hoff, J. (2003) 'A constructivist bottom-up approach to governance: the need for increased theoretical and methodological awareness in research', in H.P. Bang, *Governance as Social and Political Communication.* Manchester: Manchester University Press.

Hoffman, J. (2005) 'Internet Governance: A Regulatory Idea in Flux'. Available online at www.duplox.wzberlin.de/people/jeanette/texte/Internet%20Governance%20english%20version.pdf, accessed on 11 May 2007.

IBM (2004) interventions made by representative, Global Forum on Internet Governance, UN, New York.

ICC Member, UNICTTF (2005), Personal interview, WSIS Tunis, 14 November. Indian delegation (2005) interventions made by Indian government delegation, WGIG consultations, UN, Geneva.

International Herald Tribune (2005) 'Compromise reached in Tunis on Internet Control', 16 November.

ISOC representative (2005), intervention made at WGIG consultations, UN, Geneva.

Jensen, W. (2005) 'Recommendations of the WGIG', Public meeting on Internet Governance, Ministry of Science and Technology, 14 September, Copenhagen.

Jørgensen, R. F. (ed.) (2006) *Human Rights in the Global Information Society.* Cambridge, MA: MIT Press.

Klein, H. (2003) 'Understanding WSIS: An Institutional Analysis of the UN World Summit on the Information Society', *Information Technology and International Development, Special Issue on WSIS.* MIT Press, 1(3–4) Spring-Summer 2005: 3–13.

Kleinwächter, W. (2004) 'Beyond ICANN vs. ITU', in D. Maclean (ed), *Internet Governance: A Grand Collaboration.* New York: UN ICT Task Force Series, 31–52.

Kleinwächter, W. (2005) intervention made at WGIG consultations, UN, Geneva.

Larner, W. and W. Walters (eds) (2004) *Global Governmentality: Governing International Spaces.* London: Routledge.

Lessig, L. (1999) *Code and Other Laws of Cyberspace.* New York: Basic Books.

Mathiason, J., M. Mueller, H. Klein, M. Holitscher and L. McKnight (2004) 'Internet Governance: the State of Play', *Internet Governance Project*, available online at http://internetgovernance.org/pdf/ig-sop-final.pdf, accessed on 11 May 2007.

Mengin, F. (ed.) (2004) *Cyber China.* London: Palgrave.

Miller, P. and N. Rose (1990) 'Governing Economic Life', *Economy, and Society*, 19 (1): 1–31.

Mueller M., J. Mathiason and L. W. McKnight (2004) 'Making Sense of "Internet Governance": Defining Principles and Norms in a Policy Context', in D. Maclean, (ed) *Internet Governance: A Grand Collaboration*. New York: UN ICT Task Force Series.

Mueller, M. L., B. N. Kuerbis and C. Pagé (2007) 'Democratizing Global Communication? Global Civil Society and the Campaign for Communication Rights in the Information Society', *International Journal of Communication* 1.

Napoli, P. (2001) *Foundations of Communications Policy: Principles and Process in the Regulation of Electronic Media*. USA: Hampton Press.

The New York Times (2005) 'A compromise of Sorts on Internet Control, 16 November.

Pisanty, A. (2005) intervention by WGIG member and Director of Computing Academic Services, Universidad Autonoma de Mexico, at WGIG consultations, UN, Geneva.

Price, M. E. and S. Verhulst (2000) 'In Search of the Self: Charting the Course of Internet Self-Regulation in a Global Environment', in C.T. Marsden (ed), *Regulating the Global Information Society*. London: Routledge.

Rose, N. and P. Miller (1992) 'Political Power beyond the State: Problematics of Government', *The British Journal of Sociology*, 43 (2): 173–205.

Rose, N. (1999) *Powers of Freedom: Reframing political Thought*. Cambridge: Cambridge University Press.

Siochrú, S. Ó and B. Girard (2002) *Global Media Governance: A Beginner's Guide*. New York: Rowman and Littlefield.

Spar, D. L. (1999) 'Lost in (Cyber)space: The Private Rules of Online Commerce', in A.C. Cutler, V. Haufler and T. Porter, *Private Authority and International Affairs*. New York: SUNY Press.

The Times UK (2005) 'Tunis Talks find Internet Stalemate', 16 November.

Tunis Agenda for the Information Society (2005) UN, Tunis, http://www.itu. int/wsis/documents/doc_multi.asp?lang=en&id=2267%7C0, accessed on 11 May 2007.

Part II
The Innovation of Authority

5

Legitimacy Work: Attitudes to CSR in a Mexican and French Employers' Association

Maribel Blasco and Mette Zølner

The chapter explores how two business associations in Mexico and France construct themselves as legitimate actors. Not much is known about how private actors may come to be seen as legitimate or how they may acquire or lose legitimacy through altering their conduct (Hurd 1999: 401). Whilst literature on private authority does recognize that legitimate authority is socially constructed and, hence, that the kind and the type of actors that enjoy legitimacy are likely to vary over time and space, relatively little attention has so far been paid to variations in what is considered to be legitimate behaviour in different cultural contexts. Furthermore, little is known about the process through which private market actors construct and manage their self-representations in different contexts.

It is exactly this question of how a private actor can acquire legitimacy that is at the core of the present chapter. We propose that the institutional context in which private actors operate shapes both their ability to establish themselves as legitimate actors, and the type of appeals they make in order to achieve public recognition. By institutional context we mean social structures that have attained a high degree of resilience and which consist of three pillars: regulatory aspects that provide the legal framework for what is permissible in a given society; normative elements that introduce a prescriptive, evaluative and obligatory dimension into social life; and cultural-cognitive elements consisting of shared conceptions that frame sense-making (Scott 2003: 880). Due to the limited scope of the chapter we will not go into the regulatory aspects nor differentiate between shared normative and cultural-cognitive references in our analysis. Instead, we will focus on the roles played by various kinds of shared references in shaping the way in which private actors are expected to comply with legal regulations in different cultural contexts. We ask two questions: What, if anything, do private actors attempt to legitimize, and how do they go about doing this? We use corporate social responsibility (CSR) as a prism through which to investigate the types of appeals that private market actors make to public recognition within a particular normative and cultural-cognitive terrain.

Empirically, the notion of private authority has primarily been established and explored within Anglo-Saxon institutional contexts where private market authority has traditionally been strong (Hall and Biersteker 2002). We argue that to better understand how private market actors seek to construct legitimacy, it is illustrative to explore institutional contexts where they have low market authority as they are likely to be forced to work harder to become legitimate. We focus therefore on two institutional contexts where private market actors have traditionally suffered from a lack of public legitimacy, namely, Mexico and France. In France, this low legitimacy can be explained by a strong ideological emphasis on the common good; the low legitimacy of money when not associated with high cultural capital; and a strong egalitarian ideology. These institutionalized values place private market actors, and in particular SMEs, in a position with low legitimacy (Boyer 1996; Schmidt 1997; Mény and Surel 2001; Iribarne 2002; Pinçon and Pinçon-Charlot 2003). This negative public image coexists, however, with an assumption that French companies will observe a minimum of legal requirements, since these are effectively enforced by law. Conversely, in Mexico private market actors suffer from a bad image largely due to their role in twentieth century political events, including most recently their association with unpopular neo-liberal reforms. This unpopularity has been further exacerbated by the context of widespread social deprivation, poverty and troubled capital-labour relations. Labour and environmental regulations are poorly enforced, meaning that firms who do live up to them are the exception rather than the rule (in Peinado-Vara 2004: 5; CEPAL 2004). The Mexican and French contexts also share other institutional similarities such as a secular state, a strong Catholic and Latin tradition, high public expectations of the State with regard to social welfare provision, and conversely, a minor role for private market actors in this field. But there are also significant differences between the two countries in terms of state regulation, the scope of the welfare state, and socio-economic conditions.

As our interest is in the broader relationship between CSR and legitimacy, we will focus on the discourse of business associations rather than individual companies. We do this in order to avoid drawing narrow conclusions from factors affecting individual companies' behaviour, such as a company's life-cycle, its CEO, its company culture, its financial performance and competitive environment, etc. (Campbell 2005: 9). We have chosen two business associations that are at the forefront of promoting a social role for business in their respective societies. We assume that this role has obliged these associations to appeal more explicitly and creatively to public recognition than they would have done had they simply been following a well established trend in their respective institutional context. This criterion led us to choose in Mexico the Unión Social de Empresarios Mexicanos (USEM) which, founded in 1956, has become a key forum for discussions of social questions among business people; and in France, the Centre des Jeunes Dirigeants d'Entreprises (CJD), founded in 1938 and a pioneer with regard to ethical issues in the private sector (Ballet and De Bry 2001: 124–129). These two associations are also comparable inasmuch as they represent similar groups of businesses (small and medium-sized companies); and both have roots in Catholic Social Doctrine.[1] USEM shares its roots in Catholic Social Doctrine with several other major Mexican business associations which profess similar values (Sánchez Navarro 2000: 193), whilst the CJD is a declared non-religious organization that operates in a primarily secular business community, although business culture in France is in many ways implicitly coloured by Catholic Social Doctrine (Weber 1991).

Thus, to sum up, our comparison of USEM's and the CJD's discourse is likely to indicate similarities and dissimilarities in how business associations which resemble each other considerably in many respects appeal to public recognition through CSR in institutional contexts where private market actors have traditionally lacked legitimacy. Our analysis builds primarily on documents (books, magazines, and web-pages) in which the two associations present their visions of the socially responsible company (see also Zølner 2006). We thus explore how the two business associations appeal to public recognition in their respective institutional contexts; but we do not seek to draw conclusions about their actual CSR practices, or about whether their strategies succeed. It should be added that our investigation is still at an exploratory stage and is not intended to paint a conclusive picture of CSR attitudes in the business sector in France or Mexico; neither do we aim to comment on French or Mexican business culture more generally, as this can vary tremendously internally within each country (see Sánchez Navarro 2000: 187; Weber 1991). We are also conscious that CSR awareness and penetration vary considerably depending on company size and reach. For example, in Mexico, multinationals and large national concerns are far more likely to have an integrated CSR policy connected to their core business activities than smaller companies. CSR is, moreover, an area where attitudes are changing rapidly, and in both countries a number of national or international CSR lobby organizations and networks are active which place great emphasis on the need to integrate a more systematic social concern into core business activities (Humières and Chauveau 2001 in Peinado-Vara 2004: 4). Last but not least with this research design, we cannot draw any conclusions about the actual CSR practices employed by (selected) private market actors, or about whether their strategies succeed.

In section two below, we outline a framework for conceptualizing the relationship between CSR, private market actor legitimacy, and public recognition in institutional context. In section three, we illustrate similarities and differences in the way in which the two business associations promote a social role for private market actors in Mexico and France, respectively. In section four we discuss the implications of these observations for our understanding of private actors' legitimacy work.

'Legitimacy Work' among private market Actors

According to Hall and Biersteker, 'what differentiates authority from power is the legitimacy of claims of authority', with legitimacy defined as 'some form of normative, uncoerced consent of recognition of authority on the part of the regulated or governed'. Legitimacy is therefore seen as a form of public consent to authority which is socially constructed through a variety of different practices (2002: 4–6). Hall and Biersteker's account prioritizes how and why private actors have been 'accorded a form of legitimate authority' and on the corresponding challenges to State authority that are perceived to arise from this. Legitimacy is here treated as a motivation for behaviour in itself: a rule or institution is considered legitimate, and therefore obeyed, but the process that makes legitimacy possible becomes secondary.

Yet, as other commentators have noted, '[a] given power relationship is not legitimate because people believe in its legitimacy, but because it can be justified in terms of their beliefs' (Beetham 1991 in Ansell 2001: 8705). Consequently, rather than assuming that private market actors possess any *a priori* form of legitimacy (Hall and Biersteker 2002), we will explore the process through which private market actors reflexively construct and manage their self-representations. We call this process 'legitimacy work', a term that we adapt from Giddens' concept of 'identity work'(1991). As with identity work, we conceive of private actors' legitimacy work as being enabled and constrained by the particular institutional context in which it takes place (Giddens 1991). Private actors are at once constrained by the responsibilities, regulations, and norms that define what appropriate behaviour is for them; and on the other hand, these very structures open up opportunities for them to enhance their public image in a specific institutional context. In other words, they may accrue or lose legitimacy by adjusting their behaviour in relation to these structures.

Along these lines, private market actors may accrue legitimacy by acting in areas where the public does not expect them to be responsible, or, conversely, they can lose legitimacy and face sanctions for failing to live up to public expectations of their responsibilities. This idea is prominent in scholarship on CSR and corporate reputation, which emphasizes that a firm's legitimacy is enhanced when its social engagement is perceived to exceed the minimum level of what is expected of it.[2] Overall, the literature indicates that private market actors see CSR as an opportunity to accrue legitimacy, improve their public image, and gain political power since 'politicians, regulators, and the public at large become beholden to the corporation as a result of the good will generated by philanthropic acts' (Sánchez C. 2000: 365).

This idea rests on the notion that there is a kind of 'social contract' between private market actors and the society in which they operate, which is shaped by public expectations of how a legitimate business should act, and of the conditions under which business is entitled to 'pursue the maximization of profits' (Pava and Krausz 1997: 5). This social contract may be expected to vary from one institutional context to another, owing to differences in the regulatory elements that determine what constitutes legal behaviour for business in any given society; and in the shared normative and cultural-cognitive references that shape implicit assumptions and expectations of the role of business and its responsibilities vis-à-vis the society in which it operates (Pava and Krausz 1997: 5). Thus, for instance, non-mandatory reporting of CSR can be a means for companies to 'manage their legitimacy'; and voluntary social engagement in the form of CSR activities may be viewed as 'an ongoing means of reinforcing corporate legitimacy and managing reputation' (Clarke and Gibson-Sweet 1999: 6). Similarly, in contexts where the government is perceived to be the agency mainly responsible for ensuring social welfare, a private actor that voluntarily takes on some of this responsibility stands to gain legitimacy (Sánchez Navarro 2000).

For instance, comparing CSR in Europe and the U.S., Matten and Moon write that '[p]hilanthropy as a voluntary policy in Europe appears dispensable because these issues are not left to the discretion of corporations because they are part of the legal framework'. Because of this, they claim European companies 'are left with a far lower degree of discretion in issues of societal risk allocation [than US companies]' (Matten and Moon 2004: 7). The degree of social risk assumed by governments thus appears to be a key factor in shaping the 'minimum level' of socially responsible behaviour expected of companies (Barlett 2005: 3). We may hypothesize, then, that private market actors' capacity to accrue legitimacy through socially responsible behaviour is linked to the ways in which responsibility for social welfare is assigned, and to how the public thinks it should be assigned, among societal institutions.

The notion that CSR may function as an instrument to accrue legitimacy for private market actors in contexts where state responsibilities are being dispersed has both empirical and theoretical implications. Notably, while legitimacy is not visible in itself, its effects are. Thus, empirically, by paying attention to the types of public claims and appeals made by private market actors, and to the kind of public recognition or sanctions evoked by business activities, we may learn something about how legitimate authority is constructed in any given societal context. In terms of theory, we can sketch a framework for conceptualizing the relationship between perceived responsibilities, public recognition and legitimacy, as a basis for any authority that may be accrued by private actors.

In the following section, we will explore the legitimacy work undertaken by the CJD and USEM.

Two cases of legitimacy work: USEM and the CJD

At first glance, USEM and the CJD articulate their social engagement in rather similar ways. The explicit aim of both associations is to promote human values in business; that is, to encourage private market actors to assume a greater degree of social responsibility. On their respective webpages, USEM describes its aim as to promote human values in business and society (http://www.usem.org.mx/ September 2006); whilst the CJD claims that its ambition is to make companies more human (www.cjd.net November 2005). Both associations state that economic activity and social and societal concerns constitute a whole in the sense that economic activity cannot be considered as a realm apart from social and societal issues (CJD 2004a, b, c; Lorenzo Servitje, CEO Grupo Bimbo,

Revista USEM, 2005a). Equally, both associations present business as an instrument that must serve society. Thus, according to USEM, '[it]would be to deny the very nature of business to put men at the service of production, and not production at the service of men' (Basagoiti 2005: 18–21); and the CJD talks of 'putting business at the service of mankind' (www.cjd.net November 2005). In other words, neither USEM nor the CJD regard business as a legitimate activity in itself, but only inasmuch as it can serve social and societal aims.

Yet, while confronted with a similar need to legitimize private market activity, the two organizations actually differ in the way in which they do their legitimacy work, both in terms of what they feel obliged to legitimize and how they go about this. Some of these differences are most likely attributable to the quite different socio-economic conditions and social welfare provisions in Mexico and France. For example, while the CJD adopts a broad view that includes societal and environmental concerns when talking about private market actors' social responsibility, USEM remains focussed on poverty, social welfare, and justice. This is not surprising since, in Mexico, social exclusion and poverty are of a completely different nature and degree than in France with its well-developed social welfare state and its generally high standard of living. However, we will argue that shared references and values in a given institutional context also contribute to shaping the way in which the two business associations do their legitimacy work. In the following, we give three examples of how the Mexican and French institutional contexts constrain and enable the legitimacy work undertaken by USEM and the CJD both in terms of what they need to legitimize and how they do it.

A first difference relates to what the two business associations seek to legitimize. The CJD argues at length for why business activity not only serves the interests of private market actors, but also those of the rest of society, that is the common good (*l'intérêt général*). According to French Republican principles, the common good is incarnated by the State and must be defined rationally by the State without being influenced by private market actors or civil society, both of which are considered to act in their own self-interest. This conception implies that, unlike in the Anglo-Saxon context, the sum of individual interests does not equal that of the common good. It follows, likewise, that whereas serving the common good is positive and a source of legitimacy in a French institutional context, furthering own interests is considered to be egotistical and eventually detrimental to the common good (Mény and Surel 2001). Thus, in a context where self-interests and the common good are not considered compatible, the CJD feels the need to argue for a reconciliation of private market interests with the common good. This need is particularly well illustrated by the fact that the CJD prefers to use the concept of 'global performance' to that of 'corporate social responsibility' (CJD 1998b: 7–15; CJP, 2003; CJD 2003: 5 and 16). By using the term 'global performance', the CJD emphasizes that when doing business the economic performance of a company should always be balanced by its social and societal performance. The CJD argues, thus, that by doing business in a globally responsible way private market actors serve the common good.

Unlike the CJD, USEM does not attempt to argue that economic interests ought to be compatible with social and societal interests. Rather, it concludes that serving one's own interests is in itself tantamount to serving the common good. According to USEM, business springs from and owes its existence to social needs, and doing business is therefore perfectly compatible with social justice, not least because it generates employment, which is viewed as a human need and duty enabling investments and hence continued employment. This constitutes a just reward for goods and services provided by society. Thus, private market actors can serve society and promote the common good simply by providing employment and high-quality goods. As in the Anglo-Saxon context, the common good here equals the sum of individual interests: 'Society asks firms to be efficient for the common good, in other words, for its own good' (Basagoiti 2005: 18–21). To sum up, since the relationship between individual interests and the common good is conceived differently in the two institutional contexts, the point of departure for what needs to be legitimized is also different for USEM and the CJD.

A second notable difference relates to the way in which the legitimacy work is done. Here too, USEM and the CJD draw on quite different arguments. While the CJD material contains no overtly religious references, USEM borrows vocabulary from Catholic teachings on social doctrine. One example is USEM's ten 'Norms for the Behaviour of Businesspeople', which outline the obligation to '[...] comply with the duties of the profession not only for human motives but also because that is the vehicle which God has offered you for your sanctification'. Here, businesspeople are urged to display their Christianity through their business activities in order to fulfil their divinely ordained role. Conversely, the CJD makes exclusively secular references encouraging CSR activity both for strategic-economic and for societal motives, such as respect for future generations. The CJD considers that to do business in a socially responsible way it is necessary to have a long- and short-term perspective, and to find the right balance between economic, social, and societal concerns in the society in which one operates. This reflects the fact that although both USEM and the CJD have roots within Catholic Social Doctrine, they are respectively a confessional and a non-confessional association. USEM has an explicitly evangelical and educational aim: to disseminate the principles of Catholic Social Doctrine in the business community (*Revista USEM* 2005a). This is quite the contrary in the case of the CJD, which, although its founders were inspired by Catholic Social Doctrine, has been a declared secular association since its foundation in 1938 (Bernoux 1974; Boissonat 1999). So, while USEM appeals to the Catholic Social Doctrine and emphasizes the moral obligation to do social good, the CJD appeals to a middle way between sound economic rationality and social and societal concerns.

It follows that a source of legitimacy for USEM is Catholicism. In Mexico, the Catholic Church and confessional NGOs have retained an important social role. Throughout post-Independence Mexican history we can observe intense struggles between Church and State over various issues, including the control over welfare, which is seen as a key means of accruing legitimacy and political power (CEMEFI Nd b: 5; Hale 1996). And though the State is today regarded as the main institution responsible for social welfare (Vizcarra Bordi 2002: 3), the Church remains an important normative reference as the inspiration for and realm of private charitable initiatives (Sánchez Navarro 2000: 189). It follows that in the Mexican context, references to the Catholic Church and religious belief constitute a source of legitimacy. A voluntary engagement in social welfare by private market actors is likely to prove all the more effective as a source of legitimacy in the context of the structural reforms that have taken place recently in Mexico entailing the dispersion of State responsibilities for social welfare to non-State actors. Moreover, private market actors have been the target of a negative public discourse in rather recent history, including open hostility against them under the presidency of Luís Echeverría in the 1970s when businessmen were branded 'reactionaries', 'bad Christians', and even enemies of the people's progress. This is likely to have encouraged USEM to emphasize their Christian credentials (Story1990: 168).

In France, conversely, Catholicism is not a source of legitimacy as faith is considered to be an issue belonging to the private sphere. With the separation of Church and State in 1905, the principle of a secular State and public sphere was institutionalized. With the exception of a few confessional business organizations, trade unions and NGOs, French organizational life has fully adopted the principle of secularity. Thus, the secular CJD fits well into French associational and political life whilst its discourse can be read as a translation of Catholic Social Doctrine into secular terms. This raises the question of which sources of legitimacy the CJD can draw on in a French Republican context? Part of the answer lies in the CJD's presentation of itself as a 'think-tank' that aims to promote public causes' (www.cjd.net November 2005). Thus, the declared aim of the CJD is not to further private market actor's interests or any other particular interests, but to provide ideas that serve the common good. By presenting itself as promoting public causes and in this way setting itself above pure self-interest, CJD draws legitimacy from the Republican notion of the common good. And since the State is the traditional guardian hereof, the CJD borrows legitimacy from the State. It follows from this that to legitimize private market activity, USEM and the CJD turn to two different sources of legitimacy – the Church and the State respectively – that lend themselves to this purpose within the respective institutional contexts.

A third difference can be noticed in the business associations' conception of how to engage in social responsibility. Not surprisingly, their particular visions are closely associated with the different sources of legitimacy on which they draw. For USEM, social responsibility involves a moral commitment to take society's needs into account when doing business and in particular to help the poor and needy (Basagoiti 2005). What counts is the intention and the act of giving. As such, USEM's idea of social responsibility echoes religious commandments to do good that, when transferred to the realm of business, become philanthropy defined broadly as 'private giving for public purposes' (Ostrower 1995: 4). This is illustrated by the president of USEM, Juan Manuel López Valdivia's comment on wealth: 'Remember that the rich Epulon was condemned not for his wealth but for ignoring poor Lazarus' (cited in Basagoiti 2005: 9). Thus, while wealth is not seen as problematic in itself, USEM condemns the absence of awareness and will to help one's fellow man as a sure path to hell. Thus, according to USEM, acting in a socially responsibly manner is both a moral obligation for private market actors vis-à-vis the community and a way to achieve individual sanctification. A further way to act socially responsibly is simply to respect the law. This might sound rather unambitious, but in fact to obey the law is already to do more than most in the Mexican institutional context, where the enforcement of labour and environmental regulations is weak.

The CJD's depiction of social engagement is in keeping with the organization's secular nature and the legitimacy provided by serving the common good. Social engagement is about competently managing an economically viable company and getting the balance right between economic, social, and societal concerns (global performance, see above). As such, social engagement needs to be an integrated part of a company's strategy and it does not suffice to do social good or to protect the environment on an ad hoc basis: 'Global performance is not a series of good acts, but a global engagement and a permanent consideration' (www.cjd.net November 2005; CDJ 2004b). It follows that for the CJD, social engagement is expressed in and through the concrete management of a company. It is through a permanent effort to find the least bad solution in the best interests of all the stake-holders that a company and its managers assume their social responsibility (CJD 2002). It follows that there is no universal solution for how to perform globally and that each manager must act in the best way according to the particular circumstances and environment in which s/he operates (CJD 2003: 5 and 16). Moreover, the CJD encourages its members to be progressive and coaches them to experiment with innovative ways of engaging in social responsibilities that go beyond legal requirements. The CJD's conception of social engagement requires good management skills as it is in and through holistic management in a specific context that private market actors can assume social responsibility. Consequently, the CJD places great emphasis on business leaders' professional competence. This is for example illustrated by the CJD's legitimization of wealth as a sign of professional competence. By doing this, the CJD also draws on an additional source of legitimacy in the French institutional context: namely professional merit and excellence. A source of social recognition is to excel in one's profession, to be professionally excellent, no matter whether it is a white-collar or a blue-collar profession (Iribarne 2006: 103–111).

Private actors, public expectations, and borrowed legitimacies

Our initial questions were: what, if anything, do private actors attempt to legitimize, and how do they go about doing this? Our findings show that although private market actors in the two contexts both attempt to legitimize business as an activity capable of serving social and societal aims, suggesting a need to compensate for business' public image as being purely engaged in pursuing its own private interests, they differ in terms of which aspects of business they seek to legitimize. Whilst the CJD presents a very broad conception of socially responsible business activity as embodying concerns that transcend the national level, USEM emphasizes the positive role that business can play in society merely through carrying out its basic functions properly, i.e. providing quality goods and employment. The two organizations also diverge in terms of how they couch their social engagement. USEM borrows terminology from Catholic Social Doctrine to reconcile its social mission with profit-making; whilst the CJD remains explicitly secular. USEM's Catholic references may be seen both a means of pre-empting old claims about businessmen being bad Christians and, at the same time, as an appeal to Catholic values that are still widely held in Mexico. The favourable image of the Catholic Church, as well as the absence of any strict separation between the religious-private and the public-economic spheres enables USEM to deploy Catholic social terminology, thus 'borrowing' legitimacy from the Catholic Church. Conversely, religious appeals are not effective in the French context with its strict separation of private religious beliefs and public economic activity; as well as its emphasis on the common good. However, these beliefs enable legitimacy to be borrowed from a different source, namely, the Republican values of the common good, merit, and public service as well as a professional culture of excellence and honour. By couching its social engagement in these terms, the CJD can defend the point that an economically efficient undertaking can at the same time be socially responsible.

Thus, both in the type of appeals to legitimacy made by USEM and the CJD as well as the sources of legitimacy from which they 'borrow', we can identify differences that can be ascribed to the institutional contexts in question. Our empirical examples illustrate that shared references both enable and constrain the way in which USEM and the CJD can do their legitimacy work. In addition, our examples suggest that the socio-economic context also plays a role in shaping private market actors' room for manoeuvre in this regard. Finally, though beyond the scope of this paper, we would like to add that to acquire a broader understanding of the way in which legitimacy work is undertaken, other aspects need to be investigated as well, notably the interests, convictions, and identities of the social actors involved. Social actors can choose among a number of ways of doing legitimacy work that a given institutional context and a particular socio-economic situation opens up – or closes off. As there is rarely only one option open, social actors are likely to choose according to their priorities. Thus, if USEM adopts an evangelical and moralizing discourse, it is not only because this is viable in the Mexican institutional context, but also because its members actually are believers. In fact there is much to suggest that both organizations have a genuine social agenda motivated by strongly-held religious and social convictions.

Conclusion

The concepts of 'entanglement' and 'assemblage' (Porter; Hansen; both this volume) have been used to describe the ways in which new arrangements of authority are being constituted globally, with private actors taking on authoritative roles in ways that appear to blur the boundaries traditionally drawn between the public and the private. Our empirical findings suggest that this is not an arbitrary process. Rather, the *kinds* of entanglements or assemblages of authority that emerge are to a significant degree shaped by shared normative expectations about the proper behaviour pertaining to different social institutions in particular contexts. These expectations are, in turn, coloured by the way in which the boundaries between the public and the private have historically been drawn in a given context and the connotations that are commonly attached to these spheres. These expectations at once open up spaces within which private actors can make appeals to legitimacy; and shape the types of appeals that they can make.

What broader conclusions can we draw from USEM's and the CJD's legitimacy work? Following our definition of legitimacy work as the way in which private market actors reflectively construct and manage their self-representations, two distinct forms of legitimacy work emerge from the analysis. First, private actors may seek to generate good will and thus enhance their legitimacy by adjusting their behaviour strategically in order to comply with or exceed the minimum level of public expectations concerning their proper role. The very existence of a minimum level of public expectations offers opportunities for private actors to accrue legitimacy 'by default' by voluntarily engaging in activities perceived to be the mandate of other social institutions. Thus, for instance, firms engaging in social welfare activities in contexts where the State is regarded as the custodian of welfare and the common good may increase their legitimacy in the eyes of the public. We might speculate, then, that for a French firm to acquire greater legitimacy through CSR activities, it would have to do something over and above observing the minimum legal requirements. French firms may stand to gain little by a very overt CSR discourse since the State is perceived as primarily responsible for social welfare and lives up to this responsibility; and business is *a priori* expected to comply with a minimum of legal requirements concerning its treatment of employees and its relationship to the surrounding community. Mexican firms, on the other hand, could stand to gain considerable legitimacy merely by displaying willingness to comply even with basic legal requirements, let alone engaging in social matters.

Second, private actors may 'borrow' legitimacy from private or public institutions by couching their social engagement in the terms used by those institutions, thus obtaining a 'resonance' effect. The degree of popular endorsement enjoyed by different institutions, as well as the degree to which that endorsement may be successfully 'transferred' from one sphere of activity to another, varies according to the context. Thus, in Mexico private market actors can draw on terminology borrowed from Catholic social doctrine to justify their business activities, whilst this would be unseemly in France where religious belief is deemed a matter for one's private life – i.e. *not* one's business activities. We can see, then, that the very way in which the private-public divide is constructed in the two contexts differs substantially, with implications for the ways in which private actors can borrow legitimacy. We may then speculate that in contexts where they have low public legitimacy, private market actors seeking legitimacy may adapt their behaviour to meet or exceed public expectations; and/or 'borrow' legitimacy from other institutions, be these public or private.

The disaggregation of State authority and the dispersion of many of its former functions to other societal institutions and actors have led to much speculation about shifts in the locus of power and authority from governments to private actors (Hansen, this volume). However, we should not underestimate the continuing belief in many societies that the State is the proper custodian of the common good. We argue in the above that it is precisely the interplay between expectations of the State and its capacity to deliver that opens up spaces where private actors can, potentially, claim legitimacy. Such claims are constrained, in turn, by the sources of legitimacy that resonate positively in any given society, and which shape the extent and type of claims that can be made by those who 'borrow' from them. The resulting assemblage, or entanglement, may include private, public, or a mix of sources of legitimacy. Importantly, however, in our view any *authority* that may derive from this type of legitimacy work will strictly speaking always be public, in the sense that it is publicly recognized and endorsed.

Notes

1. Catholic Social Doctrine emerged as a movement in the early nineteenth century and was reasserted by the Pope's Rerum Novarum in 1891. Its aim was to counter social need and distress among workers in the wake of the industrial revolution. Yet though its distinctive feature is concern for the poorest as professed by Christianity, Catholic Social Doctrine goes beyond charity and presents an ideal for how to organize society. Despite variations over time and space, this ideal is characterized by the principle of subsidiarity according to which civil society (communities, corporations, organizations) was to assume State functions when appropriate (Mayeur 1986: 261).
2. In this connection, it is interesting to note that philanthropy, defined broadly as 'private giving for public purposes' (Ostrower 1995: 4), has been used historically as a means to gain social status and recognition and to 'define social distinctions and classes' (Adam 2004: 4), particularly in societies where there exists 'a mistrust of governmental power and large-scale bureaucracy' (Ostrower 1995: 8).

References

Adam, T. (2004) *Philanthropy, Patronage and Civil Society: Experiences from Germany, Great Britain and North America*. Bloomington & Indianapolis: Indiana University Press.

Ansell, C.K. (2001) 'Legitimacy: Political', in *International Encyclopaedia of the Social and Behavioural Sciences*. Amsterdam: Elsevier Science Ltd.

Ballet, J. and F. De Bry (2001) *L'entreprise et l'éthique*. Paris: Seuil.

Bartlett, J. (2005) 'Addressing concerns about legitimacy: a case study of social responsibility reporting in the Australian banking industry', in *Proceedings 34th European Marketing Academy Conference 2005*, Milan.

Basagoiti, José María (2005) 'La dirección de los negocios en tiempos de incertidumbre', in *Revista USEM*, 263, January/February.

Bernoux, P. (1974) *Les nouveaux patrons: le Centre des jeunes dirigeants d'entreprise*. Paris: Ed. Ouvrières.

Boissonnat, J. (1999) *L'aventure du christianisme social. Passé et avenir*. Paris: Bayard.

Boyer, R. (1996) 'Le capitalisme étatique à la française à la croisée des chemins', in C. Crouch and W. Streeck (eds) *Les capitalismes en Europe*. Paris: La Découverte.

Campbell, J. (2005) 'Institutional analysis and the paradox of corporate social responsibility'. Paper prepared for the conference *New Public and Private Models of Management: Sensemaking and Institutions*. Denmark: Skagen.

CEMEFI (Nd b) *Understanding Mexican Philanthropy*. Mexico: Centro Mexicano para la Filantropía (CEMEFI).

Centre des Jeunes Dirigeants d'entreprise (1998b) *Pour l'entreprise l'Homme est capital. Les combats quotidiens de jeunes entrepreneurs militants*. Paris: Vetter Éditions.

Centre des Jeunes Dirigeants d'entreprise (2002) *Manifeste pour donner un sens à la performance*. Marseille: CJD

Centre des Jeunes Dirigeants d'entreprise (2003) *Dossier thématique: Performance globale* 2004/2005. Paris: CJD.

Centre des Jeunes Dirigeants d'entreprise (2004a) *La surprenante historie de Claude-Jean Desvignes, jeune dirigeant*. Paris: Éditions d'Organisation.

Centre des Jeunes Dirigeants d'entreprise (2004b) *Charte du bien-entreprendre*. Paris: CJD.

Centre des Jeunes Dirigeants d'entreprise (2004c) *Vers un libéralisme responsable. 44 propositions pour une entreprise plus humaine*. Paris: Éditions d'Organisation.

Centre des Jeunes Patrons (2003) «Jeune Patron. Premier Cahier», *Les Cahiers Jeunes Patron*. Paris: CJP. http://www.cjd.net/ (consulted November 2005).

CEPAL (2004) *Panorama Social de América Latina 2002–2003*. Santiago: Comisión Económica para América Latina (CEPAL).

Clarke, J. and M. Gibson-Sweet (1999) 'The use of corporate social disclosures in the management of reputation and legitimacy: a cross sectoral analysis of UK Top 100 companies'. in *Business Ethics: A European Review*, 8 (1):5–13.

Giddens, Anthony (1991) *Modernity and Self-identity. Self and Society in the Late Modern Age*. Cambridge: Polity Press

Hale, C. (1996) 'Political ideas and ideologies in Latin America, 1870–1930', in L. Bethell (ed.) *Ideas and Ideologies in Twentieth Century Latin America*. Cambridge: Cambridge University Press.

Hall, R.B. and T. Biersteker. (2002) *The Emergence of Private Authority in Global Governance*. Cambridge: Cambridge University Press.

Humières, P. and A. Chauveau (2001) *Les pionniers de l'entreprise responsable*. Paris: Éditions d'Organisation.

Hurd, I. (1999) 'Legitimacy and authority in international politics', in *International Organization*, 53 (2): 379–408.

Iribarne, P. (2002) 'La légitimité de l'entreprise comme acteur éthique aux Etats-Unis et en France', in *Revue française de gestion*, 140: 23–39.

Iribarne, P. (2006) *L'Étrangeté française*. Paris: Seuil.

Matten, D. and Moon, J. (2004) ' "Implicit" and "Explicit" CSR: A Conceptual Framework for Understanding CSR in Europe'. Paper presented at 20th EGOS Conference, Ljubljana, Slovenia, July.

Mayeur, Jean-Marie (1986) *Catholicisme social et démocratie chrétienne*. Paris: Les Éditions du Cerf.

Mény, Y. and Surel, Y. (2001) *Politique comparée: les démocraties: Allemagne, États-Unis, France, Grande-Bretagne, Italie*. Paris: Monchrestien.

Ostrower, F. (1995) *Why the Wealthy Give: The Culture of Elite Philanthropy*. New Jersey: Princeton University Press.

Pava, M.L, Krausz, J. (1997) 'Criteria for evaluating the legitimacy of corporate social responsibility', in *Journal of Business Ethics*, 16: 337–47.

Peinado-Vara, Peinado-Vara, E. (2004) *Corporate social responsibility in Latin America and the Caribbean*, in Sustainable Development Department Technical Papers Series PEF-102. Washington DC: Inter-American Development Bank.

Pinçon, M. and M. Pinçon-Charlot (2003) *Sociologie de la bourgeoisie*. Paris: Découverte.

Revista USEM (2005a) No. 265, Vol. 36, May/June.

Sánchez C. (2000) 'Motives for corporate philanthropy in El Salvador: altruism and political legitimacy', *Journal of Business Ethics*, 27: 363–375.

Sánchez Navarro, J. (2000) *La ética del empresariado mexicano*. Mimeo.

Schmidt, Vivien A. (1997) 'Economic Policy, political Discourse and Democracy in France', *French Politics and Society*, 15 (2).

Scott, Richard (2003) 'Institutional carriers: reviewing modes of transporting ideas over time and space and considering their consequences', *Industrial and Corporate Change*, 12 (4):879–894.

Story, D. (1990) *Industria, Estado y Política en México: los Empresarios y el Poder.* México: Grijalvo.

USEM (http://www.usem.org.mx/, accessed on 14 September 2006).

Vizcarra Bordi, I. (2002) 'Social welfare in the 1990s in Mexico: the case of 'marginal' families in the Mazahua region', *Anthropologica*, 44: 209–221.

Weber, H. (1991) *Le parti des patrons.* Paris: Seuil.

Zølner, M. (2006) 'Young business leaders in France: Governance though values and ideas', in Martin Marcussen and Jacob Torfing (eds) (2006) *Democratic Network Governance.* London: Palgrave MacMillan.

6

Reluctant Subjects: Citizens, Consumers, and the Reform of Public Services

John Clarke and Janet Newman

The reconfiguration of public and private authority in new governance arrangements is not just a matter of 'privatization', shifting responsibilities from the public realm of state provision to the market. As argued by Hansen, and Larner, the categories public and private are produced by discourses and practices that help constitute subjects and objects in particular forms. The 'disaggregation' (Slaughter 2004) or 'dispersal' (Clarke and Newman 1997) of state power associated with neo-liberal rule involves the investment of non-state actors – including citizens – with new forms of authority alongside new forms of self-responsibility and self-rule (Rose 1999). The remaking of the boundary between public and private spheres and sectors, then, is taking place alongside the emergence of the citizen-consumer as a new instantiation of the authorized – and privatized – subject (Clarke et al. 2007). Commenting on the UK, Marquand links the enthusiasm for consumerism to wider dynamics of public service and political transformation:

> New Labour has pushed marketization and privatization forward, at least as zealously as the Conservatives did, narrowing the frontiers of the public domain in the process. Ministerial rhetoric is saturated with the language of consumerism. The public services are to be 'customer focussed'; schools and colleges are to ensure that 'what is on offer responds to the needs of consumers; the 'progressive project' is to be subjected to 'rebranding'. (Marquand 2004: 118)

The central role of consumerism in the transformation of public services can be viewed as a product of discourses and practices that re-constitute the subjects and objects of governance. Health care exemplifies the complex dynamics at stake where the reconfiguration of public and private sectors is taking place alongside new governance practices aiming to produce knowledgeable, reflexive 'citizen-consumers' (Newman and Vidler 2006a and b; Newman and Kuhlmann 2007). These new welfare subjects are authorized to challenge professional and bureaucratic power and are invested with new responsibilities for their own – and others' – care. Such processes can be understood as a global phenomenon, linked materially and discursively to the rise of a 'consumer society' and driven by supra-national institutions and transnational networks of policy transfer. However the literature from which such propositions derive tends to operate at a high level of generality and does little to assess ways in which such ideas are translated or enrolled into specific national political-cultural formations. The unity and coherence of programmes of reform in regional and national settings is still much debated while detailed studies have tended to suggest that rhetorical or discursive coherence masks considerable institutional variation in practice (Pollitt and Bouckaert 2000; Flynn 2002).

This chapter sets out to complement studies of institutional reform by providing a detailed focus on the changing identifications and relationships taking place in the intersection between public services and the people who use them. It draws on a research project which examined the shift towards a consumerist orientation in policy about public services in the UK.[1] At the time of the project, the public service reform agenda in the UK involved a double transformation based on extending the involvement of private sector providers in the delivery of public services together with expanding 'choice' for service users. The project explored the ways in which such a shift was constructed in political narratives legitimizing the modernization of the welfare state, and how such narratives attempted to address fundamental tensions in New Labour's political project. We were interested both in how service organizations adapted to such pressures and in how people understood their relationships to the public services they used (Clarke et al. 2007). Our focus here is on the attempted transformation of the UK's National Health System (NHS) around consumerism and choice.

The chapter is structured as follows. We begin by tracing the figure of the citizen-consumer in policy narratives associated with the New Labour's modernization programme in the UK, highlighting the ways in which this figure of the citizen-consumer is associated with changing relationships between private and public authority. We then consider the relationships between health services and the people who use them, stressing how people inhabit and reflect on these relationships in multiple and mobile ways. In doing so, we also explore what else is at stake in these identifications; that is, how far subjects take on the identifications associated with new forms of 'private' authority and responsibility, how far they hold on to older identifications, or indeed to what extent new 'public' subject positions may be emerging.

Constituting the 'citizen-consumer'

For advocates of a consumerist approach to public service provision – and for their critics – the relationship between citizen and consumer identities is an antagonistic one (e.g. Needham 2003; National Consumer Council 2004; Marquand 2004). The figures of the citizen and the consumer are seen to stand for wider social, political and philosophical formations, embodying the powerful and persistent binary distinction between the state and the market (a binary shared by neo-liberals and social democrats, even if their evaluation of the relative terms is different). As a result, the distinction between the citizen and the consumer carries a whole series of subsidiary binaries: public/ private; collective/individual; decommodification/commodification and so on. The state/market binary also seems to condense temporally divergent images of the social: an 'old' social of collective identifications and citizenship rights and a 'new' social of individualized and consumer-oriented identifications.

However in political and policy discourse, things have been rather less clear cut than the binary distinction between citizen and consumer distinction might suggest.[2] Both terms and a cluster of others continue to circulate in policy texts and in political statements about public services. An exemplary version was offered by Tony Blair in 2004:

> In reality, I believe people do want choice, in public services as in other services. But anyway, choice isn't an end in itself. It is one important mechanism to ensure that citizens can indeed secure good schools and health services in their communities. Choice puts the levers in the hands of parents and patients so that they as citizens and consumers can be a driving force for improvement in their public services. We are proposing to put an entirely different dynamic in place to drive our public services; one where the service will be driven not by the government or by the manager but by the user – the patient, the parent, the pupil and the law-abiding citizen. (Tony Blair quoted in *The Guardian* 24/06/2004: 1)

Here (and elsewhere) we see a proliferation of categories: citizens, consumers, parents, patients, pupils and – an interesting qualifier – 'law-abiding citizens'. There is no simple displacement or banishment of the 'citizen' in this shift to consumerism. However the meaning of citizenship and its related terms undergoes subtle reworking because of the contextualization deployed in almost all of the policy sources and New Labour statements about public services. The anachronistic character of public services – the thing that makes their reform necessary so that they can take their place in the 'modern world' – lies in the disjuncture between them and the wider social transformations, in particular the rise of the consumer society: 'Rising living standards, a more diverse society and a steadily stronger consumer culture have ... brought expectations of greater choice, responsiveness, accessibility, and flexibility' (Office of Public Service Reform 2002: 8).

The claim is that consumerism is not antithetical to citizenship because the conditions of citizenship has been transformed by the rise of the consumer society, bringing a whole new set of expectations to people's relationships with public services. Of particular note is the increasing salience of the concept of 'choice', as expressed here and in the Blair statement quoted earlier. Choice has performed multiple roles in New Labour's approach to public service reform: it is simultaneously 'what people want'; and a mechanism for driving service improvement and innovation. It is also viewed as promoting equality and facilitating the personalization of services (Ministers of State 2004: 4).

Choice has become the keyword of reform – drawing more and more services into its ambit, and opening up more and more services to the market (see, for example, Department of Health 2005; and the discussion in Clarke et al. 2006). In this view, choice is primarily understood as what the National Consumer Council's Policy Commission called 'economic choice [which] is the kind exercised in market' (National Consumer Council 2004: 26). They note that non-economic choice models and voice are also important, but the imagery (if not always the precise mechanisms) of choice that pervades New Labour discourse on public service reform is derived directly from the market model: competition between multiple providers encountering choice exercised by a 'sovereign' consumer in pursuit of individual wants.

Choice condenses both citizen and consumer subject positions, producing new hybrid forms consistent with New Labour's claims to defend public services (by modernizing them) and to renew civil society. In this new hybridized form, the 'old' social becomes transformed around an image of citizenship that is apparently more compatible with modern images of state-citizen relationships – based on responsibility, participation, and self-governance. This might be viewed as antithetical to the 'new' principle of consumer choice. However these different images and subject positions are discursively aligned in a process of re-articulation under New Labour. Stuart Hall has used Gramsci's idea of 'transformism' to analyse this alignment:

> New Labour is confusing in the signals it gives off, and difficult to characterise as a regime. It constantly speaks with a forked tongue. It combines economic neo-liberalism with a commitment to 'active government'. More significantly its grim alignment with the broad global interest and values of corporate capital and power – the neo-liberal, which is in the *leading position* in its political repertoire – is paralleled by another, *subaltern* programme, of a more social-democratic kind, running alongside. This is what people invoke when they insist, defensively, that New Labour is not, after all, 'neo-liberal'. The fact is that New Labour is a *hybrid* regime, composed of two strands. However, one strand – the neo-liberal – is in the dominant position. The other strand – the social democratic – is subordinate. What's more, its hybrid character is not simply a static formation: it is the process which combines the two elements which matters. The process is 'trans-formist'. The latter always remains subordinate to and dependent on the former, and *is constantly being 'transformed' into* the former, dominant one. (Hall 2003:19)

For various reasons – not least the data from the project that we discuss below – we would want to emphasize the phrase 'constantly being trans-formed'. Transformism is not a once and for all process: like all practices of articulation, it is vulnerable to the possibilities of rearticulation by other positions, whether the residual formulation of citizenship or emer-gent reinventions of both citizens and consumers (as ethical consumers, for example). The terms 'residual' and 'emergent' are borrowed from Raymond Williams' model of doing conjunctural analysis (Williams 1977: 121–7). New Labour works hard to make its imagined modern world – and the subjects to people it – come true, but hard work is not a guarantee of success. We have written about New Labour's approach to modernization and its construction of citizen-consumers at greater length elsewhere (e.g. Clarke and Newman 2004; Clarke et al. 2007). Here we want to concentrate on the ways in which people think about their rela-tionships to public services – and to the NHS in particular.

Identifications and relationships

We are concerned with the *changing identifications and relationships* taking place in the intersection between public services and the people who use them, and we draw here on evidence from our study collected

Table 6.1   Who do you think you are when using public services? (survey responses for health users)

Consumer	1
Customer	3
Patient	30
Service user	23
Citizen	5
Member of the public	20
Member of the local community	13
Total	97

from people who use health services.[3] Our questionnaire survey invited people to choose the words that best described their relationships to specific public services. The results (Table 6.1) suggest that, despite the current prevalence of consumerist discourse in policy texts and political speeches, it appears not to be very significant in the language people who use health service adopt to talk about themselves. These results are significant in several ways. In terms of the dominant representation of the 'new' public as consumers and customers, the extremely limited identification with these terms is striking. But so, too, is the limited identification with citizen. Very few respondents conceive of their relationship with the NHS as based in a form of citizenship. Is it possible that the 'big binary' distinction between citizen and consumer that has been so central to political discourse (and to political science) lacks any substantial popular reach around public services?

'Service specific terms' that express an internal relationship to a particular service (such as patient or service user) have a much greater reach. This may not be very surprising, given the question asks about identifications associated with using the service. But the other popular terms are ones that invoke a sense of 'membership': relationships of belonging in which people are part of something, and feel that services do – or should – belong to them. Larger collective imaginaries – the public and the local community – both carry this sense of belonging and attachment. Written commentaries on the terms in the returned questionnaires suggested that people are well able to hold different identifications alongside each other, but that these are mobilized contingently, depending on the context and character of specific interactions or encounters. People combined different identifications – and reflected on how such combinations made sense for them: for example, several linked consumerist with other forms of identification:

> I can and have been a patient and if and when I use my doctor or hospital I suppose I am a customer. As I have paid NI cons for 45 years I hope I'm a valued contributor and customer – there is a doubt in my mind though. (Newtown health user 11)

> The NHS is like any other service provider, public or private. I am therefore a customer forced to use the service but with no opportunity to take most of my custom elsewhere. The private sector does not provide many of the products only available from the NHS. (Newtown health user 21)

> I have many relatively serious conditions, and, therefore, am most definitely a patient. But I am also a consumer, having paid NI contributions for many, many years. (Newtown health user 34)

Only the second of these uses the term customer to bring out questions of choice, and does so in ways that reflect the dominant discourse about monopoly providers in public services. The others interpret 'consumer' or 'customer' as something linked to questions of payment: the service is associated with having paid National Insurance contributions or taxes. Questions about payment and entitlement occupy a complicated place in discourses about citizens, consumers, and public services. Different modes of payment form a particular focus of reflection in our respondents' comments on being a consumer. While the comments above deploy payment as indicating a consumer or customer relationship, others direct attention to the absence of an immediate 'cash nexus' in public services: 'Consumer/customer do not fit as I do not "buy". Service user is politically correct psychobabble. Citizen is not a word that appeals to me. When I need treatment I am a patient, when I do not I am a member of the public' (Newtown health user 33).

Here we can see the problem of the cash nexus being used to refuse the consumer/customer and the articulation instead of mobile and contingent identities ('when I need treatment … when I do not …'). The following example indicates a more complex field of relationships and the contingent identifications associated with them:

> I am registered as a patient with a GP practice and as such I am entitled to receive consultation and treatment and/or referral for health issues. The practice (I believe) received NHS funding for having me registered as a patient. As a member of the public my

relationship to the NHS extends beyond that of only a patient. As a long term (unpaid) carer for my elderly mother I had extensive experience of dealing with the NHS on her behalf when she became old and frail. I have been involved in voluntary work through the Carers Project on a GP initiative project. Also as a member of the public with a vote I consider a political party's policy on NHS issues when I cast that vote. (Newtown health user 13)

Here we begin to see two things. One is the complexity of relationships in which individuals may be engaged – ranging from the most individualized (as a patient) through to the wider collectivity (a member of the public with a vote). The second is the importance of reflective reasoning; this respondent is in no sense a simple bearer of dominant discursive categories, but weaves different identifications (including some that were not on offer in our list) into a compelling relational account.

The combinations of 'patient' (or sometimes 'service user') and 'member of the public' (sometimes 'member of the local community') were by far the most frequent pairings. But they implied different conceptions of 'patient' or 'service user': some dealt in conceptions of dependence and need, while others suggest a more assertive, knowledgeable or self-reliant image, closer to that found in current policy and professional discourse. We explore some of these shifting conceptions of the 'patient' in the following section.

Patient positions: Lying down or standing up?

The identification with being a patient was frequently constructed through contrasts with the idea of being a 'customer' or of 'going shopping' (Clarke forthcoming). The impersonality of market transactions was seen as the opposite of the desired relationship with health practitioners (particularly, the General Practitioner – GP):

I mean, for someone in my situation it is very, very important to have that rapport with the GP … I've had the carpet fitted this week and when I rang up a couple of companies to come in and quote for it they were just looking at doing a job for me, I was a customer for a particular item. Which you can't say with the doctor because it is not for one particular item, it's for a very widespread number of items and so as a consequence of which it's a quite different relationship than the one where you're a customer and you are going to buy something or you want a service from them. But it's generally a one off thing, you might be repeating it later, but it's generally a one off thing. (Newtown health user 2)

No, I don't want to be a customer. I want to be a patient. I want to be a patient. I think once you become a customer you are lumped with customers in a shop, customers in a petrol station, customers in a travel insurance company, whereas as a patient you have that personal relationship which is very difficult to break. That's another thing. As a patient you can't just break it like that (clicks fingers), is what I mean, but as a customer if I go to buy goods, I don't buy the goods, I go elsewhere. (Newtown Health user 3).

Not only is the relationship more personal and associated with a long term process, but the nature of the 'commodity' – health – is clearly very different from other commodities, and the nature of the transactions different from those in the marketplace. This is not particularly surprising, but what is interesting is the clarity and sophistication of the analysis on the part of 'lay' users, most of whom were well able to talk about the difference between health care relationships and those of the marketplace. Their analysis is rather different from that in contemporary policy discourse. Indeed, their view of the patient – and the doctor-patient relationship – interrupts the attempt to construct health users as consumers. There 'patient' is understood as an 'old' term, reflecting the architecture of professional power and dependency; while 'consumer' expresses the transfer of power (through choice) to the user. This old/new distinction is characteristic of New Labour accounts of modernization:

It is often said that choice and equity are in some way in opposition. I don't accept that argument. Consumers act individually but the effect of their actions is communal. The cumulative effect of individual choices increases choice for others. In this sense choice widely available is not inimical to equity, it is a driver for change for everyone. So often in state provision of services universal provision meant the equity of the mediocre. That might have been acceptable to those lying down patients of the past but it will not do for the standing up consumers of the future. What we aspire to is the equity of excellence and choice is a necessary, though not sufficient, part of that transformation. (Cayton 2003)

The question of whether choice is what 'people really want' has been at the core of arguments between the government and its critics (see, for example, Ministers of State 2004; Cabinet Office 2005; Public Administration Select Committee 2005). Our own study – like almost every other that we are aware of – exposes a degree of public ambivalence, uncertainty and contradiction around the issue of choice (see Clarke et al. 2006). For several of our respondents, choice was not seen as the 'best way forward'. While clearly committed to the objective of improving health services, they were – at best – sceptical about choice as the means of achieving it:

> I know 'consumer' and 'customer' imply choice and that is what we are supposed to want. I would consider it an acceptable achievement if everyone would have what was best in the matter of treatment as of right. There are certain cost considerations but that is another issue. 'Choice' may be a political ploy to take our eye of the ball and confuse us as to what really matters. Choice sounds a good thing – but is it? Sorry, this is one of my hobby horses! (Newtown health user 23)

> I don't quite know what choice is about, but if it's about getting the best treatment, to give you the best chance, I don't think that should be choice, I think that should be a fait accompli (Newtown health user 5).

These are voices reluctant to be colonized by the 'new' discourse of choice and consumerism. They reflect on their discursive interpellation ('what we are supposed to want') and construct rhetorical formulations, playing on the dominant discourse, even in the process of refusing it. They articulate – assertively – older discourses of equality and rights in asserting normative positions about what is right and how things should be – in short, in offering an alternative vocabulary for discussing the future of health care. These are certainly 'standing up' voices, like the consumers identified by Cayton above, but they certainly do not understand themselves as consumers – and what they 'stand up for' may be rather different from that envisaged by government. Such 'residual' values are not, it seems, in the process of being displaced by the rise of a consumer society or global consumerism. Instead, they continue to offer resources on which people draw in making sense of the transformation of public services. Williams argues that although 'residual' forms and practices were in the past, they remain effective in the present, in part because 'certain experiences, meanings and values which cannot be expressed or substantially verified in terms of the dominant culture, are nevertheless lived and practised on the basis of the residue – cultural as well as social – of some previous social and cultural institution or formation' (Williams 1977:122).

Interviews with health users confirmed that respondents perceived themselves – and wanted to perceive themselves – as patients, rather than customers or consumers. However the use of the term 'patient' did not denote the passive, dependent relationships that consumerism promises to displace:

> I am a patient and that's the word I understand … I don't feel I'm a customer of the National Health Service, or any health service for that matter. I feel I am a patient and I would like to develop my relationship with my health care professional. Because the way I view it is, being a diabetic, and any other problem I may have health wise, I'm the one whose got it and I have to lead it. The people who are around me are my team who are helping me get there. And a healthcare professional is part of my team. But I am his patient or her patient … I think customer is a very distant relationship. I don't think it is a relationship because I can walk into a shop over the road and be a customer, but not necessarily know the person who is serving me. But I think it's important that you know the person who is dealing with you as a patient. (Oldtown health user 3)

Here the word patient is not used as a default position (or, in Williams' terms, a 'residual' category), but instead was perceived as an important aspect of developing and maintaining a meaningful and productive relationship with health professionals. 'Patient' offers the point of orientation for these explorations, but its meanings are worked on through forcing it into encounters with other terms: stakeholders, partnership, and teams. Each of these is borrowed from other organizational and governance discourses as a way of trying to define the difference. But all of them are articulated through the recurrent commitment to a 'personal relationship'. Equally, there are powerful issues about what might be called 'ownership' – in which possession (my problems, my illness, my notes) is combined with responsibility (my concern) and authority ('I have to lead it'). The forms of private authority articulated by these 'patients' involved new personal capacities and orientations that might enable them to become partners with welfare professionals rather than passive welfare subjects or abstracted choice-making individuals. Such strategies of personalization and partnership bestow legitimacy on a new 'speaking voice' for the involved, responsible patient. This relational view of participation in a collaborative process is potentially significant for other emerging conceptions of health care. Concepts of 'health literacy', negotiated decision-making, and co-production have affinities with such relational and processual visions of health care (Sihota and Lennard 2004).

Remaking public and private authority: From citizens to consumers?

In this paper we have tried to unpack the ways in which the modernization of public service around the figure of the consumer fails to engage with popular identifications and relationships; with the richness and complexity of people's connections to public services; and with the material and symbolic power of the National Health Service as an institution. The discursive data from our study (admittedly a small and particular one) leads us to question the conceptual adequacy of the binary distinction between the citizen and consumer. These may look like master categories in the social sciences, where they appear to condense or embody critical social and political distinctions: public/ private; state/market; individual/collective and so on. But their lack of decisive purchase on everyday reasoning and reflection suggests that we might want to look at them again. In particular we may want to explore what is at stake in the other identifications with the public realm and public institutions that we have heard in this study. We suggest three areas worth further exploration and attention. Firstly, this data provides a simple reminder that meanings are the site of contested interpretation and translation: even the apparently medically dominated 'patient' is the focus of reworking and reinvention for people who want the identity but not necessarily the 'ruling relations' that are implied in its dominant, professionalized, institutionalized inscription (on the institutionalized inscription of ruling relations, see Smith 2005).

Secondly, we need to consider the ways in which people inhabit and reflect upon identifications in multiple and mobile ways. If they have little trouble thinking of themselves multiply (combining being citizens, tax-payers, service users, voters and kin, for example) and are mobile between such identifications (making them conditional as well as relational), it might be a good idea for social scientists to keep up with them (see Holland and Lave 2001). In particular, we might want to look more at what conditions evoke different identifications – what are the relations, practices and settings in which people position themselves as a patient or a member of the public or a citizen?

Thirdly, our study has little to say about what else is at stake in these identifications, in particular the implied, if unspoken, 'social' that they carry. Membership – whether of the public or a local community – looks like another of those ambiguous or double edged relationships that is constituted through simultaneous dynamics of inclusion and exclusion. Membership announces the sense of inclusion into a collective entity and identity while concealing its social conditionality. Who gets to be a member, and how? Both the public and community as collective imaginaries carry a complex field of relational possibilities: of centrality and marginalization; of dominant and subordinate locations; and of included norm and excluded other. The intersection of such public identities with the dynamics of difference and inequality makes them a site of contested maps of the social – in which exclusivist visions contend with imagined solidarities. There are both analytic and political implications. At a point where resurgent and exclusivist nationalisms and racisms try to narrow 'membership', we need to be attentive not just to the negative dynamics but also to how conceptions of communities, the people and the public can be the sites for inclusive and expansive imaginaries associated with discourses of solidarity, equity, fairness, and justice. Our study suggests that such discourses persist – politically, institutionally, and as parts of popular thinking. But two issues follow. What has enabled, and might enable, their persistence as more than 'merely residual'? And to whom are they extended: who are the 'we' of the community, public and people (Balibar 2002; Newman 2005)?

Remaking public and private realms: From state to market?

How might we make connections between this very specific study and wider debates about the governmental project of realigning public and private realms in the current period? We began the chapter by situating the emergence of the 'citizen-consumer' in the context of contemporary transformations of the state and processes of welfare governance. In the light of our analysis we think it is worth distinguishing three aspects of these public service reforms, each of which has implications for an understanding of the reconfiguration of public and private realms. The first centres on the methods or mechanisms involved in the shift from relatively integrated systems of public provision to more dispersed, pluralized or fragmented systems. Here the mechanisms of marketization, privatization and, increasingly, 'partnership' arrangements have attracted considerable attention. Each of these processes also involves considerable variation in practice: for example, marketization ranges from market-making through contracting to existing non-public agencies, to 'market testing' or even the construction of internal markets within public service organizations, separating purchasers and providers. Despite such variations, the process of marketization results in the extension of non-public forms of authority; that is, non-state actors being authorized to carry out functions and assume responsibilities previously the province of the state. Such 'authorized' actors range from corporations through voluntary organizations to consumers. Paradoxically, such 'authorization' is often inscribed by states in their 'meta-governance' role (Jessop 2000). For this reason, we have tended to use the concept of 'dispersal', rather than disaggregation or fragmentation, since it points to the strategic or directive capacity of states to allocate forms and positions of authority (Clarke and Newman 1997).

The second aspect involves a focus on the constructed and reconstructed character of the boundary between public and private itself. Here we encounter the transfer of functions, resources, tasks and responsibilities (predominantly) from the public realm to the private (Marquand 2004). This has been the focus of much political and institutional analysis both as a distinctive political development and as a key example of a wider global trend towards neo-liberalism (Harvey 2005). The public is often viewed as inextricably linked to collectivist, statist, de-commodifying, and (loosely) social democratic development of an expansive and expanded public realm. This assemblage can also be seen as what Leibfried and Zürn (2005) call the 'Golden Age' national constellation of the state. We are not wholly persuaded by this distinction between public and private. The supposedly 'universal' public realm conceals a variety of exclusions, marginalization, and subordinations that create a complex field of relationships rather than a singular 'public' (Warner 2002; Newman 2005). At the same time, the 'private' tends to elide at least two meanings: the private as the private sector (market-based relationship between individual contracting agents, whether persons or corporations); and the private as the private sphere (personal, domestic, familial). As a result, we suspect that there may be multiple boundary changes in play below the level of this binary conception of the public/private distinction – and they may not be of the same kind. As suggested by Hansen (this volume), in moving away from state-centred ontologies it is possible to bring into view several, multi-layered public and private realms and the production of hybrid forms and practices, as well as the mediation of and potential mobility between them. This potential mobility not only involves a shift of services and functions to the 'private' and 'not for profit' sectors, but also shifts from institutions – in whatever sector – to families, households, and individuals, newly constituted as responsible, self-governing, and reflexive subjects. This form of 'privatization' tends to be under-theorized in notions of the disaggregated, dispersed or networked state, but is an equally significant dimension of the reconfiguration of public and private authority in the remaking of welfare governance.

This takes us to the third aspect of the reconfiguration of public and private in welfare reforms that demands our attention: the forms of relationship that they imply between people and institutions (both public and private). The mechanisms of contracting, marketization, and privatization are clearly not just mechanisms: they bring with them different modes of relationship, often associated with the idea of a transition from citizens to consumers. This transition can be treated as merely reflecting wider social changes (to a consumer society, or consumer culture) or they can be seen as producing such orientations and relationships. The reflective model is visible in political and policy sources that treat the rise of the consumer society as the change imperative for public service reform. The productive model is associated with critical challenges to, and reflections on, such claims.

Our data suggests that neither position is adequate, and indicates the importance of not assuming a coherent, consistent and successful process of transformation (Clarke 2006). In the British context, New Labour's neo-liberal orientation has been compromised by the 'grit' of other perspectives on the proper relationship between public and private. These may be discursively residualized (treated as 'old' thinking); they may be coopted and subordinated in the process of articulation and 'transformism'. But they imply a need to analyse neo- or advanced liberalism as something other than a plan being 'rolled out', flattening differences of place, politics and culture (e.g. Larner 2000; Kingfisher 2002; Clarke 2004: Chapter 4). Our findings point to a rather incomplete accomplishment of the attempt to install new identifications or subjections. The persistence of other identifications and the relations they evoke need to be part of any analysis of the conjuncture of attempted transformations.

Elsewhere, we have taken up arguments with both political economy and governmentality perspectives on the rise of the citizen-consumer (Clarke et al. 2007). We want to argue for a view of transformation that is less epochal (the move from X to Y, or at least, to post-X) and is more attentive to the uneven, unstable, and unfinished character of governmental and political projects. Instead of an epochal view, then, we argue for a mode of analysis that is attentive to the co-existence of different forces, perspectives and discourses alongside – and in complex interactions with – the 'dominant'. Raymond Williams distinguished between 'epochal' analysis and 'authentic historical analysis'. In the former, attention was concentrated on the dominant tendency. In the latter, he suggested, it was necessary at every point to recognize the complex interrelations between movements and tendencies both within and beyond a specific and effective dominance ... We have certainly still to speak of the 'dominant' and the 'effective', and in these senses of the 'hegemonic'. But we find that we have also to speak, and indeed, with further differentiation of each, of the 'residual' and the 'emergent', which in any real process, and at any moment in the process, are significant both in themselves and in what they reveal of the characteristics of the 'dominant' (Williams 1977: 121–2).

'Residual' and 'emergent' formations may be drawn into subordinated or supporting roles in the dominant (for example, New Labour's attempt to equate Choice with 'equity' and 'diversity'). Such formations may be dismissed as 'old thinking' or 'impractical', but they may provide distinctive 'voicings' of social and political dissatisfactions, desires, and doubts. In doing so, they announce other ways of being in the world, other possibilities, other 'modernities'. We think it is important to keep social analysis open to practices, perspectives, and positions that are not the dominant. As a result, we want to argue against 'epochal' views that assume the successful transformations of states and the emergence of new 'privatized' subjects. While people keep open spaces of scepticism and doubt, and imagine other ways of 'progressing', how could we do anything less?

Notes

1. *Creating Citizen-Consumers: Changing Relationships and Identifications* was funded by the ESRC/AHRB *Cultures of Consumption* programme and ran from April 2003–May 2005 (grant number: RES-143–25–0008).We studied three public services (health, policing, and social care) in two places (Newtown and Oldtown). We distributed 300 questionnaires to staff and users (returns from 106 users and 168 staff = 46 per cent return rate). We conducted 24 interviews with managers; 23 with front-line staff; ten with users and held six user focus groups. The project team was John Clarke, Janet Newman, Nick Smith, Elizabeth Vidler, Louise Westmarland, based in the Faculty of Social Sciences at The Open University, UK. More details at: www.open.ac.uk/socialsciences/citizenconsumers.
2. Indeed, New Labour has demonstrated a striking enthusiasm for citizens and citizenship. It might be seen as a political and governmental project that has proliferated varieties of citizenship (and their rights, responsibilities, and locations). Some aspects of this phenomenon are discussed in Clarke 2005.
3. We collected this data in several different ways. First, we distributed a questionnaire to 50 randomly selected users in each of our two urban settings. The final question asked respondents to consider a number of possible identifications and relationships (citizen, consumer, member of the public, and so on) and to select those that they felt best reflected who they thought they were when interacting with the service in question. They could select up to two categories. They were then invited, on the questionnaire itself, to add comments about why they had chosen particular categories. This gave us an initial set of quantitative and qualitative data.

   We then used this data to design semi-structured interview schedules to test some of the emerging themes, and carried out follow up interviews with respondents who had indicated their willingness to be interviewed. The interviews, then, are not based on a random sample – they possibly represent those with more time and commitment than the norm. However we found very similar themes emerging from the questionnaires and interviews: the interviews, then, allowed us to explore in further depth themes that were already emerging from the questionnaire data. Finally, we held focus groups in each case study site drawing on members of local patient and public participation groups.

References

Balibar, E. (2002) *We, The People of Europe? Reflections of Transnational Citizenship.* New Jersey: Princeton University Press.

Cabinet Office (2005) *Choice and Voice in the Reform of Public Services: Government Response to the PASC report – Choice, Voice and Public Services.* London: Cabinet Office.

Cayton, H. (2003) *Trust Me, I'm A Patient: Can Healthcare Afford the Informed Consumer?*, Speech Delivered to the Royal College of Physicians, BUPA Health Debate, 2 September 2003, London.

Clarke, J. (2004) *Changing Welfare, Changing States: new directions in social policy.* London: Sage Publications.

Clarke, J. (2005) 'New Labour's Citizens: Activated, Empowered, Responsibilised, Abandoned?', *Critical Social Policy*, 25 (4): 447–463.

Clarke, J. (2006) 'Consumerism and the remaking of state-citizen relationships', in C. McDonald and G. Marston (eds) *Reframing Social Policy: A Governmental Approach.* Brighton: Edward Elgar Publishing.

Clarke, J. (forthcoming) 'It's not like shopping: relational reasoning and public services', in M. Bevir and F. Trentmann (eds) *Governance, Citizens, and Consumers: Agency and Resistance in Contemporary Politics.* Basingstoke: Palgrave Macmillan.

Clarke, J. and J. Newman (1997) *The Managerial State: Power, Politics and Ideology in the Remaking of Social Welfare.* London: Sage Publications.

Clarke, J. and J. Newman (2004) 'Governing in the Modern World', in D. L. Steinberg and R. Johnson (eds) *Blairism and the War of Persuasion: Labour's Passive Revolution.* London: Lawrence and Wishart.

Clarke, J., J. Newman, N. Smith, E. Vidler and L. Westmarland (2007) *Creating Citizen Consumers? Changing Publics and Changing Public Services.* London: Sage Publications.

Clarke, J., N. Smith and E. Vidler (2006) 'The Indeterminacy of Choice: political, policy and organizational dilemmas', *Social Policy and Society*, 5(3): 1–10.

Department of Health (2005) *Independence, Well-being and Choice: Our vision for the future of social care for adults in England.* London: Department of Health.

Flynn, N. (2002) *Public Sector Management*, 4th edition. Harlow: Prentice-Hall.

The Guardian 24/06/2004: 1

Hall, S. (2003) 'New Labour's double shuffle', *Soundings*, 24:10–24.

Harvey, D. (2005) *A Brief History of Neoliberalism.* Oxford: Oxford University Press.

Holland, D. and J. Lave (2001) 'History in Person: an introduction', in D. Holland and J. Lave (eds) *History in Person: Enduring Struggles, Contentious Practices, Intimate Identities.* Santa Fe: School of American Research; Oxford: James Currey Ltd.

Jessop, B. (2000) 'Governance Failure', in G. Stoker (ed) *The New Politics of British Local Governance*. Basingstoke: Macmillan.

Kingfisher, C. (ed) (2002) *Western Welfare in Decline: Globalization and Women's Poverty*. Philadelphia: University of Pennsylvania Press.

Larner, W. (2000) 'Neo-liberalism: Policy, Ideology, Governmentality', *Studies in Political Economy*, 63:5–25.

Leibfried, S. and M. Zürn (2005) 'The unravelling of the Golden Age Nation State', in Leibfried, S. and M. Zürn (eds) *Transformations of the State*. Cambridge: Cambridge University Press.

Marquand, D. (2004) *The Decline of the Public*. Cambridge: Polity Press.

Ministers of State for Department of Health, Local and Regional Government, and School Standards (2004) *The Case for User Choice in Public Services*. A Joint Memorandum to the Public Administration Select Committee Inquiry into Choice, Voice and Public Services.

National Consumer Council (2004) *Making Public Services Personal: A New Compact for Public Services*. (The independent Policy Commission on Public Services report to the National Consumer Council). London: National Consumer Council.

Needham, C. (2003) *Citizen-consumers: New Labour's marketplace democracy*. London: The Catalyst Forum.

Newman, J. (2005) *Remaking Governance: Peoples, Politics and the Public Sphere*. Bristol: Policy Press.

Newman, J. and E. Kuhlmann (2007) 'Consumers enter the political stage: the moderniser of health care in Britain and Germany', *Journal of European Social Policy*, 17(2).

Newman, J. and E. Vidler (2006a) 'Discriminating customers, responsible patients, empowered users: consumerism and the modernisation of health care', *Journal of Social Policy*, 35(2): 193–209.

Newman, J. and E. Vidler (2006b) 'More than a matter of choice? Consumerism and the modernization of health care', in L. Bauld, K. Clarke and T. Maltby (eds) *Social Policy Review 18*. Bristol: The Policy Press.

Office of Public Services Reform (2002) *Reforming our Services: Principles into Practice*. London: Office of Public Services Reform.

Public Administration Select Committee (2005) *Choice, Voice, and Public Services*. Fourth Report of Session 2004–5, Vol. 1. London: House of Commons (HC 49-1).

Pollitt, C. and G. Bouckaert (2000) *Public Management Reform: A Comparative Analysis*. Oxford: Oxford University Press.

Rose, N. (1999) *Powers of Freedom: reframing political thought*. Cambridge: Cambridge University Press.

Sihota, S. and L. Lennard (2004) *Health literacy: being able to make the most of health*. London: National Consumer Council.

Slaughter, A-M. (2004) *A New World Order*. Princeton: Princeton University Press.

Smith, D. (2005) *Institutional Ethnography: A Sociology for People*. Lanham, MD and Oxford: Altamira Press.

Warner, M. (2002) *Publics and Counterpublics*. New York: Zone Books.

Williams, R. (1977) *Marxism and Literature*. Oxford: Oxford University Press.

7
Expatriate Experts: New Zealand's Diaspora Strategy

Wendy Larner

On Tuesday 6 March 2006, along with many other New Zealanders living overseas, I received an email from KEA New Zealand (Kiwi Expatriate Association) asking me to complete the Everyone Counts New Zealand Census. Held the same day as the official five yearly New Zealand census, and co-sponsored by the Ministry of Economic Development, Ministry of Education, APN News and Media, the New Zealand Rugby Union, and the New Zealand America's Cup team, this online survey aspired to establish more precisely how many expatriate New Zealanders there are, and the nature of their connections with New Zealand. Following three initial questions about citizenship status, the first substantive question asked about their economic connections – defined as business, ownership of property, investments or other financial interests – with New Zealand. In an interview broadcast on national television Ross McConnell, the chief executive of KEA, explained the rationale for the survey: 'We want to think about New Zealand as a globally connected nation of five million rather than an isolated nation of four million stuck at the bottom of the South Pacific … that's a much more powerful way to think' (TVNZ 08 March 2006).

The New Zealand government is not alone in facilitating efforts to make formal connections with expatriate citizens who might help with the insertion of domestic organizations into global economic flows and networks. Governments across the world have begun to think about their expatriate populations in new ways. In the new 'knowledge based economy' the international competitiveness of overseas experts is expected to enhance human capital and improve economic performance by fostering greater productivity, creativity, and innovation. Consequently active efforts are now being made to link expatriate business, cultural, scientific, and policy networks to national development projects. How should we understand the recent proliferation of what are now being called 'diaspora strategies'? Is it simply coincidence that this new understanding of the role of expatriates in national development projects became visible in the early 1990s, just as globalization entered into the policy lexicons of economic development ministries around the world? If not, what, if anything, does this new emphasis on expatriate expertise and globalizing forms of development tell us about changing forms of governance in general, and the role of private authority in global politics in particular?

This paper uses a detailed analysis of the New Zealand case to examine these questions. The aim is to examine how the ambitions of the New Zealand state came to be articulated to the individual and collective experiences of expatriates, and to explore the implications of this new political-economic strategy for the nation-state. It is argued that diaspora strategies are integral to the means by which the globalizing knowledge economy is being made governmental. They exemplify how international organizations, state agencies, and individuals have all begun to think beyond national boundaries in their efforts to generate new forms of economic development. Through web pages, databases, and events, expatriate experts are being actively identified, named, and harnessed to national development projects. In the second section of the paper, it is shown that diaspora strategies not only represent a new geographic imaginary and political-economic field, they also involve the active constitution of new spaces and subjects with distinctive characteristics. These new spaces and subjects challenge existent conceptions of the nation-state. Diaspora strategies not only disrupt conventional distinctions between the domestic and the international, they are also reconfiguring public and private authority as new under-standings of nation, state, and governance all emerge.

Globalization, governmentality and diasporas

Whether theorized as structure, process or epoch, it is now widely accepted that globalization involves a move away from nation-state for-mations towards global flows and networks. While this transformation is usually regarded as a material change in the world, more recently the new emphasis on globality has been analysed as a 'governmentality' (Hindess 1998; Ferguson and Gupta 2002; Fraser 2003; Larner and Walters 2004). Nation-states, industries, regions, communities, and indi-viduals are all making efforts to advance their interests by encouraging global connectedness. Social scientists have shown that these globalizing governmentalities entail heterogeneous geographic imaginaries and political practices, expressed in the simultaneous re-ordering of territories, socialities, and subjectivities (Massey 1999; Barry 2001; Katz 2001; Appadurai 2002; Nagar et al. 2002).

Seen through this analytical lens, globalization has transformed from being a contested political-economic project aimed at attracting additional foreign direct investment, to a governmental rationality; a taken for granted 'context' in which economic activities are understood to take place. This does not mean of course, that all policymakers understand globalization in the same way. Just as welfarism was instantiated and embodied in a variety of political and institutional forms, so too is globalization. For example, the contrast between the United Kingdom government's portrayal of globalization as a monolithic process 'out there' and the New Zealand government's invoking of global connectedness is striking. More generally, Hay and Rosamond (2002) have shown how different European governments mobilize the discourse of globalization in distinctive ways. But the broader point is that policymakers, business people, and academics all largely accept that the economy is globalizing, and talk and act accordingly. It is in this context that it can be argued that globalization has become governmental both in the conventional and Foucauldian senses.

These conceptual discussions provide us with useful ways to rethink the claims about the new role of private authority in global politics. Rather than seeing the public and private as pregiven categories, and the rise of private authority as involving a shift from the former to the later, the governmentality literature would encourage us to understand both public and private as historically produced fields of action emerging from an heterogeneous array of discourses and practices that help constitute subjects and objects of governance in particular forms (Dean 1999; Rose 1999). New governmental forms are not monolithic expressions of a 'new world order' in which the ideas, practices, and institutions associated with the nation-state have been supplanted by new globalizing modes of authority (Slaughter 2004). Rather, they are specific representations of political-economic life that are worked, maintained, aligned, and made to count (Amin 2004: 225). Moreover, the processes giving rise to these governmental forms are both contested and contradictory.

Governmentality is a useful tool for this task because it emphasizes the role of particular knowledges, techniques, spaces and subjects in this process. But this is not the only approach that would help us 'denaturalize' taken-for-granted categories such as public and private by paying attention to the drawing together of particular forms of information and the devizing of strategies and techniques to mobilize organizations, groups, and individuals. Equally valuable are contemporary ethnographies of the state that allow fine-grained examinations of how particular governmental initiatives come together, the rationales deployed, the techniques mobilized, and the institutional forms that emerge. As Sharma and Gupta (2006) suggest, more than the governmentality literature, these anthropological approaches also highlight the cultural construction of states – how people perceive the state and how these perceptions are shaped by specific encounters with state processes, institutions, and officials. Seen together, these literatures encourage us to develop theoretically informed, empirically grounded, research projects that examine apparently mundane and taken-for granted aspects of governing in our efforts to understand the rise of globalizing political formations.

This chapter draws on these literatures to examine diaspora strategies as a 'litmus test' (Kuznetsov 2005) example of the discourses and techniques through which globalization is being constituted and institutionalized, and explores the implications of these strategies for both spaces and subjects. In doing so, it challenges both the fact of the diaspora and the taken-for-granted territoriality of the nation-state. Borrowing from Rose (1999), diasporas are understood as 'irreal spaces', not quite real, not quite imagined. Diaspora strategies do not mobilize self-evident groups of people who have already organized themselves according to their countries of origin. Rather, they are a new way of thinking about populations made manifest in the relatively recent 'discovery' of expatriates by a range of governments, the efforts of demographers and other social scientists to identify and count these offshore citizens, and techniques such as web-pages, databases, networking, and events through which expatriates are being mobilised. As Barry (2001: 87) argues about networks more generally, these efforts do not simply involve the representation of particular sets of social relations, but rather should be seen as involving active efforts to reorganize the social field.

More specifically, the naming and active constitution of the diaspora exemplifies the rise of a globalizing governmentality. While there has been extensive discussion of the reterritorialization of economies (under the ambit of economic globalization) and populations (under that of transnationalism), there has been less discussion of how the new spatial ontologies associated with the globalizing knowledge economy (Amin 2004) are reshaping both governmental processes and state forms. This is not an argument about the rescaling of state spaces (Brenner 2004), rather, it is to claim that diaspora strategies make manifest new conceptions of governance premised on global flows, networks, and mobility. The remainder of the paper explores these themes by asking the following questions: how was the Kiwi diaspora made visible? How has it been linked to governmental processes and state forms? What sort of space is the diaspora? What subjects are understood to inhabit this space? How are these 'irreal' diasporic spaces and subjects reshaping both state and nation? To answer these questions, the paper develops an analysis that is based on literature reviews, Internet searches, key informant interviews, and online and in person observation in London-based New Zealand expatriate association meetings.

The rise of diaspora strategies

In the policy documents of myriad international organizations, national governments and economic development agencies, diaspora strategies are now an integral part of a governmental imaginary in which entrepreneurial, globally networked, subjects create new possibilities for economic growth and in doing so contribute to the development of a knowledge-based economy. However, while diaspora policies and programmes may appear to epitomize neoliberal understandings of self actualizing individuals and globalizing markets, they are not particularly visible in the so-called heartlands of neoliberalism – the United States and United Kingdom. Rather they are found in those countries that understand themselves to have experienced 'brain drain' and so are having difficulty accessing the capital and skills needed to succeed in the global economy. Today these countries include not only the developing countries of the so-called 'South' in which diasporic relationships have long been part of development strategies, but also 'middling' developed countries of the so-called 'North' such as New Zealand, South Africa, Canada, Australia, Singapore, and Ireland.

In these 'middling' developed countries diaspora strategies are part of a broader economic strategy that involves making manifest active attempts to insert sectors, industries, regions, and individuals into global flows and networks. They are particularly evident in small 'actively globalizing' countries such as Ireland, Singapore, and New Zealand. Indeed, Kapur (2001: 22) speculates that small countries may be more open to the influence of their diaspora for the same reasons as they are often more open to trade. Moreover, figures from a recent OECD report show that New Zealand's high skill diaspora is not only the highest in the OECD on a per capita basis, accounting for 16 per cent of the total population, and 24 per cent of the highly skilled population, but is also growing at faster rate than many of its counterparts (Dumont and Lemaitre 2005). In this context, New Zealand is a useful case to examine more closely in order to understand how this new vision of globalizing networks is being constituted through new understandings of the problems of economic development, particular modes of knowledge and calculation, and new forms of interaction.

The New Zealand government discovered its diaspora in the late 1990s following a series of initiatives that made manifest the ambition to create a knowledge based economy (Larner et al. 2007). The *Bright Futures* package was launched in 1999, designed to encourage a focus on 'enterprise and innovation' in New Zealand. Elements of this package included an elite doctoral scholarship fund, the establishment of the New Economy Research Fund directed at targeted industry research, additional funding for post-doctoral scholarships, and the establishment of the Innovate New Zealand Council. One response to this package was an widely publicized open letter from a group of US-based New Zealand academics, subsequently accompanied by a submission to the Tertiary Education Advisory Committee, which argued that 'government should involve the global network of knowledge producers when doing the crucial work of developing and supporting New Zealand's academic talent' (Wilson et al. 2000: 1). As part of their proposals, these offshore New Zealanders explicitly proposed the establishment of an 'expatriate directory'.

In the lead up to the election of 1999 which saw the fifth Labour government appointed to office media attention focussed on claims that large numbers of well qualified New Zealanders were leaving the country. A full page advertisement, claiming evidence of a 'lost generation', was followed by considerable public debate and a high profile New Zealand Herald series focused on the phenomenon now being dubbed the 'Kiwi diaspora'. These years also saw a range of expatriate initiated ventures such as NZEDGE which was co-founded in 1999 by Brian Sweeney (of the public relations company Sweeny Vesty) and Kevin Roberts (of the advertising agency Saatchi and Saatchi) to raise the profile of 'global New Zealanders', the ANZA Technology Network aimed at bringing together Australian, New Zealand, and US technology companies and executives, and The Global Network of Kiwis (Gnok) founded in late 2001 also aimed at helping New Zealand technology companies enter the US market. Seen together, these diverse efforts served to make visible a previously unthought of category of New Zealanders; those who lived out of New Zealand, had little or no intention of returning, but who had retained an interest in the affairs – particularly the economic affairs – of the country.

Social scientists also played a critical role in naming and constituting the 'Kiwi diaspora'. Most visible were the demographers who found themselves engaged in a discussion about the size of New Zealand's offshore population. When asked by a journalist, New Zealand's pre-eminent demographer, Richard Bedford calculated the diaspora at some 850,000, representing 22 per cent of the national population (Collins 2001). This figure entered into general circulation, although Treasury analysts, Bryant and Low (2004), have subsequently revised his figure down to 400,000 by focussing on economically active individuals. Government officials now regularly cite the figure of one million people, including not only spouses and children, but also claiming that many expatriate New Zealanders no longer travel on their New Zelanad passports. Nor was the academic discussion just about numbers; for example, ongoing debates over 'brain drain' and the size of the Kiwi diaspora were accompanied by the emergence of 'global careers' as an object of study in New Zealand's business schools and various research projects on topics such as the economic benefits of the longstanding tradition for young New Zealanders to undertake OE (overseas experience), and expatriates motivations for staying or leaving New Zealand (see, for examples, Wilson 2001; Inkson et al. 2004).

Having been made discursively and technically visible, expatriate New Zealanders subsequently began to be actively re-enrolled in national development strategies. By the early 2000s, reflecting broader political changes involving a new focus on the experiences of other small countries, a more proactive approach to economic development made manifest in the establishment of Industry New Zealand, and a new emphasis on experimentation and pilot programmes, growing attention was being paid to expatriates in general. Rather than being 'lost' to New Zealand, discussion began to focus on the ways in which the 'Kiwi diaspora' might be encouraged to re-engage with their country of origin. Certainly, expatriate New Zealanders were highly visible at the first KnowledgeWave conference, a jointly sponsored government, University of Auckland, and private sector conference aimed at promoting a 'national debate' about the economic future of the country. Moreover, one of the high profile initiatives to emerge from this conference was the announcement of a private sector funded database of New Zealanders working in the United States IT sector. This initiative subsequently became the KEA network (Kiwi Expatriate Association) which now has chapters in London, New York, Silicon Valley, Los Angeles, New England, Washington DC, London, the Netherlands, and Sydney.

The release of the government commissioned LEK Consulting Report (2001) *New Zealand Talent Initiative: Strategies for Building a Talented Nation* further underlined the potential contribution of expatriate expertise. The report concluded that New Zealand should become a 'networked nation' in which 'New Zealand's economic prosperity will no longer be dominated by its geography, but will instead be driven by the ideas and innovations of an international talent pool' (LEK 2001: 80). It placed a high priority on the role that might be played by expatriate New Zealanders in realizing this vision. Amongst the more specific recommendations were those for a global roll of New Zealanders, a national website for expatriate New Zealanders, greater co-ordination of existent networks, and the establishment of a global 'talent club', led by the private sector and made up of elite New Zealanders.

The New Zealand Government launched a formal diaspora strategy following the second Knowledge Wave conference in 2003, which not coincidentally focussed explicitly on issues of social capital and leadership. Framed through the rationale of 'global connectedness', which now featured explicitly as one of the broader aspirations of the overarching Growth and Innovation Framework, the strategy drew together the World Class New Zealanders programme run by the Ministry of Economic Development, which is reputedly heavily oversubscribed (Frater 2004), and gave formal government support and considerable funding to the KEA programme which then subsequently relocated itself in the University of Auckland incubator. A full time director is now employed and a number of high profile initiatives underway, including the global census with which this chapter opened.

Significantly, the diaspora strategy was seen as a tactic within a wider economic strategy, rather than being an aspect of migration policy. The key ministry was New Zealand Trade and Enterprise, rather than the Department of Labour which continued to run a programme designed to encourage New Zealanders to return home (Buwalda 2005). Nor was the diaspora strategy to be simply state-driven; rather, it was seen as a collective and iterative process between government agencies and expatriate organizations. They make manifest the notion of a 'facilitative' or 'enabling' state; government's role is one of coordination and encouragement rather than control. They are increasingly explicitly aligned with initiatives such as business incubators that also bring together government actors, private sector interests, and expatriate relationships (Ellerman 2003). While KEA had been singled out for government support, the intention was that as this strategy began to cohere so too would KEA link up with other New Zealand expatriate initiatives, as well as more specialized alumni programmes such as those run by the New Zealand Treasury, the Universities, and professional associations such as ICANZ. Longer standing initiatives such as Chambers of Commerce or embassy links were also reinterpreted as providing bridgeheads into potential export markets.

Today the benefit of harnessing the 'Kiwi diaspora' to stimulate economic growth is widely accepted. Media articles and government websites regularly feature high profile expatriate 'success stories'. Initiatives underway include mentoring programmes that will allow New Zealand based firms to access export markets in places as diverse as London, Shanghai, and Dubai, the establishment of advisory boards on which expatriates feature prominently, and a proliferation of incubator schemes based on the assumption that new firms can become the basis of successful export industries if their growth is fostered by linking them up with international expertise of various sorts. These initiatives are designed to generate entrepreneurialism and innovation, and allow New Zealand and New Zealanders to better meet the 'challenges of a globalizing world'. More specifically, the ambition is that they will facilitate the transfer of technical skills, finance, and market knowledge (market standards, financial practices, corporate governance), allowing more ready access into offshore markets.

The spaces and subjects of the 'Kiwi diaspora'

The New Zealand strategy imagines the spaces and subjects of the diaspora in very distinctive forms. Expatriate New Zealanders are being cast as new sources of financial, human, and social capital. Indeed, it is remarkable how rarely the New Zealand government explicitly uses nationalistic or cultural discourses to justify its economically motivated engagement with the diaspora (cf. Walton-Roberts 2004). Expatriate New Zealanders do not appear to occupy a cultural or even a political space. As Gamlen (2005) observes, whereas diasporas are usually seen as both a resource and a constituency, in New Zealand the emphasis is overwhelmingly on the former. As we have seen in the section above, the vocabulary of the Kiwi diaspora is that of the knowledge economy. It is that of competitiveness, growth, skills, entrepreneurship, and innovation, and only rarely of community and identity. The 'Kiwi diaspora' is a globalizing economic space occupied by active and entrepreneurial subjects. Expatriates are being enrolled in development strategies in order to enhance economic opportunities for domestic actors by actively linking them into global flows and networks. In this respect, diaspora strategies also exemplify how the idea of the knowledge economy is now being harnessed as a government technology (see also Stöber, Flyverbom and Bislev, Salskov-Iversen and Hansen this volume).

This new economic space is a networked space. It is an example of the 'new, topologically and hierarchically situated economic spaces' described by Amin (2004: 219). Rather than being a singular territorially bounded space, the diaspora is imagined as being made up of multiple sectoral, functional, and geographical relationships in which some subjects might be relatively passive, whereas others might already be actively engaged in efforts to improve New Zealand's competitiveness. These diasporic relationships are territorially autonomous, not clearly part of either the host or original country. The aim of the strategy is to organize and institutionalize these relationships in ways that foster increasing participation and develop transactions among expatriates, and between expatriates and New Zealand based initiatives. Seen in this way, it could be argued that diasporic strategies are based on a vision and organizational logic of fluid, non-exclusive, institutional spaces that are made up of networks of networks. It is by constituting and accessing these globalizing economic networks that New Zealand's human, financial, and social capital will be increased.

The diaspora is a voluntary space, dependent on soft techniques and modes of governance such as credibility, reputation, image, and informality (Salskov-Iversen and Hansen this volume) The strategy relies on the ability to attract and co-opt, rather than coerce, expatriates to join these networks. Not only do members have to 'put their hands up' to participate, usually by registering on a web page, enrolling in a database, or attending an event, sometimes they even pay a subscription or entry fee. Diaspora strategies also involve those who choose to participate by giving their time and knowledge freely when they could be working as paid consultants. Nor is this just about individuals; state bureaucrats, firms, and a diverse range of intermediary organizations also join 'voluntarily' into these processes. This voluntarism explains an often made criticism of diaspora networks; namely that they are institutionally weak and organizationally diffuse. It also explains some of the financial challenges which in turn influence the ability of the network to attract members and retain participation. But the broader point is that it is that expatriates and the associated organizations not only volunteer to become members of the diasporic network, they also, wittingly or unwittingly, volunteer to become agents of the globalizing knowledge economy.

In this context, it is not surprising to find that diasporic networks are intermediated spaces. Kapur (2001:17) argues that diasporic networks are themselves 'reputational intermediaries and credibility enhancing mechanisms especially in fields based on tacit knowledge and trust based relationships'. More specifically, however, diaspora strategies require public relations campaigns to alert people to the existence of expatriate networks, the organizational capacity to identify and recruit mentors/volunteers with appropriate skills, and then they need to link these mentors/volunteers to firms and individuals who can benefit from their expertise. This requires 'outreach, organization, fundraising, project planning and implementation, technical assistance and maintaining a medium for information exchange' (Johnson and Sedeca 2004). Diaspora strategies also mobilize other intermediaries; for example, labour market intermediaries such as headhunters and recruitment agencies often play active roles. It has also been argued that new forms of expertise are emerging around these networks; for example, companies that specialize in providing business contacts and experience to firms trying to break into particular markets. Finally, it will be clear that diasporic strategies also privilege non-human intermediaries (Meyer et al. 2001). They are critically dependent on web pages and databases as a means of identifying and enrolling people.

Diaspora strategies are also exclusionary spaces. While they purport to be inclusive and democratic spaces, expatriate networks are perhaps better understood as 'clubs' (Robertson and Dale 2002). They are often narrowly based, personality driven, and controlled by specific individuals and groups. Nor is it unusual to find that they are also racialized and gendered in specific ways, reflecting the privileging of the masculine domains of financial and entrepreneurial expertise. Moreover, like networks more generally, diasporic networks may be geographically extensive but they are not necessarily well connected. Indeed, studies have shown that high skill expatriates tend to have personal and individual ties with their countries of origin, rather than strong links with fellow nationals (Meyer 2001: 100). Consequently, diasporic networks can be as much associated with patronage as with any other criteria. Nor is this exclusionary dimension an unintended consequence of the diaspora strategy. Indeed, there is an explicit discussion about the need for these initiatives to distinguish between alumni models – which involve mass mobilization – and the overachievers model which focusses on 'elite' actors and in which the targets are those who can influence corporate investment and decision making processes. Inclusion and exclusion are thus not derivative or incidental features of expatriate networks, but are intrinsic to the way in which they govern.

Diaspora strategies as private authority?

Existing discussions of diasporas tend to focus on the reterritorialization of the nation, rather than the state. One consequence is that this literature has largely been a discussion of social networks and cultural forms, and the political-economic aspects of these processes have been downplayed. Even the literature on highly skilled expatriate labour forces in global cities has focussed on informal social networks and cultural forms (see, for examples, Beaverstock 2002; Conradson and Latham 2005). State processes tend to feature in these analyses only insofar as they facilitate or inhibit long distance relationships and alternative conceptions of the nation (Basch et al. 1994). Not only does this mean that the governmental processes through which this particular way of thinking about populations has been constituted remain under-explored, but it also means that the territoriality and attributes of the state (in contrast to that of the nation) tend to be taken for granted.

The emergence of formal diaspora strategies requires us to reconsider this emphasis. While it is well recognized that links between states and expatriate populations existed in the past, these are now being systemized, and the connections are becoming both dense and multiple (Meyer and Brown 1999). Moreover, whereas previously the aim was to attract highly skilled expatriates back to their countries of origin, states now actively encourage a diasporic imagination in which there is scope for multiple affiliations and associations (Yeoh and Willis 1998). These new 'diasporas by design' (Kotkin 1992) seek to access both the expatriate expert's embodied knowledge *and* the broader contexts in which they operate. As we have seen in this discussion, this has led to a much more active mobilization of expatriates through initiatives such as investment conferences, industry and sector specific web links, the creation of expert databases, direct appeals by national leaders, short term visits by academics, mentors and industry specialists, and the explicit targeting of financial, market, and technical expertise.

The rise of diaspora strategies also suggests that discussions of globalization and governance in which it is assumed that nations and economies are deterritorializing while states remain territorially bounded require rethinking. What we see clearly in this example is that the territoriality of the state is also being reworked, confirming recent claims that the link between territory, state power, and sovereignty appears to have been broken (Sassen 1998; Hansen and Stepputat 2005). Rather than states continuing to exercise exclusive management of their populations within clearly delineated domains in an effort to confront external global economic processes, diaspora strategies involve states and non-state actors alike reaching into 'other' territories to identify and enrol 'their' expatriates in the effort to enhance economic development strategies premised on the desirability of accessing global flows and networks. Diaspora strategies thus represent a successful attempt to assert sovereignty beyond the territorial boundaries of the state and show how transnational subjects and spaces are becoming the objects of governmental interventions.

Finally, diaspora strategies highlight key aspects associated with the shift from government to governance. It is not only the nation that is being transformed, so too are state institutions and governmental forms. It is important to remember that diaspora strategies are not imposed from above. The new thinking about the role of expatriates in economic development is not emerging as either the straightforward consequence of the designs of neoliberal elites, or as an inevitable response to a globalized network economy. Rather, it is the very idea of 'globalization' that is giving rise to these new activities which are being enacted through an iterative process between government agencies, intermediary organizations, and various expatriate actors. Internationally mobile individuals are actively articulating themselves to state processes, and in turn both they and governmental processes are being rearticulated. Consequently it is not just that state agencies and hegemonic global actors are promoting diaspora strategies as a means of enhancing international competitiveness, but the state itself is coming to take new forms as a consequence of new efforts to govern through these globalizing networks of political and institutional relationships.

More generally, diaspora strategies can be seen as part of a broader process of population management (Stöber, this volume; Salskov-Iversen and Hansen, this volume) in which states have become more focused on producing subjects who are attractive to global capital. In an influential account Ong (1999) writes about a new form of 'graduated sovereignty' in which corporate entities increasingly set the terms of economic and social engagement for certain groups within the nation-state, and points to the enhanced mobility of senior managers, consultants, and various other intermediaries as one consequence of these new distinctions between populations. More recently, she has argued that these efforts are giving rise to new 'latitudes of citizenship' (Ong 2005) in which mobile bodies are differentially linked across nation-states. She compares the experiences of transnational elites, whose primary allegiance is to global flows and networks, to those of illegal migrants and refugees whose experiences of these processes are quite different. Diaspora strategies are clearly much more focussed on the former than the latter; they too privilege the 'strategic cosmopolitan as a nodal agent in the expanding networks of the global economy' (Mitchell 2003:400).

As others have argued, a number of important political issues arise from these new conceptions of transnational citizenship and population management. For example, concern has been expressed that diaspora strategies reify origins rather than residence as the primary basis of citizenship. In work on India, for example, it has been argued that diaspora strategies move definitions of Indian-ness towards a racially tinged determination (van der Veer 2005). Seen in this context, it may be no coincidence that in New Zealand diaspora strategies have begun to proliferate just as claims around increased ethnic diversity and multiculturalism have become more pressing. Certainly expatriate networks premised on relationships between members of long-standing settler populations (and sometimes those premised on indigenity) have a much higher profile than those facilitated by Indian and Chinese New Zealanders who are likely to have access to key export markets in South East Asia and China. But nor are the working class New Zealanders who have moved in large numbers to Australia over the last two decades targeted by diaspora strategies; as we have seen these are elite initiatives that privilege particular skills and talents.

While it would be easy to be cynical it is not, however, inevitable that such initiatives will lead to more exclusionary understandings of citizenship and belonging. KEA, for example, accepts members of any nationality stipulating only that those involved feel some sort of connection to New Zealand. Nor did the example of the Global census with which this chapter opened require people to be New Zealand citizens to fill it out. Thus neither origin nor citizenship is the criteria for participation in these activities. There have also been important efforts to broaden the social base of the various expatriate initiatives. Thus while diaspora strategies are helping to contribute to a broader re-ordering of populations, economies, and states, their consequences are not predetermined. Understanding more about the performative political relationships that are giving rise to new conceptions of the diaspora, the implications they have for state institutions and governmental forms, and the spaces and subjects they constitute, will allow us to think more carefully about the form and content of the so-called 'new world order' and the politics it will require.

Conclusion

This analysis of the New Zealand diaspora strategy exemplifies the ways in which networks are beginning to challenge territorial models of sovereignty (Barry 2001: 91). In the literature on diasporas the assumption has been that while nations are reterritorializing, the state itself has remained anchored to territory. But what we see very clearly here, not just in the case of New Zealand but more generally, is that these strategies take the form of state-sponsored initiatives that involve reaching out into other territories in the effort to identify and harness 'their' diasporas. Whether these are truly global networks or merely national networks writ large (Holton 2005: 213) is irrelevant. Although bounded territoriality remains an important part of the imagery of the state, the rise of diaspora strategies is significant because it demonstrates that state agencies, policymakers, and individual citizens themselves have begun to think beyond national borders and are making efforts to generate highly fluid, non-territorial forms of organization (Barry 2001; Amin 2004). Seen in this context, it could be argued that diaspora strategies are helping to contribute to a broader reordering of populations, economies, and states.

The case also has significant implications for debates about global politics in general and political authority in particular. It might be tempting to link these strategies to the rise of neoliberal globalization, and certainly they are partly shaped by political-economic elites who accept and mobilize assumptions about the desirability of global markets, entrepreneurial firms, and active individuals. However, in their blurring of public, private, technical, and popular authority (Porter, this volume), diaspora strategies do not fit neatly into existent accounts of new forms of private authority in a global world. For example, they are not an example of the government networks that are the focus of concern in Slaughter's (2004) account of the disaggregated state. She is concerned with the networks of government officials who are exchanging information, co-ordinating national policy, and working together to address common problems. Nor are they the 'epistemic communities' (Haas 1992) of professionals exercising their expertise in particular domains of policy relevant knowledge. They are may be closer to the transnational civil society networks of think tanks, nongovernmental organizations, and advocacy groups (Scholte 2002; Moghaden 2005), but while they mobilize non-state actors they remain integral to state ambitions and processes.

This suggests that analysts of the new forms of global politics may need to pay more attention to the ways in which the categories of not only public and private, but also national and global, state and civil society, citizens and non-citizens, are themselves being reworked by contemporary developments. Rather than beginning from the assumption that these concepts and categories remain territorially-bounded and mutually exclusive, it may be more useful to trace the multilayered, contradictory processes through which new political and governmental forms are being assembled in a globalizing context. This will require careful empirical work that traces the changing relationships between nation-state, sovereignty, and territory not only in terms of discursive representations, globalizing networks, transnational institutions, and multi-level agreements, but also through more quotidian analyses focussed on the taken-for-granted techniques and everyday practices through which organizations, groups, and individuals are differentially constituted and enrolled in these globalizing configurations.

Note

Thanks to Richard Le Heron, Alan Latham, Nick Gill, the editors, and fellow contributors for their comments. A longer and different version of this chapter has been published in *Transactions of the Institute of British Geographers*, 2007: 33(1).

References

Amin, A. (2004) 'Regulating economic globalization', *Transactions of the Institute of British Geographers*, 29: 217–233.

Appadurai, A. (2002) 'Deep Democracy: Urban governmentality and the horizon of politics', *Public Culture*, 14(1): 21–47.

Barry, A. (2001) *Political Machines: Governing a technological society*. London: The Athlone Press.

Basch, G., N. Glick Schiller and C. Blanc-Szanton (1994) *Nations Unbound: Transnational Projects, Post-colonial Predicaments, and Deterritorialized Nation-States*. Longhorne PA: Gordon and Breach.

Beaverstock, J. (2002) 'Transnational elites in global cities: British expatriates in Singapore's financial district', *Geoforum*, 33 (4): 525–538.

Brenner, N. (2004) *New State Spaces: Urban governance and the rescaling of statehood*. Oxford: Oxford University Press.

Bryant, J. and D. Low (2004) New Zealand's Diaspora and Overseas Population. New Zealand Treasury Working Paper 04/13. http://www.nztreasury.govt.nz/workingpapers., accessed on 11 February 2005.

Buwalda, J. (2005) Address at the New Zealand High Commission, London, 6 June.

Collins, S. (2001) 'Expats Spread Far and Wide, Not Thin', http://flatrock.org.nz/topics/immigration/expats_spread_far_and_wide.htm, accessed on 12 August 2005.

Conradson, D. and A. Latham (2005) 'Friendships, Networks and Transnationality in a World City: Antipodean transmigrants in London', *Journal of Ethnic and Migration Studies*, 31(2): 287–305.

Dean, M. (1999) *Governmentality: Power and rule in modern society*. London: Sage Publications.

Dumont, J-C. and G. Lemaitre (2005) *Counting Immigrants and Expatriates in OECD countries: a new perspective*. OECD Directorate for Employment Labour and Social Affairs.

Ellerman, D. (2003) 'Policy Research on Migration and Development'. World Bank Policy Research Working Paper 3117, August.

Ferguson, J. and A. Gupta (2002) 'Spatializing states: toward an ethnography of neoliberal governmentality', *American Ethnologist*, 29: 981–1002.

Fraser, N. (2003) 'From Discipline to Flexibilization? Rereading Foucault in the Shadow of Globalization', *Constellations*, 10(2): 160–171.

Frater, P. (2004) 'Internationalising Knowledge Flows: Pacific experiences', in *Global Knowledge Flows and Economic Development*. OECD.

Gamlen, A. (2005) 'The Brain Drain is Dead: Long live the New Zealand diaspora'. Centre for Migration, Policy, and Society, Working Paper 10, University of Oxford.

Haas, P. (ed) (1992) 'Knowledge, Power and International Policy Coordination', *International Organization*, Monographic Issue 46(1) Winter.

Hansen, T-B. and F. Stepputat (eds) (2005) *Sovereign Bodies: Citizens, migrants, and states in the postcolonial world*. Princeton: Princeton University Press.

Hay, C. and B. Rosamond (2002) 'Globalization, European Integration and the Discursive Construction of Economic Imperatives', *Journal of European Public Policy*, 9 (2): 147–67.

Hindess, B. (1998) 'Neo-liberalism and the National Economy', in M. Dean and B. Hindess (eds) *Governing Australia: Studies of contemporary rationalities of government*. Cambridge: Cambridge University Press, 210–226.

Hindess, B. (2002) 'Neo-liberal Citizenship', *Citizenship Studies*, 6(2): 127–143.

Holton, R. (2005) 'Network discourses: proliferation, critique and synthesis', *Global Networks*, 5(2): 209–215.

Inkson, K. et al. (2004) 'New Zealand Talent Flow Programme: Preliminary Results'. General report for participants and recruiting agencies. Massey University.

Johnson, B. and S. Sedeca (2004) 'Diasporas, Emigres, and Development: Economic linkages and programmatic responses'. A Special Study of the USAID Trade Enhancement for the Services Sector (TESS) Project. March 2004.

Kapur, D. (2001) 'Diasporas and Technology Transfer', *Journal of Human Development*, 2(2): 265–286.

Katz, C. (2001) 'On the Grounds of Globalization: A topography for feminist engagement', *Signs: Journal of Women in Culture and Society*, 26: 1213–34.

Kotkin, J. (1992) *Tribes: How Race, Religion and Identity Determine Success in the New Global Economy*. New York: Random House.

Kuznetsov, Y. (2005) 'Promise and Frustration of Diasporas: "How to" of mobilization of talent abroad for the benefit of countries of origins'. Presentation at a World Bank Workshop 'Transforming Brain Drain into Brain Gain', Buenos Aires, Argentina, 26–27 April 2005.

L.E.K. Consulting (2001) 'New Zealand Talent Initiative: Strategies for Building a Talented Nation'. www.beehive.govt.nz/innovate/lek.pdf, accessed on 05 April 2004.

Larner, W., R. Le Heron and N. Lewis (2007) 'Co-constituting "After Neoliberalism?": Political projects and globalizing governmentalities in Aotearoa New Zealand', in K. England and K. Ward (eds), *Neo-liberalization: States, Networks, People.* Blackwell Publishers (accepted, forthcoming).

Larner, W. and W. Walters (2004) 'Globalization as Governmentality', Special edition of *Alternatives* (eds M. Dean and P. Henman), 29(5): 495–514.

Massey, D. (1999) 'Imagining Globalization: Power-Geometries of Time-Space', in A. Brah, M. Hickman and M. MacanGhaill (eds), *Global Futures: Migration, Environment and Globalization.* Basingstoke: St Martins Press.

Meyer, J-B. (2001) 'Network Approach versus Brain Drain: Lessons from the diaspora', *International Migration*, 39(5): 91–110.

Meyer J-B., D. Kaplan and J. Charum (2001) 'Scientific Nomadism and the New Geopolitics of Knowledge', *International Social Science Journal*, 53(168): 309–321.

Meyer J-B. and M. Brown (1999) 'Scientific Diasporas: A new approach to the brain drain'. Paris: UNESCO MOST Discussion paper No 41, www.unesco.org/most/meyer.htm, accessed on 10 May 2004.

Mitchell, K. (2003) 'Educating the National Citizen in Neoliberal Times', *Transactions of the Institute of British Geographers*, 28(4): 387–403.

Moghaden, V. (2005) *Globalizing Women: Transnational feminist networks.* Baltimore: The Johns Hopkins University Press.

Nagar, R., V. Lawson, L. McDowell and S. Hansen (2002) 'Locating Globalization: Feminist (re)readings of the subjects and spaces of globalization', *Economic Geography*, 78(3): 257–285.

Ong, A. (1999) *Flexible Citizenship: The cultural logics of transnationality.* Durham: Duke University Press.

Ong, A. (2005) 'Splintering Cosmopolitanism: Asian immigrants and zones of autonomy in the American West', in T-B. Hansen, and F. Stepputat (eds), *Sovereign Bodies: Citizens, migrants and states in the postcolonial world.* Princeton: Princeton University Press.

Robertson, S. and R. Dale (2002) 'Local States of Emergency: the contradictions of neo-liberal governance in education in New Zealand', *British Journal of Sociology of Education*, 23(3): 463–482.

Rose, N. (1999) *Powers of Freedom: Reframing political thought.* Cambridge: Cambridge University Press.

Sassen, S. (1998) *Globalization and its Discontents.* New York: New Press.

Scholte, J. A. (2002) 'Civil Society and Democracy in Global Governance', *Global Governance*, 8: 3: 281–304.

Sharma, A. and A. Gupta (eds) (2006) *The Anthropology of the State: A Reader.* London: Blackwell Publishing.

Slaughter, A-M. (2004) *A New World Order.* Princeton and Oxford: Princeton University Press.

TVNZ (2006) Interview with Ross McConnell, Chief Executive KEA, Broadcast on Television New Zealand 8 March 2006.

Van der Veer, P. (2005) 'Virtual India: Indian IT labour and the Nation-State', in T-B. Hansen, and F. Stepputat (eds), *Sovereign Bodies: Citizens, migrants and states in the postcolonial world*. Princeton: Princeton University Press.
Walton-Roberts, M. (2004) 'Globalization, National Autonomy and Non-resident Indians', *Contemporary South Asia*, 13(1): 53–69.
Wilson, M. et al. (2000) Submission to the Tertiary Education Advisory Commission.
Wilson, M. (2001) 'The Concerns and Issues of the 'Generation Lost': Beyond the Brain Drain'. Press Release July 2001, http://www.nzedge.com/hot/braindrain_poole.html, accessed on 14 February 2005.
Yeoh, B. and K. Willis (1998) ' "Singapore Unlimited": Configuring Social Identity in the Regionalization Process.' WPTC-98-08, www.transcomm.ox.ac.uk/working_papers.htm, accessed on 10 May 2004.

8
Globalizing Webs in Public/ Private and Translocal Interfaces

Dorte Salskov-Iversen and Hans Krause Hansen

In their proclaimed efforts at 'modernizing' themselves, public sector organizations, also at the sub-state level, are not only appropriating – and being subjected to – a number of private sector ways of thinking and ruling, notably managerialization, marketization, and entrepreneurialism. Increasingly, they also envision the new information and communication technologies (henceforth referred to as ICT) as a means and an object of public sector modernization. The focus on ICT as a key factor in these processes is premised on two interlaced assumptions: ICT as an instrument of rationalization and direct intervention in specific public sector practices and routines; and ICT as a vehicle for knowledge sharing about how best to manage and organize the public sector. In both cases, ICT facilitates networking across professional, organizational, sectoral, and jurisdictional borders, including borders that sever the 'public' from the 'private', the 'local' from the 'global'.

Together, all these transborder flows constitute a bewildering and ever-growing grid of what we term *globalizing webs*. These webs bring together otherwise disconnected actors and spaces through mediation, and articulate the heterogeneous and complex landscape of organizations, networks, communicative forms, practices of enrolment, and alignment. Such emerging arrangements can be viewed as an instantiation of disaggregation and entanglement of authority (Slaughter 2004; Hansen this volume; Porter this volume), involving linkages and mechanisms – human and non-human – that 'translate' knowledge from one point to another (Latour 1986; Law 1986; Rose and Miller 1992; Law and Hetherington 2000; Dicken et al. 2001; Kendall 2004). On closer inspection, these arrangements hold out interesting opportunities also for sub-national government institutions intent on innovating their authority in global governance.

When local governments 'internationalize' it comes in all shapes and sizes, in one or several policy areas: affiliation with transnational associations and networks; participation in transnational best practice, benchmarking, and award schemes; applying for EU project funding; and keeping abreast with international professional literature. Here, we are particularly concerned with transnational networking in the field of 'e-modernization', i.e. reforming the public sector through ICT in order to meet the needs of globalization and the multiple demands of the information age: e-literacy, e-access, e-business, e-governance, and/or e-democracy. In the public sector, harnessing ICT depends on the expertise and resources of private and transnational actors, which, in turn, breeds transboundary fora of deliberation, knowledge sharing, advocacy and policy formulation, cutting across traditional demarcations between the local and the global, between the public and the private sectors. E-modernization is an emerging arena of global governance. Sub-state units such as city and regional governments actively contribute to the making of the cross-border flows that constitute this arena; these units are important players in a fast changing urban organizational architecture (Sassen 2002: 1), which effectively redefines the strategic outreach of the units and organizations involved. Our focus here is on how city *governments* try to reassert their authority in this system, and on the subsequent ascendance of transboundary organizational forms the authority of which is worthy of being studied in its own right.

The paper is divided into two main sections. In the first section we take a more detailed look at the cities of Bromont in Canada and Miraflores in Peru – and at two networks that link them up.[1] Bromont and Miraflores cannot claim representativeness – this is beyond the research design. What unites them is their proactive search for and involvement in transnational networking. Nor do these vignettes lead to a comparison. Rather, they serve the purpose of generating insights into the mediated nature of each and every connection. In the second section we draw particularly on the literatures of organizational innovation, governance, governmentality, and actor-network theory to discuss the role of e-modernization and its derivatives, such as e-innovation, and speculate about the implications of these developments, including the formation of globalizing webs and the role of mediation, for the construction of authority across different government levels.

City governments in global dialogue: E-modernization and new transnational platforms

Today, the main thrust of public sector reform in the OECD is organized by the concept of modernization (OECD 2005). It aims at improving public sector performance and making government more efficient, open, and responsive, much like its precursor New Public Management. The need to 'modernize' developed at the same time as the idea of the 'information society' began to give renewed impetus to public sector reforms, and, increasingly, the two have become intertwined. Indeed, according to some scholars, it is the complex of ICT centred developments that together constitute 'the most general, pervasive and structurally distinctive influence on how governance arrangements are changing in advanced industrial states today' (Dunleavy et al. 2006: 478). In the emerging economies, the last decade has seen similar processes blending public sector modernization ideals with ICT and information society visions, also in Latin America. The effects of these modernization discourses are specific to each locality. Globally dominant discourses tend to follow contextually defined logics, latching on to local dynamics and becoming harnessed for local projects and networks. In the vignettes below we look into how these dynamics are being played out when two city governments log onto the world wide web of transnational e-modernization networks.

For reasons that will become clear below, Bromont and Miraflores have orbits that do not intersect naturally. They are completely unrelated except for the fact that their respective trajectories are both 'a movement of the digital era in society at large' (Dunleavy et al. 2006: 469). We chanced upon them in the context of the Global Cities Dialogue (GCD), a transnational network of city governments of which they are both members. Importantly, the GCD counts among its partners a host of other types of organizations that are highly active in the field of e-modernization. These include private actors such as The Global Business Dialogue on electronic Commerce (GBDe) – a CEO-driven arrangement composed of leading enterprises and economic organizations, as well as the Technology Empowerment Network (TEN), founded by a World Economic Forum Community of IT companies, organizations, and other leaders offering their expertise to identify and support projects based on the use of the new ICT. In 2004 the GCD adopted the URB-AL Network 13 'Towns and the Information Society'.

The Network 13 is a project network organized within the framework of the URB-AL programme – phase II of the European Commission, aimed at bringing together European and Latin American municipalities in a common effort to explore the opportunities offered by ICT for local governance. The network members meet to exchange knowledge and develop project ideas, facilitated by externally recruited moderators. Approved projects receive grants from the EU, co-financed with a minimum of 30 per cent by the project partners, who often include other actors such as local business and NGOs. The GCD and URB-AL Network 13 share the same vision about 'information society', and the promises it holds out to governments, citizens, and businesses.

The last decade has seen a virtual mushrooming of similar initiatives designed to enable different types of transnational networking in the field of e-modernization. The initiatives embrace a multiplicity of actors, both as initiators and participants, including supranational – notably the EU – national and subnational governments, transnational ICT and consultancies, and international institutions and organizations, such as the UN and the World Bank, as well as new, 'multi-stakeholder partnerships' operating globally (See Flyverbom and Bislev this volume; Flyverbom and Hansen 2006). Saliently, the recently concluded UN World Summit on the Information Society (WSIS) also reflects this thinking. This UN Summit was the first ever to allow the participation of local governments, complete with a special series of preparatory meetings, and with summits in Lyon (2003) and Bilbao (2005) focussing entirely on the role of cities and regions. As one might have expected, a large number of GCD and URB-AL Network 13 members participated in the two summits, including representatives from Bromont (in 2003) and Miraflores (in 2005).

The City of Bromont

The City of Bromont, with a population of about 5,000, is located in Canada, in Québec's Eastern Townships. It is a small but wealthy community, living off tourism and knowledge intensive industries. However, like other parts of Canada this area is feeling the effects of rural depopulation. Its decision to proactively engage e-society reflects the City's concerns with these developments and is part of a broader policy of ruralism aiming specifically at ensuring that attractive citizens stay and that the right sort of new people move in. Ironically, developments like 9/11 have given small communities like Bromont a new lease of life, the City management notes, because this has 'brought home to an increasing number of the very kind of people that the city would like to retain that these things don't happen in Bromont. Technology, then, is one of the answers to making Bromont an attractive City' (Interview in Bromont 2004).

It was the arrival of a new mayor in 1998 that propelled thinking about how to work strategically with e-governance to modernize and develop both the administration and the local community. It was the new mayor that conceived the vision to leverage Bromont through ICT, to harness ICT to mobilize the city's untapped resources, or in the words of its official mission statement, 'to permanently transform the way citizens govern themselves, communicate and live'. In early 1999, the mayor invited a group of citizens to develop a local development strategy capable of preparing Bromont for taking charge of its own destiny. An important result of this initiative was the launch in January 2000 of an ambitious e-project, the non-profit organization Bromont Collectivité Ingénieuse, with the goal of integrating information technology into the Bromont community. More specifically this meant to develop an on-line city and an ICT culture in and among Bromont's citizens, in part by implementing a local citizens' portal. The realization of the project was made possible by a public-private partnership – Bromont Ville Branchée – consisting of provincial and municipal governments, large corporations (IBM, Videotron, Mouvement Desjardins), and local companies (Volt Design, Cabana, Com, Idèmo Communication, D2 Marketing, and Artopex) as well as provincial and local educational (Sherbrooke University and Granby College), health-care institutions, and local organizations.

The partnership was stitched together in collaboration with CEFRIO, a Québec information technologies integration transfer centre (www.cefrio.qc.ca 2007) – just as it was CEFRIO that conceived of the idea of raising the money via a partnership construction. CEFRIO initiates action-research and innovation projects that engender knowledge of the transformation through ICT of organizational systems in the education, health, public services, and industrial sectors, and its main financial partner is the government of Québec. Both the City of Bromont and CEFRIO stress that their eventual cooperation was a pure coincidence. With hindsight, Bromont's e-strategy owes its conception and eventual success to a combination of 'the people factor' – i.e. the mayor and a very well educated population – and a series of coincidences, all of which are nonetheless in various ways connected to wider societal developments, notably the emergence of a multitude of actors all dedicated to the e-cause.

At this point it is relevant to briefly reflect on the wider political context in which the Bromont experience is embedded. By international standards, Canada is known as a world e-champion. Ever since international e-benchmarking schemes began to attempt a global hierarchy of e-nations, Canada has come out on the top, even if competition has become tougher in the last couple of years. In the most recent spate of e-benchmarking reports, Canada featured prominently in several of them. Thus, Canada is ranked as number one for the fifth year in a row in Accenture's sixth and, at the time of writing, most recent global e-government benchmarking report from 2005, with the US and Singapore as number two and three.[2] Throughout, though with varying intensity, the Canadian federal government and state governments have engaged very enthusiastically in promoting the Canadian e-agenda, taking pride in the positive reputation effect of Canada's e-record (interview CEFRIO, November 2004). With regard to the Bromont Ville Branchée, CEFRIO's role was to find partners for the project, connecting Bromont with CEFRIO's network, crucially, CEFRIO's contacts in the Québec Federal Government. The latter agreed to support the Bromont project financially because it could use the ideas and experiences to be gained from the Bromont project to improve the digital performance, including the web communication, of its Department of Finance. According to CEFRIO, the Ministry needed a best practice, a guaranteed success capable of demonstrating to its internal and external stakeholders the potential of ICT. And tiny, well-organized and well-educated Bromont seemed capable of delivering (interview with CEFRIO November 2004).

As part and parcel of its ambition to be an online city, Bromont has sought and received external recognition of its initiative, both in Québec, in Canada, and abroad. Its reputation as a very active networker in Canada and abroad was further cemented when it became a member of GCD in 2003. Thus, in 2003, it was identified and showcased as one of the finalists by Canadian Information Productivity Awards as a groundbreaking e-government city. In October 2004, the director of the Bromont Ville Branchée project featured in Direction Informatique, an ICT journal, as the Québec ICT personality of the month. The Bromont Ville Branchée has three times distinguished itself at the French Villes Internet Award (www.villes-internet.net/label04/flash/main.htm 2007). In 2003 it received a 4-@ label out of five, in 2004 and 2005 it got a 5-@ label, even though, as a non-French participant, it was *hors concours*.

Becoming internationally exposed and the membership of GCD were never planned. But it started due to a series of coincidences, with key people in the City of Bromont via the intervention of CEFRIO being connected to the Villes Internet Concours. And this was what motivated the City to be represented at the World Summit of Cities and Local Authorities on the Information Society in Lyon in December 2003, and this also paved the way to the membership of GCD. An early evaluation of Bromont's engagement in the GCD suggests that Bromont is not a very active GCD member. While there are no signs that Bromont is back-tracking on its e-strategy or planning to discontinue its focus on enhancing its e-capacity, there are signs that Bromont may not be using e-modernization and ICT as aggressively as before to leverage its reputational clout and to communicate its particular vision of its locality. Indeed, Bromont appears to have entered a new cycle, responding to different signals in Canadian politics, not least at the federal level. The city is clearly busy developing its emerging record as a seasoned and astute networker, capable of identifying and connecting the right actors, making different institutions collaborate, spotting opportunities – a skill the city has acquired not least through its ambitious e-governance initiative (interview with CEFRIO November 2004). Precisely because Bromont's ICT project was not about technical innovation in the narrow sense of the term, its lessons can be transferred to other areas and contexts.

The City of Miraflores

Miraflores is a relatively affluent municipality in the City of Lima, currently counting around 100,000 inhabitants. Like Bromont, its membership of the GCD is fairly recent, and so are its activities in the context of URB AL Network 13 and other transnational networks. In contrast to the vast majority of Peruvian municipalities, the municipality of Miraflores has for a number of years been heavily engaged in the cause of e-modernization. Miraflores has received very little support from the shifting Peruvian governments, whose attention to e-modernization has been very scarce, reflecting the extremely fragile and unstable institutional environment in the country. And, as the mayor of Miraflores states, 'things are moving so fast in the field of ICT that we simply cannot wait for initiatives and decisions made at the national level, we have to do it ourselves' (Interview with Miraflores 2004).

Miraflores rightly considers itself a pioneering municipality in Peru when it comes to e-modernization. The first *cabina pública*, the Peruvian term for public internet access point, later to become one of Peru's most recognized contributions to information society in Latin America and referred to as a worldwide best practice by international organizations (Hilbert and Katz 2003), was set up in the district of Miraflores by the *Red Científica Peruana*, a network of researchers and engineers, as early as in 1994.

In the late 1990s, a group of reform-minded politicians came into power in Miraflores and began to work with innovative and highly skilled administrators and engineers in order to implement ICT systematically in Miraflores. Since then, it has been the objective to increase the range of communication channels between the government and citizens; to promote the exchange of knowledge and enhance transparency and curb corruption; to increase participation and foster citizen empowerment; and, importantly, to improve the high priority issue area of public safety and security. Today, citizens are enabled to 'interact and express their opinion concerning ongoing projects and activities of the municipality at any time (24 hours throughout 7 days). Any question – which mainly concerns administrative matters, is replied to within 48 hours' (www.miraflores.gob.pe 2005). The basic rationale is to improve the cooperation between the municipality, business, and citizens by enhancing trust in the city administration. In line with this ambition, public tenders, acquisitions, and municipal budgets are now published at the municipal website.

The City has also tried to simplify administrative procedures, based on the idea that the use of ICT allows a 'user oriented approach, combined with a reduction of administrative costs, improving the offer of more cost-effective services'. Online procedures for the payment of taxes, the delivery of documents and certificates, licences and permissions, as well as new forms of security prevention and management based on internet technologies have been implemented. The City has completed a wireless network system spanning the area around the Town Hall and the central business district. This and many of the above mentioned initiatives were presented on various occasions at the General Assembly Meeting of the GCD in November 2004 hosted by Miraflores.

Miraflores' e-modernization initiatives have been undertaken in a context that differs substantially from Bromont. Miraflores is one of approximately forty autonomous municipalities of Lima – a number which is fluctuating as political districts have been added, annexed, divided, and merged with the rapid expansion of the city. Urban planning has been extremely difficult if not absent due to the fragile, opaque and shifting character of the political structure and institutions in Lima and in Peru in general (De Soto 1986). Like other Latin America countries, Peru has always had great difficulties in achieving and sustaining democratic regimes organized around political parties in the North American and European sense of the term, and military influence over civil matters has been heavy (Levitsky and Cameron 2001). Urban politics in Lima has been shaped by fluctuating political groupings and organizations. One of the most important in the 1990s was *Somos Lima* ('We are Lima') created and organized by Alberto Andrade. Not really a party, but an organization with a vague agenda built up around Andrade's person, the *Somos Lima* was redubbed *Somos Perú* to serve as a launch pad for Andrade's candidature for the national presidential elections in 2000.

When Fernando Andrade, Alberto Andrade's brother, was elected mayor of Miraflores in 1996, there was a growing awareness about the potentiality of ICT in public administration, but in parallel to this there was also an increasing focus on democratization and decentralization. Today, the City of Miraflores speaks of a 'development deficit', caused by the political and institutional weakness and fragility of the Peruvian political system at all levels, and by the scarce public resources coming from taxation and other incomes.

In order to be better equipped to meet these challenges, Miraflores emphasizes, it is important to seek allies, and these come in two fundamental ways: as new ICT, and as networks involving knowledge sharing and access to funding. Proactive initiatives on the part of the City of Miraflores to counter and influence the conditions and prospects of its citizens and the area are not to a very large extent supported by external actors, be they national government, foreign investments, etc. Such initiatives come from below, from the technologies, activities, and networks in which the municipality and its citizens participate, and from participation in transnational activities. Interestingly, according to the ITU (ITU 2006), in its so-called Digital Opportunity Index, Peru is among the major beneficiaries when it comes to leveraging ICT, ranking 5 after India, China, Russia, and Hungary.

Miraflores has only been a member of the GCD since 2003. As mayor Fernando Andrade expressed in an interview with us (2004): 'Until last year we did not know anything about all these international activities, it is a completely new theme to us, but since then we have jumped on the train, and this is a fast running train'. While until recently very focussed on the collaboration with other municipal governments within Greater Lima and Peru, Miraflores now wants to speed up 'the integration of all Peruvian communities within the Information Society at regional and international levels', and it is looking forward to 'intensifying the cooperation with other municipalities within the GCD in the field of e-democracy, e-voting, e-inclusion, and e-learning'. Thus, in November 2005, Miraflores' Mayor was among the official speakers at the II World Summit of Cities and Local Authorities on the Information Society in Bilbao, Spain. And in October 2006, GCD's Steering Committee elected Miralflores as Overall Vice Chair City.

Public sector (e)-modernization, (e)-innovation and globalizing webs

In the above we have seen how e-modernization, with varying intensity and for varying periods of time, can connect very different local governments. As a connector, e-modernization is, in part, assembled and managed by transnational organizational forms, providing different yet partially overlapping platforms – on-line and off-line – for networking, exchanging knowledge, learning, and joint project development. The analysis leads towards an unfolding of the concept of globalizing webs and the power dynamics inherent in this type of social mode.

At this point, it is helpful to consult Jane Fountain's work on the transformative effects and potentialities of new ICT on the structures and practices of government and the relationships between government, civil society, and the market (Fountain 2001; 2006). With the caveat that the Internet in itself provides none of the social skills that translating the technology into useful action requires, Fountain is particularly interested in the burgeoning of interorganizational networks. Importantly, the multiplicity of networked connections correlates with the arrival of new ICT and the perceived need for different types of innovation across traditional functional and jurisdictional boundaries. Networked connections and networked governance do not replace hierarchy or bureaucracy as much as they have added another organizational mode, creating both tensions between competing logics and opportunities for rationalization of scarce resources, learning and incorporation of new knowledge (Newman 2001; Hartley 2005; Fountain 2006).

In both Bromont and Miraflores, there is evidence of the local modernization project being strongly ICT-centred. To paraphrase Fountain, the local state is very much sought reconstructed 'as organizational actors enact new technologies to reshape relationships in the state and the economy' (Fountain 2001: 201). Furthermore, in both cities e-modernization is clearly related to a discourse of innovation – how to be a learning government, capable of acquiring, creating, transferring, modifying, and applying new knowledge – which arguably represents a new phase in the perennial pressures for efficiency and improved performance. The vast and continuously changing ICT field constitutes a veritable goldmine of potential improvement, which is also born out by the massive increase in both accomplished and expected spending on ICT in the public sector across the globe. In this vein, subscribing to e-modernization has become synonymous with subscribing to e-innovation. To this end, networking is of the essence.

While both cities can be seen to be subjected to and to respond to developments related to 'the digital era in society at large' (Dunleavy et al. 2006), they do so in radically different circumstances. Unsurprisingly, therefore, the networked arrangements that can be observed on the ground in the two cities are qualitatively different. There is of course a sense in which this observation is trivial, but it still warrants mention, in particular in regard to the way in which external sources of authority are being mobilized and tapped. In Bromont, we see the City government confidently engaging a multitude of indvidual and institutional players at different levels and across domains. Bromont relatively effortlessly plugs into an already existing and fast developing web of flows dedicated to harnessing ICT, creating contacts, synergies, and innovation. The City of Miraflores, by contrast, relies on its ability to identify, stir, and mobilize elusive, unobtrusive, and highly informal networks of local entrepeneurs, in and outside the City Hall. It is essentially a very bumpy and bottom-up process and it is only when Miraflores chances upon the transnational ICT community that it connects to a more encompassing e-modernization vision.

The development of new combinations of new or existing ideas and skills – innovation – does not take place in isolation. Organizations intent on innovating must ensure extensive interaction with their environment, the innovation literature reminds us (Fagerberg 2004; Hartley 2005). This observation requires close attention not only to how particular ideas and skills are generated, appropriated and edited (Sahlin-Andersson 2001) in local settings, but also to how they are mediated across organizational, institutional, and national boundaries. Global Cities Dialogue and URB-AL are cases in point. In our studies of these and other transnational networks, it has struck us that mediation plays a major role in shaping the organizational practices applied, defining the issues, and framing the actors. This is an aspect which is relatively under-researched in literatures on transnational networks. Mediation in this sense captures how new media technologies pave the way for new types of connectivity, modes of organizing, and not least, new ways of thinking and acting towards issues of public concern. If we claim that, in any society, the basic units of individuals, groups, and organizations are linked by networks, then it is logical to claim that, in any *contemporary* society, media networks make up the core infrastructure of such links (van Dijk 2005: 146). Importantly media networks are not only the medium through which governance may be exerted, but also an object of governance (Singh 2002: 13).

To better reflect the mediated character of the innovation dynamics in networks, we have proposed the notion of 'globalizing webs'.[3] Inspired by Barry's work (2001: 12), we argue that globalizing webs are not fixed organizational entities, but orderings in flux in an environment increasingly shaped by the new ICTs (Deibert 1997), which facilitate transnational connectivity, fluidity, complexity, and virtuality in ways we have not seen before. If social, political, and economic orderings in time and space will always flow from a complex network of localized, technical devices and practices, the new ICTs make it possible to link in novel ways calculations and actions at one place with calculations and actions in another place. For these connections actually to be realized, they need processes of 'translation' and 'association' (Rose and Miller 1992). Translation in this sense resonates the movement from place to place, and, by implication, alignment or association of sorts between the nodes of these processes. In this manner, globalizing webs become a lens for studying knowledge as it travels, and the new technological innovations capable of connecting the different nodes in the webs.

The data presented in the above reveal little about whether the knowledge gained from being transnationally networked has de facto spurred (e)-modernization on the ground in Bromont and Miraflores. Nor is there any evidence that being well-connected leads to novel and improved practices. That said, the two vignettes give us an idea of how the political and administrative leaderships in Bromont and Miraflores use and thus co-constitute globalizing webs as an integrated part of their efforts at innovating, in part through e-modernization, their respective communities. These webs enable them to latch onto a wide range of actors who develop, share and co-produce knowledge about how best to govern and how to innovate. The diversity of the actors enrolled suggests that membership is not conditional on subscription to exactly the same issues. What unites these actors is that they can creatively draw on the same discourse when articulating the challenges and opportunities they face.

Globalizing webs question established distinctions between the inside and the outside of the nation-state, between what is perceived as the local and the global, the public and the private. Instead these webs bear out claims that states are not unified but disaggregated actors (Slaughter 2004; Hansen and Salskov-Iversen 2005a), disrupting and reconfiguring one of the pillars of modern political imagination, the boundedness of state authority (See also Barry 2001: 20; Larner this volume). Moreover, when contrasted with the political networks, knowledge networks, epistemic communities, and transnational discourse communities usually associated with political globalization and referred to in much recent research, including our own (e.g. Hansen et al. 2002; Stone 2002; 2003), globalizing webs stand out due to their relative indeterminacy, incoherence, mobility, plus their emphasis on and use of new ICT. Importantly, in these webs, processes of innovation, e-modernization and transnational connectivity are interlaced and, to a large extent, viewed as reinforcing one another

While the research design of this study does not allow a systematic assessment of the connections between our cities and their transnational networks, it is nevertheless tempting, and useful, to speculate on how they could be described using the classical Granovetter categories of broad, narrow and weak, strong ties (Granovetter 1973; Powell and Grodal 2004: 61). It is our contention that the links we are looking at are both broad and weak, unstable, and defy top-down managerial control. Developing and accessing new knowledge by harnessing broad and weak ties at the transnational level does not automatically translate into innovative practices in the local organization, and even if it does, it may only be a few individuals that know about these links. And yet, precisely because of the virtual dimension of these ties, they can often be accessed and used by others than those members of the organization who *go global* and establish the ties. The globalizing web, therefore, is not unlike a 'rhizome' (Deleuze and Guattari 1987), which is capable of connecting any point to any other point, regardless of the specific characteristics of each point, much as Kearney's 'globalizing reticula' (Kearney 1996:126).

At this point, we need to re-engage the question of authority. The city governments of Bromont and Miraflores depend not only on their formal, institutional state status, but also on the chain of actors that make up their total networks. When these organizations tap into the symbolic resources of the globalizing webs of which they form part, they recognize other types of actors – be they companies, transnational networks, partnerships – just as they appropriate the amorphous discourse of innovation and excellence in the field of e-modernization. The authority work going on here is quite noticeable: one effect of these processes is that they confer authority on many non-state or hybrid actors because of the recognition, legitimacy, and prestige they have already gained as suppliers, astute networkers, and knowledge brokers, as for instance in the field of e-modernization.

The Global Cities Dialogue is a salient example of these dynamics. Far from the OECD league, it belongs to a big and steadily growing band of transnational organizations and networks. They exist in all policy and issue areas, working at arm's length from traditional government where they compete for attention and recognition as authoritative voices. They reflect a growing preoccupation with participating 'at a distance' in the global economy (Larner and Heron 2004; Larner this volume), their role is to offer knowledge, and their authority depends on the translation of knowledge for its impact. Such actors also include private companies and hybrid arrangements that offer public sector organizations participation in best practice, benchmarking and award schemes, all of which reflect an increasing interest in making global comparisons, as well as aspirations of global competitiveness. Serving as 'agencies' of external verification, these actors are themselves recognized as invested with authority to the extent that public sector organizations are enrolled into their activities, and importantly, they enable the latter to reaffirm their own authority if a reputation effect can be gained (Hansen and Salskov-Iversen 2005a; b; c).

The process of 'double recognition' hinted at here can be further illuminated. According to a diffusion model, the transmission or diffusion of ideas can be explained by pointing to an initial 'broadcast point' possessing a kind of *a priori* authority. The idea of diffusion entails rather passive receivers. On the other hand, the idea of translation implies a much more active process of reception, one which is relational and entails the possibility that ideas can be edited in the process of travel (Latour 1986; Powell et al. 2005). The GCD and similar organizational forms do not possess the kind of a priori authority implied in the diffusion model. Their authority is not something that is possessed, but is rather the consequence of the actions of a chain of agents each of whom translates, or better transforms, a given set of ideas or pieces of knowledge in accordance with their own intentions and projects. In short, the conceptual movement from authority in a diffusion model to authority in a translation model means to view authority 'not as a cause of people's behaviour but as the consequence of an intense activity of enrolling, convincing and enlisting' (Latour 1986: 273). To the extent that organizational forms such as the GCD manage to enrol, enlist, and align social actors to their purposes, they will gain authority. However, any process of enrolment will always entail the probability that competing organizations are doing a better job, or that social actors will resist or have other objectives than those stipulated by the authority in question. If the construction of authority relies on the translation of ideas and the successful enrolment and subscription to these ideas, it will always be imperfect and can always fade away.

If we turn to the URB-AL programme, the dynamics are somewhat different. URB-AL is basically an EU project network, aiming at rolling out a particular world view – the EU's – and a common framework of action, not only in Europe, but also in Latin America, by means of mutual agenda-setting, policy formulation, and learning. Despite their differences both the GCD and URB-AL exemplify a technique of governance, which is on the rise and relies on its ability to attract and co-opt rather than to coerce. In the EU, this technique is known as the Open Method of Coordination, institutionalized at the Lisbon Summit in 2000.

Concluding reflections

The cities of Bromont and Miraflores provide evidence of how very unlike cities, in part through their subscription to the same transnational fora, are part and parcel of the diffuse project of modernizing and innovating the public sector by appropriating the new ICTs, applying them and integrating them into their organizational infrastructure, strategies and discourse. Throughout, their respective national governments have been conspicuous by their absence, though to varying degrees. Instead, we have seen a number of other actors stepping in, including Global Cities Dialogue and URB-AL, whose authority depends on their capacity to successfully enroll and mobilize others in the pursuit of their goals.

Enrolment and mobilization, in turn, necessitate translation processes that align the objectives of the two networks with the projects of other actors, including those of Bromont and Miraflores. This is of the essence for the construction of authority and when acting at a distance. Crucially, for those who sign up, the prize is not only knowledge but also identity and reputation gains. Being projected across national boundaries is increasingly appreciated by also subnational government instutions as it allows them to reassert their authority, not least locally.

Globalizing webs constitute a kind of fluid organizational arrangement, with a loose and mobile alignment among participants that involves the production of knowledge, relies on mediation, and implies the construction and entanglement of many types of authority. Put another way, the existence of these arrangements may be seen as an instantiation of how public authority disaggregates and becomes entangled with other forms of authority, such as private, technical, popular, and hybrid forms (Porter, this volume). Underlying such a claim is an understanding of authority as relational and as something that has to be made (Rose and Miller 1992; Latour 1986; Law and Hetherington 2000). This position suggests that the construction of authority is not always contingent on the accumulation of wealth, control over territories, and the exercise of physical means of violence, or delegation. Thus, the present study has illustrated how the effectiveness at enrolling others to one's project can be crucial for the construction of authority: 'Those who exercise the greatest power are those who enrol many others with more resources than themselves, and, more importantly, those who enrol others who are even better at enrolling others than themselves' (Braithwaite and Drahos 2000: 482). The question of enrolment is thus key to various transnational organizational forms that create, share, and provide knowledge and expertise about different issue areas. These organizational forms bring together national public sector organizations, international organizations and networks, private companies, and civil society organizations in loosely structured and crosscutting setups. As peddlers of knowledge and expertise about specific issue areas, their authority is premised on the involvement of their members and target groups, as well as on their ability to shape the preferences of others through interaction, dialogue, and persuasion 'at a distance'.

Notes

What eventually became this chapter has been presented at two different venues, both of which were crucial for the development of our argument. A very early version was presented at *The Reinventing the Public Conference* at the Open University, the UK, 15–16 April 2005, organized by Janet Newman and John Clarke. We remain grateful for the thoughtful comments we received, not least from the designated discussant, Wendy Larner, and from Janet and John. A later version was presented at the *International Studies Association Workshop on Accomplishments and Challenges on Private Authority and Private Governance*, Chicago 27 February 2007, convened by Tony Porter. We would like to thank the participants at this workshop, and in particular the discussant on our paper, Thomas Conzelmann, for their constructive comments. Finally, we would also like to express our gratitude to the people we interviewed during our visits to Mireflores and other Peruvian organizations, Bromont and CEFRIO, Montréal.

1. Our account is based on interviews with key municipal officers and politicians in the two localities, on conversations with officials in charge of the Global Cities Dialogue and the URB-AL Network 13 – two transnational networks – on participant observation at two annual meetings and workshops; as well as on documentary research and on studies of other accomplished networkers and networks, all conducted from 2003–2006 (Hansen and Salskov-Iversen 2005a;

b; c; Flyverbom and Hansen 2006; Hansen and Hoff 2006; Salskov-Iversen 2006a; b).

2. For other international benchmarking schemes, see *World Economic Forum's annual Global Information Technology Report* 2006–2007 (see http://www.weforum.org/en/initiatives/gcp/Global%20Information%20Technology%20Report/index.htm), ranking Canada as number 11; *the UN's 2005 Global E-Government Readiness Report* (see http://www.unpan.org/egovernment5.asp) ranks Canada as number 8 while the same report's index on E-participation ranks Canada 4. *The 2006 e-readiness rankings* (prepared in collaboration with the IBM Institute for Business Value and the Economist Intelligence Unit, see http://www.eiu.com/site_info.asp?info_name=eiu_2006_e_readiness_rankings), which sets out to measure a blend of public and private initiatives that yield meaningful improvements for private citizens, businesses and government, ranks Canada as number 9.

3. Our accounts of 'globalizing webs' draw on Hansen and Salskov-Iversen 2005b; c.

References

Barry, A. (2001) *Political Machines Governing a Technological Society*. London: Athlone Press.

Braithwaite, J. and P. Drahos (2000) *Global business regulation*. Cambridge: Cambridge University Press.

Deibert, R. J. (1997) *Parchment, Printing and Hypermedia – Communication in World Order Transformation*. New York: Columbia University Press.

Deleuze, G. and F. Guattari (1987) *A Thousand Plateaus. Capitalism and Schizophrenia*. Minneapolis: University of Minnesota Press.

De Soto, H. (1986) *El otro sendero*. México D.F: Diana.

Dicken, P., P.F. Kell, K. Olds and H.W-C.Yeung (2001) 'Chains and Networks, Terrritories and Scales: Towards a Relational Framework for Analysing Global Economy', *Global Networks*, 1(2): 89 112.

Dunleavy, P., H. Margetts, S. Bastow and J. Tinkler (2006) 'New Public Management Is Dead – Long Live Digital-Era Governance', *Journal of Public Administration Research and Theory*, 16: 467–494.

Fagerberg, J. (2004) 'Innovation: A guide to the Literature', in J. Fagerberg, D.C. Mowery and R.R. Nelson *The Oxford Handbook of Innovation*. Oxford: Oxford University Press.

Flyverbom, M. and H.K. Hansen (2006) 'Technological Imageries and Governance Arrangements', in H.K Hansen and J. Hoff, *Digital Governance//Networked Societies Creating authority, community, and identity in a globalized world*, Nordicom/Samfundslitteratur, Copenhagen, 79–108.

Fountain, J. E. (2001) *Building the Virtual State: Information Technology and Institutional Change*. Washington DC: Brookings Institution Press.

Fountain, J. E. (2006) 'Challenges to Organizational Change: Multi-Level Integrated Information Structures (MIIS)'. *National Cenrte for Digital Government Working Paper* No. 06-001. Pre-publication version of contribution to D. Lazer and V. Mayer-Schoenberger (eds) *Information Government*. Cambridge, MA: MIT Press.

Granovetter, M. (1973) 'The Strength of Weak Ties', *American Journal of Sociology*, 78(6): 1360–1380.

Hansen, H. K., D. Salskov-Iversen and S. Bislev (2002) 'Discursive globalization: transnational discourse communities and New Public Management', in M. Ougaard and R. Higgot (eds) *Towards a Global Polity*. London: Routledge, 107–24

Hansen, H.K. and J. Hoff (eds) (2006) *Digital Governance//Networked Societies Creating authority, community, and identity in a globalized world*. Copenhagen: Nordicom/Samfundslitteratur.

Hansen, H.K. and D. Salskov-Iversen (2005a) 'Remodeling the Transnational Political Realm: Partnerships, Best Practice Schemes and the Digitalization of Governance', *Alternatives*, 30(2): 141–164.

Hansen, H.K. and D. Salskov-Iversen (2005b) 'Globalizing Webs: Translation of Public Sector e-Modernization', in B. Czarniawska and G. Sévon (eds) *Global Ideas. How Ideas, Objects and Practices Travel in Global Economy*. Brussels: Liber, 213–232.

Hansen, H.K. and D. Salskov-Iversen (2005c) 'Public Sector Innovation: E-Modernization and Globalizing Webs', in M. Veenswijk (ed) *Organizing Innovation. New Approaches to Cultural Change and Intervention in Public Sector Organizations*. Amsterdam: IOS Press, 134–143.

Hartley, J. (2005) 'Innovation in Governance and Public Services: Past and Present', *Public Money & Management*, 25(1): 27–34.

Hilbert, M. and J. Katz (2003) *Building an Information Society in Latin America*. Santiago de Chile: CEPAL.

ITU (2006) *Digital Opportunity Index*, available at http://www.itu.int/osg/spu/statistics/DOI/index.phtml.

Kearney, M. (1996) *Reconceptualizing the Peasantry. Anthropology in Global Perspective*. Boulder: Westview Press.

Kendall, G. (2004) 'Global networks, international networks, actor networks', in W. Larner and W. Walters (eds) *Global Governmentality – Governing international spaces*. London: Routledge, 60–65.

Larner, W. and R. Heron (2004) 'Global Benchmarking. Participating 'at a distance' in the globalizing economy', in W. Larner and W. Walters (eds) *Global Governmentality – Governing international spaces*. London: Routledge, 213–232.

Latour, B. (1986) 'The powers of association', in J. Law (ed) *Power, Action and Belief*. London: Routledge & Kegan Paul.

Law, J. (1986) 'On the methods of long-distance control: vessels, navigation and the Portuguese route to India', in J. Law (ed.) *Power, Action and Belief*. London: Routledge & Kegan Paul.

Law, J. and K. Hetherington (2000) 'Materialities, spatialities, globalitites', in J.R. Bryson, P.W. Daniels, N. Henry and J. Pollard (eds) *Knowledge, Space, Economy*. London: Routledge.

Levitsky, S. and Cameron, M.A. (2001) 'Democracy without Parties? Political Parties and Regime Collapse in Fujimori's Peru'. *Paper* published by Congress of the Latin American Studies Association, Washington DC 66 pages.

Newman, J. (2001) *Modernizing Governance: New Labour, Policy and Society*. London: Sage Publications.

OECD (2005) *Modernizing Government. The Way forward*, OECD: OECD Publishing.

Powell, W. and S. Grodal (2004) 'Networks of Innovation', in J. Fagerberg, D.C. Mowery, and R.R. Nelson *The Oxford Handbook of Innovation*. Oxford: Oxford University Press.

Powell, W., D. Gammal and C. Simard (2005) 'The Circulation and Reception of Managerial Practices in the San Fransico Bay Area Non Profit Community', in B. Czarniawska and G. Sévon (eds) *Global Ideas. How Ideas, Objects and Practices Travel in Global Economy*, Brussels: Liber, 233–258.

Rose, N. and P. Miller (1992) 'Political Power beyond the State: Problematics of Government', in *British Journal of Sociology*, 43(2): 173–205.

Sahlin-Andersson, K. (2001) 'National, international and transnational constructions of New Public Management', in T. Christensen and P. Lægreid (eds) *New Public Management: The Transformations of Ideas and Practice*. Aldershot: Ashgate.

Salskov-Iversen, D. (2006a) 'Learning Across Borders: The Case of Danish Local Government', *International Journal of Public Sector Management*, 19(7): 673–686.

Salskov-Iversen, D. (2006b) 'Global Interconnectedness: Danish Local Government in Network Society', in H.K. Hansen and J. Hoff (eds) *Digital Governance//Networked Societies Creating authority, community, and identity in a globalized world*. Copenhagen: Nordicom/Samfundslitteratur.

Sassen, S. (2002) *Global Networks/Linked Cities*. New York: Routledge.

Singh, J.P. (2002) 'Introduction: Information Technologies and the Changing Scope of Global Power and Governance', in J.N. Rosenau and J.P. Singh (eds) *Information Technologies and Global Politics*. New York: State University of New York Press.

Slaughter, A-M (2004) *A New World Order*. New Jersey: Princeton University Press.

Stone, D. (2002) 'Knowledge networks and policy expertise in the global polity', in M. Ougaard and R. Higgott (eds) *Towards a Global Polity*. London: Routledge.

Stone, D. (2003) 'The "Knowledge Bank" and the Global Development Network', in *Global Governance*, 9(1): 43–61.

Van Dijk, J. (2005) *The Deepening Divide. Inequality in the Information Society*. Thousand Oaks: Sage Publications.

Internet sources

www.cefrio.qc.ca, accessed on 20 May 2007.

http://www.eiu.com/site_Info.asp?Info_name=eiu_2006_e_readiness_rankings, accessed on 4 June 2007.

www.miraflores.gob.pe, accessed in November, 2005.

http://www.unpan.org/egovernment5.asp, accessed on 4 June 2007.

www.villes-internet.net/label04/flash/main.htm, accessed on 4 June 2007.

http://www.weforum.org/en/initiatives/gcp/Global%20Information%20Technology% 20Report/index.htm, accessed on 4 June 2007.

Part III
The Mediation of Authority

9
Place Branding – How the Private Creates the Public

Birgit Stöber

In a globalizing world places compete more than ever with one another to attract residents and employees, investors and tourists. One instantiation of this situation is the proliferation of *place branding*. The practice of branding has it roots in business, particularly marketing and public relations. But in recent years it has begun to pervade other domains, including the state, across different level of government. While corporate branding aims at helping companies develop an identity and image and consumers identify with specific companies, place branding assists national, regional, and city governments and other organizations to forge images and patterns of identification between places and people, be they (future) citizens, shoppers, tourists, investors, businessmen (and women), their own public sector employees and politicians (and those of other public sector institutions), etc. This chapter sets out to examine some of the ideas, processes, and mechanisms that have made the branding of places an increasingly important feature of *urban* politics. Drawing on studies of place branding, governmentality, and new urban governance, this chapter will argue that place branding – exemplified by the case of Berlin – is more than a simple and rational adaptation to the demands of globalization. Rather, as a power practice, it rests on particular beliefs and governance techniques, which differ from previous modes of place marketing and promotion. Such beliefs and techniques do not only involve the entanglement of public and private authority, but they also assign a pivotal role to media and discursive processes.

The introductory section illustrates some of the forces and dynamics at play in city branding as evidenced by the city of Berlin. It does so by focussing on some of the organizational formats and practices involved in the branding of post 1989 Berlin. In the second section, this paves the way for a more general discussion of place branding and what makes it distinctive from *place marketing* and *place promotion*, both of which have a long track record, often involving collaboration with the private and public sectors. However, with the intensification of public sector reforms since the 1980s, new modes of management and strategic communication have come to the fore (Hansen et al. 2001), including place branding, which draw heavily on the professionalization of private sector experiences and the emergence of new media technologies. This is the springboard for the analysis in the third section, in which place branding is unpacked as a soft power practice that depends for its effects on the involvement of both public and private authority; and on media and discursive processes. The final section reflects on the implications of place branding – when viewed as a soft power practice – for urban governance.

Partnering for branding: The case of Berlin

The long, dramatic, and widely, even globally, projected and mediated history of Berlin makes it an interesting place to investigate the shifting meanings of a place. As this chapter is primarily concerned with the most recent cycle of Berlin's efforts at managing its reputation, I will start out by briefly describing the constitution and framing of Berlin's current *branding* work, with Berlin Partner as the empirical focus. Berlin Partner is a public-private partnership organized as a limited company (*Gesellschaft mit beschränkter Haftung GmbH*). It is the result of a merger in 2005 of the Business Development Corporation and Partner für Berlin (PfB[1]). While Berlin Partner cooperates closely with the State Senate of Berlin, fifty-five percent of the company is owned by the private sector.[2] It employs around 75 staff, most of whom have been trained in economics or business administration and come with experience from the financial sector, business and industry or lobby organizations (Kalandides 2006), just as most of the members of its supervisory board are business leaders. The business mindset is indeed stressed when Berlin Partner introduces itself: 'Business thinking is built into our structure; flexibility allows us to provide tailor-made services suited to your needs' (www.berlin-partner.de 2007).

Since 2003, PfB and, from 2005, its predecessor, Berlin Partner GmbH, have been commissioned to re-imagine Berlin, to provide the City with another image, and eventually, another reputation and another identity. Berlin Partner moreover provides support for investors and helps Berlin-based companies to identify and tap into foreign markets.

What is today Berlin Partner has evolved from initiatives that date back to 1950 when the City of Berlin was already divided into two zones – a Western zone (i.e. from the French, British, and American zones) and a Soviet zone, but without a wall between them. This was when *Berliner Absatz-Organisation GmbH* (BAO) was founded as a subsidiary of the Berlin Chamber of Industry and Commerce with the aim 'to counteract West Berlin's insular nature' and 'to create economic ties between West Berlin and the rest of the Federal Republic' (www.berlin-partner.de 2007). This strategy seemed even more relevant after the construction of the Wall between East and West Berlin in the late summer of 1961. In 1977, BAO was separated from the Berlin Senate Department for Economics and the Berlin Business Development Corporation was set up with the principal task to focus on the City's business promotion activities. With the fall of the Berlin Wall in late 1989, Berlin's situation changed drastically not only politically, but also economically, socially, and culturally. While the Western part of the city lost the financial support previously granted to it by the West German government to retain firms, East Berlin soon faced a virtual collapse of its industrial and trading base just as its state-subsidized manufacturing sector proved sadly inept at responding to the dramatic pace of change (Häußermann and Colomb 2003: 200). While Berlin has undergone an extraordinary economic transformation since the Reunification, and while hopes were high not least with regard to the benign consequences of a foreseen expansion of the service sector, the overall level of employment did not increase, rather, it dropped markedly. Thus, from 1991 to 2001, Berlin lost more than 150,000 jobs in the traditional industries, and saw its unemployment rate rise temporarily to almost 20 per cent.

After the decision in 1991 to move the German capital back from Bonn to Berlin it was deemed necessary both by representatives from Berlin's business community and local politicians to prepare not only long-established citizens and companies, but also newcomers such as potential visitors and investors for the new German capital. Hence, in 1994 a private limited company named *Partner für Berlin* (PfB) was founded with the task to promote *Das Neue Berlin* 'as a product in and of itself' (Ward 2004: 248).[3] Over the years PfB enlisted more than 130 shareholders from the private sector, granting them privileged access to Berlin's business community and the City's relevant network. These partners contributed to half of PfB's budget. Since the City had commissioned PfB to design and implement urban marketing activities for Berlin the City provided the other half of the budget, but without being a direct shareholder. The formation of this organizational model probably owed some of its success to the personal connections between, on the one hand, the chief executive of PfB up until 2001 – a well-known civic leader and, in the early 1990s, a Senator for Urban Development – and, on the other hand, the Berlin Senate and Berlin's business community (Häußermann and Colomb 2003: 203). PfB's task was to address both image creation *and* identity building. Communication towards the local citizens of Berlin was indeed a priority for PfB. Thus, from 1995–2005, PfB organized the annual event *Schaustelle*, which was essentially an organized tour, targeting the citizens of Berlin, of the numerous construction sites in the city. PfB's work has been widely acclaimed, not only in Berlin and Germany, but also abroad, particularly because of its novel use of advertisements in the media, exhibitions and several image campaigns.

Throughout, these initiatives focussed exclusively on the bright aspects of the post-1989 New Berlin and, importantly, on the potential of certain sectors such as science, culture, and creativity. This strategy of 'history-less' marketing was deliberate:

> We are not a historical organization (…). Primarily, we are interested in the development after 1989 und the opportunities generated from this. Our job as a marketing organization for Berlin is neither to point out the city's history nor the existing problems. (…) Our job is to fore-ground positive impulses, and to visualize them. The communication of advantages is our job. Disadvantages are known enough through the press. (Interview with the Berlin Partner marketing manager 2004)

In mid 2005, the Berlin Business Development Corporation and PfB merged and became Berlin Partner GmbH.

Engaging creativity

In the last hundred years, Berlin's images have changed from the 1920s image of a both glamorous and wicked Berlin to the image of the power centre and quintessence of Nazi Germany, followed by the image of a devastated and divided city representing the Cold War time par excellence. Today, Berlin is 'one of the more visible and dramatic partic-ipants in a broader evolution of and by cities (…) toward a competitive realm of the virtual in which image-city competes against image-city' (Ward 2004: 250). One of these images is the image of Berlin as the Creative City and Cultural Metropolis, as evidenced by the Berlin Partner advertisement shown in Figure 9.1. In this section I will unfold Berlin's claim to being both creative *and* visible.

Figure 9.1   Charging Berlin

Notes: 'Berlin changes every day. Creativity is a way of life here and people are always experimenting and setting new trends. We at MTV will definitely feel at home here' (Catherine
Mühlemann, CEO MTV Germany, author's translation).

Source: By courtesy of Berlin Partner. http://www.berlin-partner.de/hauptstadt 2007.

The advertisement in Figure 9.1, is part of a wider testimonial campaign initiated back in 2001 by PfB.[4] Launched in several printed media,
such as *Time Magazine, Business Week, Newsweek,* and *Der Spiegel,* as well
as on Berlin Partner's website, the advertisement captures some of the
key characteristics of the work currently undertaken by Berlin Partner.
Firstly, the visual representation of the cooperation underscores the
strong private sector dimension of the Berlin Partner organization. The
logos of the MTV is featured prominently. Secondly, both the visuals
and the related text emphasize the focus on Berlin's creative and cultural
industries. And thirdly, the advertisement itself is an example of the
vital importance of visual media in place branding activities.

It is in part through international campaigns like this one that Berlin
Partner goes about staging Berlin not only as a major capital city and
decision-making centre, but also as a strategic site for young and creative
industries. By envisioning Berlin as a location for young and creative
industries, the partnership has targeted a niche that gains more and

more attention in present-day city branding activities. Recent developments suggest that culture, including the informal cultural sector, and media are fast becoming serious business (Krätke 2004). There is evidence that the Berlin Partner's strategy has had some success. Since the late 1990s, several regional corporate headquarters, including BMW, Daimler-Chrysler, Siemens, and Universal Music, the world's largest record company, have come to Berlin. It was probably Universal Music's relocation that led MTV Deutschland to move from Munich to Berlin in 2004 to a nearby warehouse in the eastern harbour area (Ward 2004: 252). It was shortly after MTV became a partner of Berlin Partner that MTV's CEO Catherine Mühlemann was asked to participate in the above image campaign to promote the Creative Capital City. Since this campaign aimed not only at promoting the city, but also at highlighting the settlement of MTV in Berlin, the synergetic offer was kindly accepted.

The focus on MTV as a new corporate resident in Berlin brings out the internal German urban competition between cities like Munich, Berlin and also Hamburg (*The Economist* 2007). Another indication of the prevailing competitive mood was presented in the summer of 2004 at a press conference where Catherine Mühlemann and Berlin's mayor stressed their mutual interest and belief in the city's future as an important player in the international (business) world of music. Here the impending arrival to Berlin of another corporate trophy, *Popkomm*, an international fair for the music and entertainment industries founded in Köln, was referred to at great length.

Today, when places compete, an increasingly often cited proxy for their alleged attractiveness and potential is their cultural resources and particular creative economies, which in turn reflects the ever more significant international trend to focus on the production and dissemination of images, symbols, and styles. Hence, culture is no longer simply viewed as topping (see Lindner and Musner 2005: 27): witness the publication of the first report ever on 'the cultural economy' of Berlin in 2005. Unsurprisingly, the City was more than grateful when the UNESCO in January 2006 awarded Berlin the title of 'City of Design' – as the first city in continental Europe.

In this vein, the focus on the creative city 'can be seen as the newest place-marketing product, employed in the struggle between cities to attract investors' (Lund Hansen et al. 2001: 852) – not only in Berlin, but also in many other cities, irrespective of size and current brand value.[5] It is obvious that culture and creativity have become 'key concepts on the agenda of city managers, development agents and planners, who are desperately searching for new grounds in city development with dwindling city budgets' (Kunzmann 2004: 384). Many of them have adopted the thoughts of Richard Florida, an American economist and sociologist, who became known for developing the concept of the creative class (Florida 2002) and evaluating urban regions according to their track record in technology, talent, and tolerance, ranking them 'on everything from the number of patents per head to the density of bohemians and gays, [and] on their respective shares of immigrants' (Peck 2005: 746). What transpires in much urban policy making and planning, and certainly also in Berlin, is that members of the creative class are seen as a key driving force behind economic development of post-industrial cities (Jensen 2005: 9).

Of equal importance is 'the critical infrastructure' (Zukin 1995) of people who implement cultural economy ideas and frame new ways of life by offering images by which we define ourselves and our place in the world and differentiate ourselves from 'them'. Among the members of this 'critical infrastructure' are 'the politicians and developers seeking to make economic or political profit by selling lifestyles, "community", or the "uniqueness" of place' (Mitchell 2000: 83). Thus, in the case of Berlin, the role of the City Mayor, social democrat Claus Wowereit, should not be underestimated. He came into office in 2001 despite out- ing himself during the campaign with the phrase: 'I'm gay and that's a good thing!' (www.spiegel.de 2006), and was re-elected in September 2006 for another period of five years. According to the German news maga- zine *Der Spiegel*, the voters 'credited him with enhancing Berlin's image as a hip, tolerant, cultural city. [...] and under his watch the city has increasingly become a magnet for artists, fashion designers, writers, and high-profile exhibitions' (ibid).

Thus, spending both substantial energy and amounts of money in order to participate in the competition for inhabitants, investors, and tourists has become the order of the day for both cities and countries. In Copenhagen for instance, the official inward investment agency of Greater Copenhagen, Copenhagen Capacity, shares many traits with its counterpart in Berlin. Established in 1994, Copenhagen Capacity operates as 'an independent organization financed by the Greater Copenhagen Authority (HUR) and with a Board of Directors consisting of regional politicians and businesspeople' (see http://www.copcap. com). Interestingly, both agencies' home pages refer to prizes awarded by fDi, the specialist global foreign/inward investment magazine owned by the Financial Times Group. While Berlin is hailed as the 'European City of the Future-Germany 2006/2007' due to its 'excellent promotional strat- egy, clearly explained investment incentives, overall attractiveness to

FDI [Foreign Direct Investment], heritage, hospitals, housing and universities' (www.businesslocationcenter. de 2007), Copenhagen is awarded the 'Scandinavian City of the Future' (www.copcap.com 2007). On Copenhagen Capacity's website we can find details on the ranking procedure:

> More than 150 cities and regions are competing in order to be the 'title city of the future' and it is an independent panel of judges who ranks the locations from 28 individual criteria across seven main categories. All leading Scandinavian cities have been in competition. Copenhagen has done well in all seven categories. (www.copcap.com 2007)

An even more extensive survey is the basis for the (since 2005) annual Anholt City Ranking Index. In 2005, Berlin was ranked tenth (and London first). In 2006, Sydney came out on the top as the world's favourite city brand. This time round, the list was dominated by US entries while Berlin, the only German city featured, came out as number twenty. In 2005, the survey's participants[6] had described Berlin as a safe and modern city with good infrastructure, affordable flats, and well educated people. While the fall of the Wall and Reunification were the most often associated events, more than one third of the interviewees in Mexico, Spain, and China, spontaneously associated Berlin with the name of Adolf Hitler. The fact that Berlin is still so strongly associated with negative aspects of its history is a major problem for Berlin as a brand, and Simon Anholt, the brand practitioner and man behind the index, recommended the city fathers to try to highlight even more the capital's numerous attractive aspects (www.citybrandsindex.com 2007). This is exactly what *Berlin Partner* and its predecessors have been striving to do since 1994, focussing exclusively on the New Berlin, and thus distancing it from its recent past. However, despite the progress made, there are limits to what a place brander can do. And even relatively consolidated and widely recognized positive brands may prove unstable when new competitors – cf. the new American entries in the Anholt City Ranking Index – enter the branding game, or when faced with crises, scandals and other developments that question the images on which such brands rest: witness the implications of the recent cartoon debacle in Denmark.[7]

Place branding – what's new?

Understanding what's new about place branding requires an understanding of its history and in particular its defining qualities compared to place marketing and place promotion. Early attempts at attracting the attention of outsiders primarily took the shape of selective images of geographic localities to a target audience (Ward and Gold 1994: 2). For example, already during the age of colonial expansion, West European and East Coast American newspapers were full of advertisements aimed at persuading people from the 'old world' to venture into the unknown. Part of the aim was to create an attractive image and, in doing so, the results were remarkably consistent. Such representations are not new and have always been linked to the strategic use of communication. As Zukin (1995: 16) remarks, for centuries 'visual representations of cities have "sold" urban growth. Images, from early maps to picture postcards (...), have been imaginative reconstructions – from specific points of view – of a city's monumentality.' Yet many of these early practices of promoting or marketing places, however carefully designed they may occasionally have been, did not amount to the comprehensive strategic interventions that we can observe today and which would fall under the heading of *place branding*. They were, as Kavaratzis (2005: 330) points out, often 'intuitive and randomly undertaken by various individuals and organizations that had an interest in promoting the place'. Today, however, the promotion and marketing of places have become directly associated with particular forms of professional knowledge and expertise and the invocation of particular life styles and cultural forms; with specific representations of the role of private actors and territorial authorities in a globalizing world; with new modes of managing and governing; and last, but not least, with particular technological developments, which have set the stage for new ways of using the media in the representation of places. In order to better appreciate the nature and rise of place branding, and the associated move from place promotion and marketing towards, let me briefly revise the main changes.

First, the simultaneous focus on image *and* identity building is new. In traditional place marketing, the point of departure is understanding the demands of the 'outsider' – the customer. In other words, place marketing rests on an 'outside-in' logic. So does place branding, but at the same time it embraces an inside-out approach. It is as much a means to change relations 'inside' as it is a means to impact on the relations with the outside – precisely because the inside is constituted by the outside and vice-versa (Jensen 2005: 13).

Second and third, and closely related to the above, come the general professionalization and inclusion of private expertise in place branding practices plus the emergence of new organizational formats underpinning branding campaigns, such as public-private partnerships. In fact, urban branding can be understood as one aspect of the new orientation from the public sector towards the market (Krantz and Schätzl 1997: 469), articulating urban governments' reorientation towards 'more flexible forms of market principles in public policy, or "New Urban Management"' (Jensen, 2005:15). In a similar vein, Jessop has described the situation as following:

> The city is being re-imagined – or re-imaged – as an economic, political, and cultural entity which must seek to undertake entrepreneurial activities to enhance its competitiveness; and (…) this reimag(in)ing is closely linked to the re-design of governance mechanisms involving the city – especially through new forms of public-private partnerships and networks. (Jessop 1997: 40)

Fourth, place branding is also characterized by a different kind of packaging and by a much stronger focus on visual material. This has not only to do with greater availability of new media technologies, but also with the general recognition, backed by scientific expertise, that human beings encounter places through perceptions and images (Kavaratzis and Ashworth 2005: 507). In other words, people make sense of places or construct places in their minds through their consumption and appropriation of various types of media in which places are being constructed and exposed, such as films, novels, paintings, news reports and so on.

Fifth, withholding unattractive or unpleasant aspects is new. In contrast, the editorial of the Copenhagen tourist magazine *Illustreret Turist-Tidende* from 1914 reads as follows:

> Copenhagen is a lively city – not merely in the sense that its inhabitants are a merry and bright race, but the city in itself has a smiling and bright, almost festive air. It is full of variety and colour, the only exception being certain suburban districts where one meets that colourless, dreary monotony so well known from most of the worlds great modern cities. (*Illustreret Turist-Tidende*, 1914, Nr.1)

The last sentence in particular would be rather unthinkable in a tourist information publication today, but it made sense at the time of early city marketing when documentary trends were very dominant. Mentioning the ugly suburban districts of Copenhagen was not merely an 'unintentional honesty'. Rather, 'colourless, dreary monotony' was synonymous with being one of 'the world's great modern cities' – in other words, ugly suburbs elevated Copenhagen into the league of modern cities of importance. Today's brand campaigns, on the contrary, 'want to focus the public mind by marginalizing bad publicity, ignoring negative aspects of the place, and accentuating positive aspects of the destination' (Ooi 2004: 111). In the context of urban competition, places have to be attractive, without dark spots and problems. Therefore, urban branding appears as 'a sort of evocative story telling aiming at "learning" its recipients to see the city in a particular way' (Jensen 2005:12). In other words, positive and seductive voices dominate.

Together these five developments suggest that place branding is more than a rational marketing activity. As van Ham (2002: 263) points out, branding 'does not take place in a power vacuum; behind the PR and image stands the power of practice'. It is to this that I will turn in the next section.

Place branding as a power practice

Place branding is a soft governance technique on the rise, across different levels of government. Crucially, it depends for its effects on the authority constructions that underpin it. The issue of authority comes to the fore when you investigate who has the right to (re)present a particular place and who creates what kind of image of a particular place. In general, brands are built on factors like trust (van Ham 2002: 264) and credibility. As noted in the above, place brands in particular are very complex and are very difficult to manage and document, both because the spectrum of relevant factors that influence the perceived value of particular places is very wide and because so much of what goes into it is beyond the control of any one government institution.

It is against this background that recent years have seen a veritable mushrooming of ranking exercises. The key quality of rankings is that they allow very complex information to be communicated and mediated in multiple contexts and across distances. The 'knowledge' generated by these exercises can and do serve several purposes. Rankings are initiated and published regularly by consultants and the media (as for instance the Anholt City Ranking Index and fDi), by government institutions and international organizations – or in combinations thereof. It is evident that there is a market for rankings and that politicians, consultants, and entrepreneurs consider these rankings of strategic value (McCann 2004). Both the producers of rankings and those who commission and pay for these rankings can exercise considerable power. Rankings establish a discursive frame that facilitate and legitimize initiatives on 'objective', 'factual' grounds. To Hansen and Salskov-Iversen (2005: 146) these kinds of rankings are part of particular governance techniques, namely the *techniques of performance* that 'present themselves as ways of restoring trust, [...], and enhancing innovation and change.'

By availing themselves of the services of independent and professional ranking experts, governments and other public sector institutions invest their own authority with that of external expert knowledge. In this sense, we can speak of mutual recognition and a shared production of authority. If anything, this brief visit to Berlin reminds us of the pivotal role played by the media in place branding activities, both because of the discursive processes they facilitate and because they themselves are resourceful actors whose particular ways of framing, researching and reporting on specific issues can invest e.g. a City's claim to excellence with authority, or seriously derail any such efforts. When public sector institutions proactively go about engineering their reputation, and, as part and parcel of this, either proactively enter their institutions in various ranking schemes or await the results of leading ranking exercises it 'may also be an indication of how public-sector institutions are reasserting their power and how they are playing more proactively and confidently the governance game' (Hansen and Salskov-Iversen 2005: 143). However, as we saw in the case of Berlin, ranking can be a risky business and less conducive for the (re)building of trust when the results are ambiguous or downright negative.

Ranking is closely associated with the general *rapprochement* between political and business communities (Hubbard and Hall 1998: 9; Jessop 1997). So are other techniques and organizational set-ups involved in place branding, notably many of the initiatives that flow from various public-private partnerships (see Flyverbom and Bislev, this volume). Together they remind us of how important an ingredient branding has become in territorial politics. Recent research on urban politics and development highlights that inter-urban competition has become a major driver of urban economic growth policies, which in turn implies a larger role for private sector interests than previously (Cochrane and Jonas 1999; Desfor and Jørgensen 2004: 482). Partnership arrangements have become the centrepiece for boosting 'entrepreneurialism' as well as the involvement of a wide variety of 'stakeholders', specifically profes-sional marketing firms, in order to attract external funding, investment, and employment sources (Harvey 1989: 7; Kavaratzis, 2005: 336).

Place branding through partnerships and ranking rests on the power of discourse and mediation, having both 'external' and 'internal' dynamics and mechanisms. On the one hand, it aims at generating overall economic and political advantage for the location in question by attracting people and money from the outside. On the other hand, it aims at stimulating a sense of belonging amongst (corporate) citizens working and living there. By implication, there is a strong focus on visual material in these processes. Once a particular place brand has been forged, it is being distributed through media such as magazines, newspapers, posters, film or television. From this perspective, then, place branding takes the shape of identity projects, relying heavily on mediation and with a strong focus on 'imagineering' (Teo 2003) specific locations and generating exciting experiences and stable patterns of loyalty.

Studies of governmentality help us view place branding as a practice of power or governance, or, in governmentality language, as a governmental technology and political rationality. Place branding as a 'technology of government' (Rose and Miller 1990; Dean 1999) means viewing it as a heterogeneous instrument of intervention in public sector organizations and society. It is not least through this technology of government that public sector organizations are currently seeking to modify internal organizational processes and strengthen their position vis-à-vis citizens, with a specific view to improving organizational identity, image, and reputation. Regarding place branding as a 'political rationality' suggests that governments' concern with place branding is located within a wider discursive field in which new conceptions of the role of government are articulated. In this field, the couplet of 'management' and 'entrepreneurship' is strongly articulated in a discourse that trumpets the role of government in the mould of 'New Public Management' (see Clarke and Newman, this volume; Salskov-Iversen and Hansen, ibid). This discourse has introduced private sector management thinking and practices to the public sector through performance measures (e.g. 'value for money' and 'closeness to the customer'), and marketization (e.g. 'consumer choice' and 'contracting out'). From this perspective, the proliferation of place branding is related to the increasing emphasis on management and entrepreneurship – i.e. the political rationality of 'managerialism' – in the public sector.

More generally, the concept of 'advanced liberalism' (or neoliberalism) has been used to capture the tendency to develop 'markets' where there used to be public provision; to employ indirect means of regulation such as evaluation and auditing; to disperse and decentre the management of risk; and to form multiple and new types of agency with the capacity of ruling within the framework of a 'decentralized' and 'participatory' liberal democracy (Rose and Miller 1992; Dean 1999; Larner and Walters 2004).

Together, increased competition, decentring of authority away from rule-based, centralized bureaucratic hierarchies and traditional 'taken for granted' authority towards loosely coupled, decentralized public and private agencies drawing on the expertise of consumer-conscious citizens and other 'stakeholders', have turned public administration into 'risky business'. In fact, place branding might be viewed as a kind of 'risk management' (Dean 1999) – a governmental technology which assumes that proactive identity and image management is crucial for the survival of public sector organizations. This kind of 'risk management' can be found in different versions. During the late 1980s and early 1990s, many OECD cities, including Berlin, faced serious economic problems due to 'the triple problems of de-industrialization, a falling tax base, and declining public expenditure' (Kavaratzis 2005: 330). In this era, 'we witnessed the re-emergence of political structures and ideologies based around the notions of privatization and de-regulation' (ibid). In this context, 'entrepreneurial cities' deserve special attention because of 'their self-image as being proactive in promoting the competitiveness of their respective economic spaces in the face of intensified international (and also, for regions and cities, inter- and intra-regional) competition' (Jessop 1997: 28). On the national level, another version of place branding as 'risk management' can be observed. Both Germany – before the FIFA World Cup in 2006 – and Denmark – after the Cartoon Crisis in 2005/2006 – have spent money and expertise in order to promote their respective countries in the face of different types of reputation crises. In both cases, private consultancies have been involved and authorized to develop new images and suitable place branding campaigns (see www.land-of-ideas.org 2007 or www.em.dk 2007).

Concluding remarks

The case of Berlin sheds light on key aspects of place branding, notably the entanglement of public and private authority as well as the role of mass media and discursive processes. This chapter set out to analyse the complex phenomenon of place branding and the assumption on which it is predicated, namely that in 'a globalized world, every place must compete with every other place for its share of the world's wealth, talent, and attention' (www.placebrands.net). We have seen evidence of how urban politics increasingly has become a politics of growth, driven by intense inter-urban competition. Few places can afford to be non-places or bad places (i.e. suffering from either having no reputation at all or having a bad reputation). Unlike that which certain globalization scholars claim, place matters since it is the specificity of particular places that is crucial for perpetuating processes of capital accumulation (Harvey 1989; Hubbard et al. 2004). In this lens, *places* are constructed and experienced as material artefacts, represented in discourse, and used as representations in themselves. Their brand values are permanently being negotiated and inevitably caught up in power struggles between the multitude of actors whose support and endorsement are required for the claim to a certain image of any place to have a positive, disciplinary effect on (corporate) citizens, employees, investors, tourists, etc.

Media are pivotal to the conduct of public and private life, and, in the case of place branding, this becomes very clear. Here we find a complex and mutually reinforcing relationship between the media representations and the efforts made by cities to boost their competitiveness. The MTV example shows the double character of the media – simultaneously a key player in the local creative economy and a professional image producer commissioned to instil a new identity into Berlin. The Financial Times Group's fDi Magazine reminds us of how the media can function both as a messenger of city images while at the same time operating as a profitable private business which, through its ranking activities, obtains influence, power, and authority.

In sum, branding Berlin is premised on the successful engagement of a network of organizations and high-profiled, strategically positioned individuals in the private sector. By partnering with the City of Berlin, or subjecting it to various types of external verification, such as ranking, these actors invest the City with the authority they enjoy as prestigious, entrepreneurial, and creative private sector actors or 'objective' experts. Sometimes, but not always, the relationship is reciprocal in the sense that in exchange for their investment, these private sector actors also gain reputation wise from engaging with the City. Sometimes, the price for teaming up with the public sector is less of a symbolic nature and primarily pecuniary. Either way, the considerable role played by business in reconstructing city and country images, and thus paving the way for new identities and new reputations, has been met with critical voices because it challenges prevailing notions of democracy. In other words, there are signs that the conspicuous and powerful presence of private authority in what many consider the preserve of democratically elected politicians and their bureaucracy may fail to generate the legitimacy on which the success of an ambitious branding project like Berlin's ultimately rests. Even if the data contained in the Berlin case say little about the actual democratic effects of bringing branding to the centre stage of urban politics, it nevertheless seems appropriate to end this chapter with some of the critical comments that this development has given rise to.

In the case of Berlin, the concerns and ideas of a global corporation like MTV and a relatively small number of (primarily) young and successful people employed by the music, fashion, and design industries arguably do not reflect the realities of the vast majority of Berlin's 3.3 million inhabitants. Berlin's City Administration of Culture estimates the number of people working in the creative economy to be around 100,000, a figure which is dwarfed by the city's unemployment rate, which, at 16.3 per cent (March 2007),[8] remains stubbornly unaffected by the creative economy vision. Also, the sheer amount of public money invested up front in public-private partnerships in order to brand Berlin has become a contested issue (Häußermann and Colomb 2003: 215): why indeed should the tax payer in Berlin pay for a 40 second film clip on MTV or a glossy advertisement in a life style magazine focussing on a very specific segment of Berlin's economy such as the young business community? What kind of place images are produced by the private organizations and consultancies involved in place branding? How do these place branders communicate their ideas of the public spaces they are supposed to brand? How are these actors held accountable for their initiatives to the citizens of Berlin whose image and identity they set out to engineer? What happens when the private creates the public? Other observers, though, have noted that the techniques and rationality of branding, in particular those associated with the potential of the new media's inherent visuality, may open up new democratic spaces, for instance by accommodating social and ethnic groups whose voice is rarely heard in the conventional political processes (Zukin 1995).

Thus, place branding not only reflects broader changes in the ways in which governments operate. It directs our attention to the linkage between changing practices of power and governance: the re-imagination of the city ties in with specific representations of the role of the place in a competitive social order, as well as with the processes of redesigning the ways in which authority, particularly in the public sector, is exercised and managed.

Notes

1. This chapter is based on interviews, e-mail correspondences and the study of websites.

2. Berlin Partners Holding – Capital City Marketing Ltd. holds a 40 per cent share of the company. 15 per cent are shared equally between three other organizations: Berlin Chamber of Small Business and Skilled Crafts (HWK), Berlin Chamber of Industry and Commerce (IHK), and UVB Confederation of Employers and Business Associations of Berlin and Brandenburg. With 45 per cent of the shares, Investment Bank Berlin is the main shareholder.

3. Ward (2004: 248) points out that the motto *Das Neue Berlin* is a '1920s phrase re-used by the Berliner Festspiele'.

4. Despite the organizational changes, the main image campaigns originally created by PfB are still in use, though with subtle changes. The advertisement in Figure 9.1 is still run, but while PfB used it to promote Berlin as The Creative City, Berlin Partner uses it under the heading 'Capital City Marketing: events/projects'.

5. For another example, see Creative London, which is part of the London Development Agency, established in 2003; and Creative Spaces, a collaborative initiative started in December 2004 by Creative London and its Toronto counterpart launched to develop strategies to enhance and develop their respective creative industries (www.creativelondon.org). See also Salskov-Iversen and Hansen, this volume.

6. 17,502 people aged 18–64 in 18 countries were asked to judge 30 cities in terms of culture, tourist appeal, standard of living and international status.

7. In September 2005, the Danish newspaper *Jyllands-Posten* published cartoons depicting the Islamic prophet Muhammad. In response, Danish Muslim organizations staged protests and a group of Danish Imams lobbied decision-makers in the Middle East. As a result, a large consumer boycott of Danish products was organized in several Middle East countries. For weeks, there were numerous protests against the cartoons all over the world, some of them extremely violent.

8. http://www.arbeitsagentur.de/RD-BB/RD-BB/A01-Allgemein-Info/Publikation/pdf/Aktueller-Monatsbericht-1002.pdf

References

Cochrane, A. and A. Jonas (1999) 'Reimagining Berlin. World City, National Capital or Ordinary Place?', *European Urban and Regional Studies*, 6(2): 145–164.

Dean, M. (1999) *Governmentality: power and rule in modern society*. London: Sage Publications.

Desfor, G. and J. Jørgensen (2004) 'Flexible Urban Governance: The Case of Copenhagen's Recent Waterfront Development', *European Planning Studies*, 12(4): 479–496.

The Economist: 'Reinventing Hamburg. A city always ready for the next deal'. 17 March 2007, 382(57).

Florida, R. (2002) *The Rise of the Creative Class: And How It's Transforming Work, Leisure, Community, and Everyday Life*. New York: Basic Books.

Hansen, H. K., R. Langer and D. Salskov-Iversen (2001) 'Managing Political Communications', *Corporate Reputation Review*, 4(2): 167–184.

Hansen, H.K. and D. Salskov-Iversen (2005) Remodelling the Transnational Political Realm: Partnerships, Benchmarking Schemes and the Digitalization of Governance, *Alternatives*, 30(2), 141–64.

Harvey, D. (1989) 'From Managerialism to Entrepreneurialism: The Transformation in Urban Governance in Late Capitalism', *Geografiska Annaler. Series B, Human Geography*, 71(1): 3–17.

Häußermann, H. and C. Colomb (2003) 'The New Berlin: Marketing the City of Dreams', in L.M. Hoffman, S.S. Fainstein and D.R. Judd (2003) *Cities and Visitors. Regulating people, markets, and city space*. Oxford: Blackwell, 200–218.

Hubbard, P., R. Kitchin and G. Valentine (eds) (2004) *Key thinkers on space and place*. London: Sage Publications.

Hubbard, T. and P. Hall (1998) *The entrepreneurial city: geographies of politics, regime and representation*. Chichester; New York: Wiley.

Illustreret Turist-Tidende, 1914, Nr.1. København.

Jensen, O. B. (2005) 'Branding the Contemporary City – Urban branding as regional growth agenda?'. Plenary paper for Regional Studies Association Conference *Regional Growth Agendas* Aalborg, 28–31 May 2005.

Jessop, B. (1997) 'The entrepreneurial city. Re-imaging localities, redesigning economic governance, or restructuring capital?', in N. Jewson and S. MacGregor (eds) *Transforming Cities. Contested Governance and new Spatial Divisions*. London: Routledge, 28–41.

Kalandides, A. (2006) 'Fragmented branding for a fragmented city: Marketing Berlin', available at http://www.geography.dur.ac.uk/conferences/Urban_Conference/Programme/pdf_files/Ares%20Kalandides.pdf (accessed 10 April 2007).

Kavaratzis, M. (2004) 'From city marketing to city branding: Towards a theoretical framework for developing city brands', *Place Branding*, 1(1): 58–73.

Kavaratzis, M. (2005) 'Place Branding: A Review of Trends and Conceptual Models', *The Marketing Review*, 5 (4): 329–342.

Kavaratzis, M.and G. Ashworth (2005) CityBranding: an effective assertion of identity or a transitory marketing trick?, *Tijdschrift voor Economischeen SocialeGeografie*, 96(5): 506–514.

Krantz, M. and L. Schätzl (1997) 'Marketing the City' in C. Jensen-Butler, A. Shacher and J.van Weesep (eds) (1997) *European Cities in Competition*. Aldershot: Avebury, 468–493.

Krätke, S. (2004) 'City of Talents? Berlin's regional economy, socio-spatial fabric and 'worst practice' urban governance', *International Journal of Urban and Regional Research*, 28(3): 511–529.

Kunzmann, K. R. (2004) 'Culture, Creativity and Spatial Planning', *Town Planning Review*, 75(4): 383–404.

Larner, W. and W. Walthers (eds) (2004) *Global Governmentality. Governing international spaces*. London: Routledge.

Lindner, R. & L. Musner (2005) 'Kulturelle Ökonomie, urbane 'Geschmackslandschaften' und Metropolenkonkurrenz', in M. Baumeister et al. (2005) *Stadtbilder und Stadtrepräsentationen. Informationen zur modernen Stadtgeschichte*. 1/2005, 26–37.

Lund-Hansen, A., H.T. Andersen, E. Clark (2001) 'Creative Copenhagen: Globalization, Urban Governance and Social Change', *European Planning Studies* 9(7): 851–869.

McCann, E. J. (2004) ' "Best Places": interurban competition, quality of life and popular media discourse', *Urban Studies*, September 2004, 41(10): 1909–1929.

Mitchell, D. (2000) *Cultural Geography. A critical introduction*. London: Blackwell.

Ooi, C. (2004) 'Poetics and Politics of Destination Branding: Denmark', *Scandinavian Journal of Hospitality and Tourism*, 4(2): 107–112.

Peck, J. (2005) 'Struggling with the creative class', *International Journal of Urban and Regional Research.* 29(4): 740–770.

Rose, N. and P. Miller (1992) 'Political Power beyond the State: Problematics of Government', *The British Journal of Sociology*, 43(2): 173–205.

Teo, P. (2003) 'The Limits of Imagineering: a Case Study of Penang', *International Journal of Urban and Regional Research*, 27:545–563.

Van Ham, P. (2002) 'Branding territory: Inside the wonderful worlds of PR and IR theory', in *Millennium*, 31(2): 249–269.

Ward, J. (2004) 'Berlin, the Virtual Global City', *Journal of visual culture*, 3(2): 239–256.

Ward, S.V. and J.R. Gold (eds) (1994) *Place Promotion: The Use of Publicity and Marketing to Sell Towns and Regions*. Chichester: John Wiley & Sons.

Zukin, S. (1995) *The Culture of Cities*. Oxford: Blackwell.

Internet resources

www.arbeitsagentur.de/RD-BB/RD-BB/A01-Allgemein-Info/Publikation/pdf/Aktueller-Monatsbericht-1002.pdf

www.berlin-partner.de, accessed 11 April 2007; 25 March 2007; 17 April 2007.

www. Businesslocationcenter.de/en/A/seite0.jsp, accessed 16 April 2007.

www.copcap.com/composite-9325.htm, accessed 16 April 2007.

www.creativelondon.org, accessed 25 March 2007.

www.citybrandsindex.com/press-20051206ger.asp, accessed 5 March 2007.

www.em.dk/sw17043.asp, accessed on 10 April 2007.

www.land-of-ideas.org accessed on 10 April 2007

www.placebrands.net, accessed on 1 March 2007.

www.spiegel.de/international/0,1518,437943,00.html, accessed on 24 September 2006.

10
Global Politics, Local Action: the Discursive Politics of Mediation

Lilie Chouliaraki

This chapter addresses a relatively under-researched dimension of the link between global politics and private authority, namely the dimension of mediation. To be sure, mediation as an agent of global politics has already been theorized in terms of how transnational media networks operate as 'agenda-setters' in the context of international politics or as 'self-referential agents' of an elite public dialogue in the global landscape of information (Hjarvard 2002: 91–7). Yet, less attention has been paid to the question of how such transnational information networks may operate as agents of 'global civil society', that is how they may shape beyond-the-West forms of cultural resonance and promote public action for populations and groups who are underprivileged, living in poverty or with war.

It is, in particular, the mediation of suffering in Western media that best throws into relief this problematic. The media today enable, indeed, an unprecedented visibility of distant misfortune: from the entrenched battlefield reports of the Iraq war to the amateur videos of the Asian tsunami, we are constantly confronted with images of the suffering 'other'. Yet, the question remains. Does the global mediation of suffering enable care and responsibility for faraway others – what theorists also call cosmopolitan citizenship?[1]

My argument is that, despite the celebration of transnational media networks as agents of global connectivity, the cosmopolitan attitude of a 'global civil society' depends on more than the technological capacities and institutional powers of mediation. The idea and ideal of cosmopolitanism crucially depends on the discursive politics of mediation, as well. By discursive politics of mediation, I refer to the processes by which media technologies use the resources of language and image in order to tell the story of distant suffering and, thereby, tend to shape public dispositions towards the sufferer among television audiences.

"

Using a number of news broadcasts in western European media, I show that such dispositions encompass a number of ethical proposals for audiences, ranging from indifference and apathy, where the suffering other appears to belong to a different world from the spectator, to responsibility and care, where the sufferer appears as a cause for emotion and even action on the part of the spectator. Instrumental in the disposition of responsibility and care vis-à-vis the sufferer is the way in which the news broadcast accommodates the voices and actions of private authority, such as human rights NGOs, political personalities or celebrity activists, so as to motivate local interest for a distant cause among diverse media publics. This is because these private authority agents carry a strong moral message (Hall and Biersteker 2002), which may not only catch the audiences' attention but also offer each individual spectator a proposal as to what to do about the suffering she/he watches (Calhoun 2001; 2005). The presence of private authority in media discourse, in short, introduces the practice of social solidarity in the everyday life of the western spectator – a practice that can make a difference in the sufferer's conditions of existence and is, therefore, constitutive of the disposition of cosmopolitan citizenship under conditions of global mediation.

In exploring the articulation of moral private authority with processes of global mediation, this chapter demonstrates that the divide between the 'global' and the 'local' is not fixed once and for all but constantly negotiated in the discursive politics of the news, whereby distant events may become causes for local action with a potentially global effect. The chapter similarly challenges the divide between the 'public' and 'private', by showing that processes of mediation constantly blur the two spheres, both in individualizing the public call of moral authority, say, in the face of the activist or the celebrity, and by addressing each individual spectator as a private person with emotions and with a will to act upon the injustices of the world.

My argument unfolds in three moves. First, I critically discuss the thesis of global connectivity in media and social theory and I propose that, rather than insisting on the certainties of an abstract debate, we should approach practices of mediation in their historical specificity as objects of concrete and systematic analysis. Second, I demonstrate that the distribution of public dispositions towards distant suffering in western European television is hierarchical and that this hierarchy depends on the distribution of the symbolic resources, language, and image that news broadcasts use in their reports on distant suffering. Public dispositions to global suffering appear to be shaped by the degree to which the news establishes proximity towards and offer option for reflection and action upon instances of human misfortune and it is here that the importance of private authority voices comes into play. I finally, claim that the public discourse of cosmopolitanism is a specific type of discourse that, under the legitimacy of moral private authority agents, manages to combine emotion for the sufferer with the ethical demand for justice, thus bringing into media discourse a politics of social solidarity. The question of global civil society, I conclude, far from 'simply' a matter of global governance institutions, is also a matter of the mediation of messages of social solidarity, in ways that penetrate the everyday lives of spectators and convince them to take local action that, in making a real difference in the lives of distant sufferers, may have global effects.

Mediation and global connectivity

The role of television as a global agent of civic responsibility lies at the centre of the debate on cosmopolitan politics in media and social theory, where the media are seen to establish new forms of global connectivity and sociability. This is so in two respects:

In the *celebration of communitarianism* version of global connectivity, television introduces the spectator into a broad community of fellow-spectators simply by engaging her in the act of simultaneous viewing. This is a vision on the mass media as early as McLuhan's idea of the 'global village' (1964), according to which television establishes a spectatorial 'feeling in common' based more on the activity of viewing and less on the content of the spectacle. Yet there is a deep pessimism in this line of thinking. Whereas images bring spectators together in new forms of sociality and connectivity, the question of what these images show or how their content affects the spectator remain unaccounted for. This is because it is not the connectivity to the spectacle of the 'other' on screen that counts as the purpose of mediated experience, but the connectivity to fellow spectators. What this view of mediation as tele-sociality misses out is an orientation towards the distant 'other'. Closely connected to this view is the argument about compassion fatigue. Compassion fatigue takes its point of departure in the spectator's everyday life under conditions of safety and comfort, and accuses television of over-burdening spectators with news of human pain and misfortune. This overdose of misery, the argument has it, ultimately renders suffering banal, unimportant, and irrelevant to the spectator's own world (Peters 2005).

In the *democratization of responsibility* version of global connectivity, on the contrary, television's news from around the world increases the spectator's awareness of the existence of others people and, thereby, also increases her concern for the misfortune of the distant sufferer (Thompson 1995; Tomlinson 1999). The constant flow of images and information on screen, the argument has it, inevitably opens up the local world of the spectator and enables the reflexive process by which the spectator comes to recognize non-local realities as a potential domain of her own effective action. It is the interplay between the visibility of the 'other' and the reflexive action of the spectator in response to the 'other' that contains here the promise of cosmopolitanism. This optimistic account of the ethical force of mediation goes as far as considering the media to be changing democracy today towards a deliberative model, whereby audiences use media information to form judgements about distant events and undertake public action in the local contexts of their everyday life. Despite its forceful rhetoric, however, this optimistic version proposes no specific perspectives as to how such forms of public action may be realized. Rather than asking how exactly the image of the 'other' may lead to effective action, the 'democratization of responsibility' argument ultimately turns to wishful-thinking; audiences, we are told, must turn their sense of responsibility *into a form of moral-practical reflection* because this is *the best – the only option we have* (Thompson 1995: 265).

To sum up, the paradox of technology seems to haunt both celebratory narratives of mediation: technology connects, but how and who connects with whom remain unaccounted for. In order to understand how cosmopolitanism is shaped as a mutual feeling of togetherness with fellow-spectators or as responsibility to the distant 'other', we need to keep separate the conceptual space between watching and acting. This is the space of mediation as discourse and it is to a discussion of the qualities of this space that I now turn.

Mediation and the hierarchy of news

My own argument is that the potential of mediation to cultivate a cosmopolitan sensibility is neither de facto possible nor a priori impossible. The potential of mediation to shape a cosmopolitan sensibility has its own historical and social conditions of possibility. What we need to do in order to investigate these conditions of possibility is to investigate empirically how television narrates instances of human suffering through specific regimes of meaning, which construe the spectator in particular relationships of proximity and agency vis-à-vis the sufferer – what we may also call 'regimes of pity' (Chouliaraki 2006: 70–1). The research practice I am exercising is one of phronesis, an Aristotelian practice that approaches ethics as the situated enactment of values, rather than as abstract principles of conduct. Situated ethics is a form of critical investigation of the norms of public conduct that, without altogether abandoning the normative perspective, provisionally brackets this perspective in order to assess how the meanings of right and wrong are constituted in particular examples of news on suffering (Aristotle 1976: 1140a: 24, 1140b: 12, and 1144b: 33–1145a1; Flyvbjerg 2001: 110–28).

Two particular dimensions of the spectator-sufferer relationship are instrumental in the analysis of how mediated connectivity is produced in meaning. These are the dimensions of *proximity – distance* and *watching – acting*. How close or how far away is the spectator placed vis-à-vis the sufferer? How is the spectator 'imagined' to react vis-à-vis the sufferer's misfortune – look at it, feel for it, act upon it? By use of a Foucualt-inspired Discourse Analytic methodology, the Analytics of Mediation, I have studied closely a range of news broadcasts from the global channel BBC World, and two national European channels, the Greek and the Danish state broadcast corporations (Chouliaraki 2006: 70–96).

Three categories of news emerge out of this study. Each category reports on various instances of suffering around the world by combining the language and image of television in different ways. Consequently, each category of news proposes its own ways through which the spectator should engage with the scene of suffering and its own options for possible action upon the sufferer's misfortune:

i. *adventure news*, a class of news which blocks the production of pity;
ii. *emergency news*, a class of news which produces a demand for action upon the suffering; and
iii. *ecstatic news*, an extraordinary class of reports on suffering that manages to bring the globe together in the act of simultaneous watching.

These differences construe a hierarchy of news that corresponds to a broader hierarchy in global relations of power and reflects the historical fact that some places and, therefore, some human lives, deserve more news time, more attention, and more resources than others. Far from simply confirming this piece of well-established sociological knowledge, Foucauldian analytics helps us to trace down how this hierarchical production of news takes place in its discursive detail.

Adventure news

The category of adventure news is illustrated by three pieces of news, 'shootings' in Indonesia, a 'boat accident' in India, and 'biblical floods' in Bangladesh.[2] Their common feature is that their value was not prioritized in their respective news broadcast. The fact that, for example, forty children on their way back from school were drowned in the boat accident in the Indian province of Orissa, was not 'breaking news' or in any way part of the news networks' headlines. The status of these pieces of news reflects the fact that television accommodates a selected number of world misfortunes within less-than-a-minute report slots. I use, therefore, the Bakhtinian term *adventure* to describe this category of news that, like the early Greek romance he critically discusses, fails to provide a framework for understanding the events it describes and renders their broadcasting a chain of random and isolated 'curiosities' that make no affective demand on the spectator. Three semiotic features constitute news as an adventure:

- Brief descriptive narratives that only register 'facts' (e.g. forty children drowned in a boat accident in the Indian province of Orissa),
- Singular spacetimes that restrict the spectator's proximity to suffering (use of maps and photos rather than on location reportage);
- The lack of agency that de-humanizes the sufferer and suppresses the possibility of action in the scene of suffering (sufferers are numbers, e.g. *forty*, and nobody appears to act upon their misfortune).

These features, the minimal narration of suffering, the establishment of radical distance from the location of suffering, and the refusal to humanize the sufferer, come to interrupt the connectivity between spectator and sufferer and fail to make an ethical demand on the spectator. Yet these features should not be regarded as lying outside the enactment of the moral mechanism of mediation itself. The interruption of connectivity is a variation of this enactment and a moral claim in its own right. Suffering without pity, then, is itself an ethical option available to the spectator, which construes the sufferer in discourses of insurmountable cultural difference, as an 'other', and thereby keeps the spectator in her/his own zone of comfort, free from the moral obligation to engage with the sufferer's misfortune.

Emergency news

I here examine prime time news on a rescue mission for illegal African refugees who were caught in a storm in the Mediterranean sea on their way to Southern Europe, on a famine crisis in the poor Argentinean province of Tucuman leading young children to emaciation, and on the 'death by stoning' sharia verdict against the Nigerian Amina Lawal, a young woman who gave birth to a child outside marriage.[3]

All these figures of suffering share one feature that was absent in adventure news. They call for immediate action. It is this demand for immediate action on distant misfortune, which produces the regime of pity that I call emergency news. As opposed to adventure news, the enactment of pity as emergency entails complex news narratives, with multiple connections between safety and danger, and novel possibilities of action both for the participants in the scene of suffering and for the spectator. In this respect, I consider emergency news to be a complex regime of pity that best throws into relief the possibilities, as well as limitations, of public action that are today available to the western spectator.

I would describe the distinction between adventure and emergency news in terms of three major shifts in the representation of suffering:

• The move from visually static and verbally minimal descriptions with low affective power, to visually and verbally complex narratives with increasing degrees of affective power;
• The move from singular and abstract spacetimes (the map) to concrete, specific, multiple, and mobile spacetimes. Spacetimes place suffering in the order of lived experience and often give suffering historical depth and future perspective. They may also connect suffering with the zone of safety and propose a particular type of action to the spectator herself. It is, in fact, only in the example of the news on the Nigerian convict that such connectivity between suffering and safety is established, offering a valuable proposal for the spectator to express practically her solidarity towards the victim of the sharia law;
• The move from non-agency (numerical sufferer; absence of other agents) to conditional agency (active and personalized sufferer; presence of benefactors and persecutors). Conditional agency implies that the sufferer is only able to be active in a limited and ineffective way, hence the need for external intervention. Yet, the very fact of acting endows this sufferer with a quality of humanness that we do not encounter in adventure news. Again, it is particularly the Nigerian Amina Lawal who is signified as a full historical figure – at the same time, a cultural 'other' and a human being just like 'us'.

Ecstatic news

I reserve the term 'ecstatic' for media events such as the tsunami catastrophe or the terror attacks of the September 11th – the latter of which I have analysed as a prototyical case of this category of news (footage from Danish National Television). I use the term 'ecstatic' to refer to a constitutive undecidability that brings such pieces of news and their spacetime together in a unique and rare relationship to one another. 'Ecstatic' time breaks with the ordinary conception of time as a succession of now moments and presents us with *truly historic* time: 'moments when a minute lasts a lifetime, or when a week seems to fly by in next to no time ... what Heiddegger calls "ecstatic temporality"' (Barker 2002: 5). This formulation of the ecstatic perceptively captures the spectator's shock and disbelief at the moment of the second plane crash on the World Trade Center, a moment when a minute seems to last a lifetime.

Although ecstatic news shares with emergency news the demand for action, the two categories differ drastically in their overall representation of suffering and, therefore, in the way each organizes the ethical relationship between the spectator and the sufferer. I describe the distinction between emergency and ecstatic news in terms of three major shifts in the representation of suffering:

- The generic move from news broadcast to live footage. This is the move from a conventional news narrative, punctuated by single, finite, and unrelated pieces of news, to a constant flow of images and verbal narratives with various degrees of affective power. This flow enables the spectator to engage in multiple topics of suffering, and so to empathize, to denounce, and to reflect upon the suffering;
- The move from the emergency chronotope, that is from concrete, specific, multiple, and mobile spacetimes, to an ecstatic chronotope. This entails a temporality that places suffering both in the order of 'lived' experience and in the order of historical rupture; and a spatiality that connects this specific suffering to the globe as a whole, making 'humanity' the simultaneous witness of that suffering;
- The move from conditional agency to sovereign agency. Sovereign agency construes each actor in the scene of suffering as a thoroughly humanized and historical being – somebody who feels, reflects, and acts upon her fate.

This construal of the sufferer as a sovereign being is instrumental in further construing the relationship between western spectator and sufferer as a relationship of *reflexive identification*, whereby the spectator engages with the misfortune of the sufferer continuously, intensely, and multiply (Nichols 1991: 156–58). It is this relationship of identification that, subsequently, enables the emergence of a 'universal' moral stance vis-à-vis the September 11th event and, at least partly, legitimizes the political project of 'war against terror' that followed these terror attacks.

In summary, each and every news piece on suffering is organized around a set of values that appears to be evident and natural but, when placed in comparison to one another, reveal their complicity in sustaining the hierarchy of places and of human life that media critics denounce. These positions represent a key aspect of the information divide in the discursive space of mediation. Although the landscape of global news flows is infinitely complex, this typology captures a significant bias in the intersection between global and national news flows. It tells us that, despite the expansion of mediation technologies, all news flows are eventually subject to a process of selection and symbolic particularization that defines whose suffering matters for the western spectator (Rantanen 2002; Boyd-Barrett and Rantanen 1998). If cosmopolitanism, the ethical disposition that connects the spectator with the distant sufferer, depends on the capacity of television's symbolic practices to produce proximity with the sufferer and propose action on her misfortune, then the question is: which proximity? whose action?

The discourse of cosmopolitan citizenship

To answer this, let me now briefly return to the narratives that celebrate the global connectivity of mediation. The positive version of this narrative, which celebrates the 'democratization of responsibility' through the act of television viewing, finds justification in the empirical reality of ecstatic news. The pessimistic version of this account, which narcissistically favours the bond among spectators at the expense of our moral connectivity with distant sufferers, finds justification in the empirical reality of adventure news. But can these two types of news provide us with the sense of proximity and the options for action that are necessary for a cosmopolitan disposition? Does adventure and ecstatic news provide us with a view of public space, where the spectator connects to the sufferer through a relationship of emotional and practical engagement? The answer is no. None of them is able to construe the public space of television as a space of cosmopolitan agency, because their model of the public is their very own community, the community of western civil life.

The communitarian public of adventure and ecstatic news

Adventure news is paradigmatically associated with the compassion fatigue argument. The argument of compassion fatigue, let us recall, blames television for bombarding the spectator with images of human misfortune and, consequently, holds television accountable for weakening the spectator's sensibility towards distant suffering. Yet, rather than finding the cause of compassion fatigue in the omnipresence of images of suffering, adventure news demonstrates that compassion fatigue is related to the systematic absence of certain sufferers as human beings from the viewing community of western spectators (Tester 2001: 54–71; Cohen 2001: 192). This inadequacy of television to represent certain sufferings as deserving the spectator's emotion and action results in excluding certain places and human lives from the public space where the spectator belongs to and feels able to act within. The main implication of this exclusion is that, in the name of tele-sociality and the spectator's benign desire for comfort, television blocks the possibility of public action beyond the spectator's familiar community of belonging.

Ecstatic news is paradigmatically associated with the 'democratization of responsibility' thesis, which takes its point of departure in television's capacity to connect dispersed locales into a community of spectators. In this respect, ecstatic news clearly demonstrates the effectivity of television to create a global audience, but it simultaneously shows that this aggregate function is reserved for those rare pieces of news that have a historical significance for the West. In the September 11th live footage, television offered the western spectator multiple engagements with the terror attacks. Yet, this therapeutic connectivity worked to rationalize the move from a thinking of terrorism as a story about 'others' to a thinking that such terrorism is real possibility for somebody like the western spectator herself. The community of ecstatic news, global as it may be in its scope, in fact addresses the fears of the European who may now imagine that similar attacks are imminent in Madrid or London. As a consequence, the space of identification and action in ecstatic news is the space where the spectator already belongs to. In what Butler calls *a narcissistic preoccupation with melancholia*, the shared vulnerability of ecstatic news is the vulnerability of the West, leaving out places and populations whose suffering from terror preceeds and follows the western experience by many and by far (2004: 30–1).

Adventure and ecstatic news, in their different ways, appeal to a spectatorial community that is already constituted as a public space. This public space is either the familiar and safe space of collusive denial, where no call to the cause of a distant 'other' disturbs the spectator, or it is the space of common vulnerability, where the spectator's commitment to the suffering 'other' is natural because the sufferer is somebody like her. It is precisely by virtue of this shared feature, namely that they address the West as an already constituted community, that neither adventure nor ecstatic news is able to contribute to the ethical question of how a space of public action towards distant suffering may be constituted in the process of mediation itself.

The problem with evoking the West as an already constituted community of spectators is that these types of news simultaneously evoke a set of pre-existing assumptions implicit in any communitarian bond, as to whose misfortune matters and what there is to do about the misfortune. The communitarian bond, in other words, organizes the content of mediation around the concerns and interests of specific viewing publics, which may transcend the national but do not encompass the global; they are resolutely western. The West, in this perspective, is not a 'universal' context of viewing and action but a particular public, a micro-public, that co-exists with other such micro-publics in the global information landscape. The western claims to care and responsibility vis-à-vis the distant sufferer compete with similar claims of alternative news flows, which equally appeal to their sense of commitment and care for their own sufferer. Today, more than ever, it is important to compare these competing claims to humanity and pity across micropublics of public, because such comparison may shed valuable light onto overlaps and incompatibilities as to whose suffering matters most to whom around the globe.

The public space of pity in emergency news

Between adventure and ecstatic news, the category of emergency news covers a middle space that does not completely efface the sufferer nor does it render the sufferer thoroughly sovereign. It is not that emergency news does not evoke the West as the imagined community where the spectator belongs to. It is rather that emergency news presents the western spectator with a demand for engagement that does not exclusively follow from the pre-commitment to implicit obligations; from the communitarian bond. Neither the apathetic spectator of adventure news, nor the over-engaged spectator of ecstatic news, the spectator of emergency news moves through a number of plausible positions of agency vis-à-vis the distant sufferer. She intensely watches the rescuing of the African sufferer, sheds a tear for the misfortune of Argentinean children or protests for the death verdict of the Nigerian convict.

Free from the 'contractual' relationship to suffering, these pieces of news pose the question of commitment as a problem to be solved and render distant suffering a case to be judged as worthy of action by the impartial spectator. In opening up a range of positions from whence the judgment of suffering is now possible, emergency news simultaneously opens up a space of engagement that may lie beyond the spectator's local horizon for feeling and acting. This means that, rather than restricting public space to the West as a given community, television now addresses the public as an undefined entity.

The 'undefinedness' of the public points to the fact that mediation does not always assume a given public but may also call a public into being, at the moment when it presents the spectator with a cause for engagement (Dayan 1999: 743–765; Barnett 2003: 54–80). In appealing to the spectator as a philanthropist towards Argentinean children or as an activist protesting against Amina Lawal's verdict, emergency news throws into relief this pedagogical dimension of mediation as shaping the spectator's conduct towards a cosmopolitan disposition. The spectator is now the member of a world bigger than the West, who develops her self-identity and disposition to act upon this world in response to visions of the public that television itself proposes. This is why the more we insist on examining the nature of mediation, which emergency news enacts vis-à-vis an undefined and always evolving public, the closer we get to the conditions of possibility for cosmopolitanism; for public action upon humanity (Chartier 1999; Barnett 2003: 100–104).

The 'universal' morality of emergency news

Emergency news evidently confirms the point that global visibility cannot alone guarantee public action upon humanity. But it does more than this. Emergency news further demonstrates that the move from a communitarian to a cosmopolitan sensibility requires a specific kind of public discourse. This is a discourse that assumes no prior ties between spectator and sufferer and, therefore, evokes the idea of public agency precisely at the moment of addressing it. Which is then the quality of mediation that characterizes emergency news?

Emergency suffering is an ambivalent condition that construes the question of commitment to the cause of suffering in an indeterminate and fragile manner. Emergency news offers no proper distance from where the spectator contemplates the suffering, nor does it propose a proper humanness which characterizes the sufferer on television. The humanness of the Nigerian convict, for example, remains suspended between a condition thoroughly 'universal', her motherhood, and thoroughly 'alien' to the western experience, her life, or rather, the threat to her life under the sharia rule. Similarly, the spectator's judgement vis-à-vis African refugees or Argentinean children constantly hovers between these sufferers' desire for life, compatible to the spectator's own, and their fate, radically different from anything the western spectator is likely to experience. Emergency news then presents the humanness of the sufferer as an inherently unstable condition and it is this very instability that sums up the paradox of cosmopolitan action. The possibility of cosmopolitanism lies in the impossibility of representing the condition of distant suffering as suffering proper (Silverstone 2004: 444–6).

This impossibility, however, is at odds with the dominant discourse of ethical conduct today, which is eloquently condensed in Ellis' words *'you cannot say you didn't know'*. What does this dominant discourse – with all the suppressed guilt that it uncomfortably stirs up for the spectator – tell us? Rather than acknowledging the indeterminacy inherent in the mediation suffering, this dominant discourse assumes that, once confronted with the spectacle of suffering, the spectator reacts with a compassionate reflex. The 'democratization of responsibility' argument, for example, clearly assumes that the spectator of the news, in general, is automatically under the moral obligation of the sufferer – on the condition that she/he makes her dramatic appearance on screen.

At this point, however, we can see that it is strictly the spectator of emergency news that may be endowed with such ethical capacity. This is because the spectator of emergency news is the only one to be offered a concrete engagement with the moral values around suffering that claim to have a 'universal' status, in our culture (for an account of the historical origins of the politics of pity see Arendt 1963: 75). In philanthropy, the moral horizon of the spectator is based on the value of common humanity, which moves the spectator's heart in empathy at the sight of children in need. In denunciation, the moral horizon of the spectator is based upon the value of justice, which turns the spectator against the violation of human rights by the sharia law. In the aesthetic register, the moral horizon of the spectator is based upon fantasy and fear as 'universal' faculties of the spectator's engagement with human destiny and the powers that rule human life. These 'universal' values, articulated as they are in a dispersed and discontinuous manner, make up the conditions of possibility for a public ethics in western television.

At the same time, these 'universal' values of suffering do not stand on their own. Because each piece of news struggles to accommodate its own specific realities of suffering – the misery of refugees, the emaciated bodies of Argentinean children, or cruelty in the streets of Nigeria – there is always a struggle between the 'universal' truths of humanity, casting the suffering in an enabling proximity, and the detail of singular sufferings, inevitably evoking a certain distance from the scene of misfortune.

Confronted with these 'twilight' presences on screen, the spectator also becomes an ambivalent figure herself. Neither a true philanthropist who compassionately cares for stranded refugees or emaciated children, nor a proper activist who engages in a practical politics of justice, the spectator is also captured in a fragile, if not impossible, representation. Contradictory as this may sound, the spectator's fragility is not a bad thing. On the contrary, I wish to argue, it is precisely this paradoxical and fragile condition that we need to preserve if we wish to sustain the idea of cosmopolitanism not only as a programmatic utopia of mediation but also as a political reality of contemporary public life.

The key is to draw attention to the internal hierarchy of emergency news that affects the quality of each particular and, consequently, also affects the combination of the particular with a 'universal' discourse of action. Whereas all emergency sufferings appear to be concrete and specific for the spectator, only some pieces manage to represent suffering in terms of multiple and dynamic contexts of activity or as mobile and practically accessible terrains of action. Similarly, the human presence of the sufferer across emergency news ranges from an undifferentiated mass of 'miserables' to an individual with a personal biography and a cultural history. Whereas the African refugees story capitalizes on spectacular images and keeps the story firmly outside a discourse of explanation and public action, the Argentinean crisis appeals to the ideal of 'our' common humanity but tells us nothing about what the crisis is about or how it might be overcome. It is only the news on the Nigerian convict that manages to articulate suffering as a public cause of action for the spectator, by connecting the concrete reality of a death by stoning verdict with the discourse of human rights and the imperative of social solidarity.

This suggests that for the spectator to be confronted with the call for effective action, action that can make a difference in the sufferer's fate, only a certain articulation of the particular and the 'universal' is appropriate; only a certain type of fragility of the sufferer is powerful enough to present her to the spectator as a cause for concern. The capacity of Nigerian convict news to place pity for the sufferer in a historical context and to articulate pity with a demand for justice renders its representation of suffering the clearest instance of cosmopolitan politics in the typology of news.

The cosmopolitan disposition: Historicity and reflexivity

What differentiates the Nigerian case from the other two pieces of emergency news is that it goes beyond bringing a story into the public spotlight and begs the question of 'why'. It is the question of why that makes Amina's suffering appear as a dynamic and open event worthy of public commitment.

This is not a 'grand' why referring to the structures of society or the traditions of religion. It is a 'modest' why embedded in the news as dispersed historicity. This means that this news incorporates relevant fragments of the trajectory of events around the Nigerian court case, such as the hint to a potential conflict between the secular government of the country and the Islamic law or the reference to a similar Amnesty campaign thanks to which another convict had eventually been acquitted in Nigeria. By pointing to the tensions and potentialities that are inherent in the development of the story, references like these simultaneously establish the multiple, specific, and mobile connectivities between the space-times and actors of suffering and the spectator. Who has acted or should act at which place and point in time so as to make a difference to Amina's life organize a regime of pity that does not explicitly moralize the spectator into a politically correct activism but subtly confronts the spectator with the consequentiality of her own actions?

To be sure, the Nigerian piece of news is precisely this: a single piece of news inserted in the flow of a longer broadcast. It can only provide glimpses of the event it represents. It can, under no circumstances, determine the nature, causality or outcome of Amina Lawal's suffering. Nevertheless, by begging the question of why, this piece of news does offer to the spectator the space to reflect upon the cause for action that it proposes. This is what Boltanski calls a 'politics of justice' (1999: 5). As opposed to the politics of pity, where the urgency to bring an end to the suffering always prevails over considerations of justice, in the politics of justice the sufferer never simply 'happens to' suffer but is always subject to a test of fairness, to the question of whether her misery is justified. Why should a woman that had her baby outside marriage be convicted to death? Why should inhumane practices against women take place without us speaking out in favour of human rights? It is these questions of the justification of suffering that the spectator is called to contemplate.

A crucial feature of why questions is that they are not simply propositional; they do not simply formulate issues. They are also performative; they enact a certain disposition towards the ethical and political issues that the news articulates. Why questions, in other words, at once express and construe the reflexivity of the spectator – the capacity of the spectator to consider herself as a speaker who responds to the suffering she watches in front of an undefined public. In the Amina Lawal news, the reflexive response of the spectator is multiply incorporated in the news narrative. First, it is linguistically formulated in the news voiceover through references to the unfairness of the verdict and the shock of the international public opinion; second, it is visually displayed in the top-right screen graphic 'no to death by stoning'; third, it is – crucially – embodied and enacted via the interview of the Amnesty International activist who speaks about the petition for Amina's life and the need for everybody to denounce 'practices of humiliation, stoning, mutilation'. Both the verbal and the visual semiotic modes, then, take part in the staging of this piece of news as a cause for public action.

Cosmopolitan politics: Social solidarity

This form of action speaks in the name of an international public opinion that uses agencies such as Amnesty International in order to monitor the will of governments to act upon world suffering and injustice. Foucault, among others, forcefully advocated such a form of militant international citizenship, reclaiming the right of the governed to act within the sphere of those who are governing: 'Amnesty International, Terre des Hommes and Medecins du Monde', Foucault states, 'are initiatives that have created this new right – that of the private individual to effectively intervene in the sphere of international policy and strategy' (Foucault 1984/2000: 474–75).

Isn't the call for action in the name of Amina's life, made possible precisely by the presence of Amnesty International? This is because, in its capacity as an human rights NGO, Amnesty International is both the carrier of global civil society values and a powerful political agent that monitors the democratization process around the world. To use Kaldor's words, Amnesty enacts cosmopolitanism in a dual sense: as a moral sentiment but also as a political project (Kaldor: 2000; but see also Archibugi and Held 1995; Archibugi, Held and Koehler 1998 for the role of NGO's in cosmopolitan politics). This felicitous ambiguity in the agency of Amnesty enables the representation of Amina Lawal's news to combine a politics of pity with the claim to justice. By representing Amina as a woman treated with injustice and by representing the spectator's agency in the concrete form of the petition, Amnesty International introduces in the news broadcast the practice of social solidarity (Calhoun 2001: 164).

Social solidarity refers to a bond of mutual commitments that, as Calhoun explains, is not based on 'similarities of pre-established interests or identities' (essentially, the communitarian bond), but rather includes 'the citizens' engagement in shared projects of constituting a better future' (Calhoun 2001: 170–174). Calhoun's concept of social solidarity does not only uncouple people's bonds of commitment from their specific interests as already existing groups; it further connects this sense of commitment with the political and humanitarian vision of a 'better future' for a group of people who, because they remain undefined, can potentially extend beyond their own community and encompass care for the future of 'others', too. This cultural definition of social solidarity is a necessary dimension of any cosmopolitan project, because cosmopolitanism is not only about technological or economic development. It is also about the voice of global institutions, which, in addressing world sufferings and poverty, have the power to stretch the concerns of various publics around the globe beyond local perspectives and, thereby, to constitute these publics as non-communitarian publics.

The option of social solidarity that television enables via the voice of private agents with moral authority is an important discursive proposal for the spectator, in the context of this discussion. This is because, necessary as these global agents may be in terms of their economic impact and political activism, they would not contribute to cultivating a cosmopolitan attitude among broad media publics unless their message is mediated; unless, that is to say, they make visible and explicit their commitment to the world-beyond-the West and unless they communicate their practice of social solidarity to such publics in a clear, systematic, and repetitive manner. The legitimacy and effectiveness of cosmopolitan politics crucially depends on the global mediation of the voices of Amnesty International as well as other NGOs, the United Nations, Nelson Mandela, Bono, and the Live Aid artists, because all of these agents carry the expertise, the authority and, not least, the celebrity aura necessary to push the ethical cause of suffering through to vast television publics. In so doing, these voices also have the power to perform the ideal identity of the cosmopolitan citizen for the 'undefined' publics of television around the world, and to call this public into being at the moment that they call upon it. Unless this form of performative politics of solidarity is in place, transborder broadcasting may still operate within a logic of border-setting, rendering the de-territorialization of news flows and their re-territorialization in local contexts of viewing and action the two sides of the unequal relationship between 'us' and the 'other' (Morley 2003: 8).

Indeed, pieces of news such as the Nigerian one are admittedly rare, both in national and transnational television. National television may increasingly draw on transnational broadcasting in its news reports, but it does so in a manner that addresses the spectator as a national citizen within the communitarian logic of its own body politic (Barnett 2003). In a similar manner, transnational broadcasting may have emerged as a strong player in the arena of international politics, setting agendas and giving voice to the disempowered, but it is questionable if it does so in ways that cultivate a politics of social solidarity beyond the West (Silverstone 2006).

If the cosmopolitan politics of emergency news tells us anything, this is that social solidarity in the realm of mediation may be an exception but it is definitely a possibility. It is, in my view, a key question in the agenda of social research today to investigate, rather than to celebrate, whether transnational news flows reproduce the spectator's communitarian concerns in the zone of safety or whether they cultivate new connectivities between spectator and distant sufferer.

Conclusion

In this paper, I discussed a hierarchical typology of news on distant suffering that consists of adventure, emergency, and ecstatic types of news. I showed that, far from the direct outcome of globalizing technologies of communication, the possibility for cosmopolitanism appears to reside in one class of news only, emergency news – news that entails a proposal of action at a distance, using global voices of moral authority to turn distant suffering into a cause for our care and responsibility. Given the urgent ethical and political dilemmas of our world, the study of how mediation articulates with moral private authority is essential in our attempts to study the formation of cosmopolitan publics.

Notes

1. I draw on a social theory definition of cosmopolitanism as *an orientation, a willingness to relate with the Other* (Hannerz 1996: 103). In International Relations, Archibugi's definition of cosmopolitanism is very close to mine: *The cosmopolitan perspective sets out from the assumption that it is necessary to give equal value to human life, irrespective of whether an individual belongs to 'our' or to 'another' political and social community* (2001, http://www.ssrc.org/sept11/essays/archibugi.htm).
2. The 'shootings' and the 'boat accident' pieces come from BBC World, 31 August, 2002, floods in Bangladesh news comes from national Greek television, 23 July, 2002.
3. Greek national television: 23 July, 2002 for the African rescue news; 8 November, 2002 for the economic crisis in Argentina and the death-by-stoning verdict in Nigeria.

Bibliography

Archibugi, D. (2001) *The Cosmopolitan Perspective, Terrorism & Cosmopolitanism* http://www.ssrc.org/sept11/essays/archibugi.htm (accessed November 2005).

Archibugi D., D. Held and M. Köhler (1998) *Re-imagining Political Community: Studies in Cosmopolitan Democracy*. Cambridge: Polity Press.

Archibugi D. and Held D. (1995) *Cosmopolitan Democracy: An Agenda for a New World Order*. Cambridge: Polity Press.

Arendt, H. (1963/1990) *On Revolution*. London: Penguin.

Aristotle (1976) *Nichomachean Ethics*. Harmondsworth: Penguin.

Barker, C. (2002) *Alain Badiou: A Critical Introduction*. London: Pluto Press.

Barnett, C. (2003) *Culture and Democracy*. London: Edinburgh University Press.

Boltanski, L. (1999) *Distant Suffering. Politics, Morality and the Media*. Cambridge: Cambridge University Press.

Boyd-Barrett, O. and T. Rantanen (eds) (1998) *The Globalization of News*. London: Sage Publications.

Butler, J. (2004) *Precarious Life*. London: Verso.

Calhoun, C. (2001) 'Imagining Solidarity: Cosmopolitanism, Constitutional Patriotism and the Public Sphere', *Popular Culture*, 14 (1): 147–72.

Calhoun, C. (2005) 'A World of Emergencies: Fear, Intervention and the Limits of Cosmopolitan Order'. 35th Annual Sorokin Lecture, University of Saskatchewan, Canada (available at http://www.artsandscience.usask.ca/ sociology/seminars/ Yearly%20Sorokin%20PDF/35th%20Annual%20Sorokin%20Lecture.pdf).

Chartier, R. (1999) *The Cultural Origins of the French Revolution*. New Jersey: Princeton University Press.

Chouliaraki, L. (2006) *Spectatorship of Suffering*. London: Sage Publications.

Cohen, S. (2001) *States of Denial*. Cambridge: Polity.

Dayan, D. (1999) 'The peculiar public of television', *Media, Culture & Society*, 23 (6): 743–765.

Flyvberg, B. (2001) *Making Social Science Matter*. Cambridge: Cambridge University Press.

Foucault, M. (1984/2000) 'Confronting Governments', in J. D. Fabion (ed), *Essential works of Foucault 1954–1984. Vol.3*. London: Penguin.

Hall, R.B. and T. Biersteker (2002) *The Emergence of Private Authority in Global Governance*. Cambridge: Cambridge University Press.

Hannertz, U. (1996) *Transnational Connections*. London: Routledge.

Hjarvard, S. (2002) 'The study of international news', in K. B. Jensen (ed) *A Handbook of Media and Communication Research*. London: Routledge, 91–7.

Kaldor, M. (2000) 'Cosmopolitanism and Organized Violence'. Paper for Conference on 'Conceiving Cosmopolitanism', Warwick, 27–9 April, 2000.

McLuhan, M. (1964) *Understanding Media*. London: Routledge.

Morley, D. (2003) 'What's "Home" Got to Do with It?: Contradictory Dynamics in the Domestication of Technology and the Dislocation of Domesticity', *European Journal of Cultural Studies*, 6 (4) (2003): 435–458.

Nichols, B. (1991) *Representing Reality*. Bloomington and Indianapolis: Indiana University Press.

Peters J.D. (2005) *Courting the Abyss. Free Speech and the Liberal Tradition* Chicago: University of Chicago Press.

Rantanen, T. (2002) *The Global and the National*. London: Rowman and Littlefield.

Silverstone, R. (2004) 'Media Literacy and Media Civics', *Media, Culture and Society*, 23 (3): 440–449.
Silverstone, R. (2006) *Media and Morality*. Cambridge: Polity.
Tester, K. (2001) *Compassion, Morality and the Media*. Milton Keynes: Open University Press.
Thompson, J. (1995) *Media and Modernity*. Cambridge: Polity Press.
Tomlinson, J. (1999) *Globalization and Culture*. London: Sage Publications.

11
Conclusions: The Making of Authority in Global Politics – Towards the Engagement of Practice and Micropolitics

Hans Krause Hansen and Dorte Salskov-Iversen

The concept of private authority, introduced by scholars of international relations and international political economy in the late 1990s, constitutes a rich approach to investigate the changing role of business and other non-state actors in global politics. Drawing on insights from this spate of research and inspired by studies of governmentality and institutions, this book has explored the constitution of authority in a variety of contemporary political arenas, on and across different sectors. This concluding chapter returns to the three conceptual lenses offered in Chapter 1 – the disaggregation, innovation, and mediation of authority – and spells out and discusses key insights from the preceding chapters.

The concept of disaggregation serves the purpose of examining the dispersed, fragmented, yet often entangled character of authority, providing us with glimpses of the very practical ways in which rule is coordinated, consolidated or contested. The concept of innovation serves as an entry point to explore the ways in which the contemporary making of authority relies on beliefs and techniques of modernization and change, and how these processes are necessarily shaped by the dynamics of and interactions between specific social and political contexts. The concept of mediation highlights the role of technologies and discourse in the making of authority and in the constant blurring and reconfiguring of the divisions between the public and the private, the national and the international, the global and the local.

The three lenses nuance our understanding of recent developments by relativizing the either/or categorizations, which in much previous research have arguably prevented alternative conceptualizations of how authority operates today. Future analyses of the production of authority may gain from incorporating a focus on multiple levels, domains, and sectors. As Dicken et al. (2002: 90) have pointed out in their study of the deeply relational character of the global economy, the automatic privileging of 'one particular scale over others', or 'specific organizational loci of analysis' can often become an obstacle to understanding. It may neglect or even dismiss as relevant other important factors, and it may provide a shortcut to questionable justifications for particular political strategies and actions.

Following this relational view in our accounts of authority in global politics we have stressed the invariably multiple and contextual nature of circumstances that impact and generate (new understandings of) the making of authority. Previous studies have focussed mostly on the role of non-state actors in the making of and compliance with private international rules of various sorts. By examining the materialization of the 'private' in public authority, by exploring 'hybrid' constellations on the rise that link actors and activities across levels and domains, and by scrutinizing some of the mediated practices that underpin them, we have probed into the complex mechanisms and mutually defining relationships that in specific social contexts and issue areas constitute and rework what is contested or accepted as authoritative. Further research on the production of authority in global politics will be enriched by a more systematic and empirically grounded investigation of the everyday activities, mechanisms, and practices, discursive and non-discursive, human and non-human, that underpin the processes of making and contesting authority. This may be a promising launch pad for the next sequel of studies of the politics of disaggregation and hence of the politics of association and alignment.

Everyday forms of disaggregation and techniques of entanglement

We began our journey with Tony Porter's investigation of the disaggregation of public authority, exemplified by the cases of the privatization of airport and border security, the regulation of global finance and the unauthorized downloading of songs. Challenging positions that view the disaggregation of public authority as relatively insignificant, as well as those that ignore the role of media technologies in the making, linking and contestation of different forms of authority, Porter develops three propositions:

i) some issue areas, like airline and border security, are closer to traditional public authority than others, and are therefore likely to be less disaggregated;
ii) disaggregation is affected by the presence and absence of technological systems, including processes of mediation through networks;
iii) disaggregation is affected by the demands of non-state actors with whom the state has come to share its power over issues traditionally viewed as the preserve of state power.

Porter's comparison of the extent of disaggregation of public authority in the issue areas under scrutiny produces some support of the first proposition, but not as much as one might have expected, and particularly not when this proposition is assessed against the backdrop of the second and third propositions. In fact, the introduction and operation of technological systems and mediated networks, and the emergence of demands from the wider public, highlight the important roles played by private, popular and technical forms of authority, as well as a variety of techniques and mechanisms that link these forms to one another and to public authority. For example, the introduction of new surveillance technologies in airports greatly increases government reliance on the industries that produce this technology and on the technical knowledge involved to make it work. The reliance on private and technical authority is complemented by public political debates that draw on competing discourses of popular authority – *pro or against more surveillance in times of global terrorism?* – enabling and constraining the use of these surveillance measures in important ways.

Porter's investigation thus suggests that not only does the disaggregation of authority involve the transformation of authority from a more state-centric public form to increasingly mediated private, technical, or popular forms of authority. It also suggests that these forms are entangled with one another, producing highly complex patterns of authority. Such complex patterns are further investigated by Olsen, Flyverbom and Bislev, Larner, and Salskov-Iversen and Hansen. Olsen argues that transnational networks of organizations issuing and promoting voluntary standards are on the rise. He introduces the concept of meta-governance to describe how the standards guiding government auditing are increasingly developed 'beyond the state' by hybrid organizations strongly influenced by (multinational) private accountancy firms. His study, in other words, provides us with compelling evidence that in this field state authority is clearly moving towards more disaggregation. But this may also very well be the case for other forms of authority, as Olsen rightly states: 'For public and private sector organizations alike, the costs of being influential through the transnational regulatory network is likely to be that they, in turn, are being influenced by the other organizations in the network'. Simultaneously, and in very practical ways, these arrangements rest on the entanglement created by institutional entrepreneurs capable of spotting, designing, and managing their interconnections. These entrepreneurs are skilful people with experiences from both the public and private sectors at national and international levels. They link up otherwise disparate, sometimes competing, organizations by working as brokers and network designers at the interfaces of the organizations.

Flyverbom and Bislev explore the processes of disaggregation and entanglement in the emerging field of Internet governance, demonstrating how the development of 'multi-stakeholder participation' as a technology of ruling allows governments, international organizations, the private sector and civil society groups to come together around an issue of common and rapidly increasing concern. The authors argue that myriad technical and private sector bodies take decisions with far-reaching consequences for the shape and development of the Internet, and that this emerging field is a model case of the development of a highly 'entangled' mode of public and private authority. Specifically, the authors show how the WSIS process has both spurred a reconfiguration of the involvement of different actors and led to a clash between different modes of governance, in particular intergovernmentalism and self-regulation. Importantly, the WSIS process paved the way for a general acceptance of 'multi-stakeholder participation' as a key governmental technology, entangling participants in a web of interrelations. By representing governments, international organizations, the private sector and civil society groups as 'stakeholders', this governmental technology has been able to operate through strategies of cooperation and consensus, bracketing at least for a while otherwise incompatible political positions.

The questions of how authority disaggregates and gets entangled, and what constitutes the boundaries of disaggregated authority and its modes of connection to particular sectors or spheres are also brought up in other chapters of the book. Larner invites us to pay more attention to the ways in which new political forms are being constructed. A key feature of some of these new forms, notably those assuming the form of diaspora networks, is that, while they mobilize non-state actors at great distances and in this way challenge territorial models of public authority and sovereignty, they also remain an important part of the ambitions and initiatives of local and national governments. We may say that public authority itself is assuming new forms as a consequence of the efforts to govern through these globalizing networks of political and institutional relationships. A similar proposition is made by Salskov-Iversen and Hansen who investigate the 'globalizing webs' connecting various public sector institutions operating at different levels and across different sectors in the field of e-modernization. It is in this way that very dissimilar cities, in part through their engagement in the same transnational fora, contribute to and in different ways shape the diffuse project of modernizing the public sector. The authority of these transnational fora depends on their capacity to successfully enrol and mobilize others in the pursuit of their goals. For those who sign up, the effect – and eventual authority – of their enrolment depends on the degree to which they can access useful knowledge and contacts. At the level of urban politics, Stöber's analysis shows how the project of branding Berlin to a large degree is predicated on the success of the City government to engage a network of organizations and high-profiled, strategically positioned individuals in the private sector. By partnering with the City of Berlin and subjecting it to various types of external verification, such as ranking exercises sponsored by companies, these actors invest the City with the authority they enjoy as prestigious, entrepreneurial and creative private sector actors or 'objective' experts.

The above studies all avoid taking for granted that public and private organizations are unitary actors operating in sharply deliminated sectors and domains. In this way, they highlight the fluid, entangling and mutually defining interactions between the multiple actors that constitute and change what is authoritative. The studies reported here thus provide a supplement to literatures on private authority in international affairs and global governance that have primarily focussed on the large scale shifts in power from states to markets and civil society domains, and from public sector actors to private and civil society actors. Drawing on the above findings, we therefore recommend future investigations of the rise of hybrid formations of authority to look more into some of the mechanisms and practices that link together organizations across the 'public' and 'private', 'national' and 'international' spectra.

This will require more focus on the 'institutional entrepreneurs' and other important 'brokers', including 'partnerships', that operate at the intersections of organizations and networks and on multiple levels, tying things together. By implication, it would also require more attention to the practical forms of meta-governance, that is, the governance of governance. If the state remains a significant, organizing force and distinctive authority for meta-governance in the sense that it has 'the capacity to require partnerships to take place, to direct them and to evaluate them' (Clarke 2004: 115), it may also be the case that these capacities increasingly are located and developed elsewhere, e.g. amongst 'non-state partners'. In other words, if governments on various levels have become more engaged in organizing the self-organization of partnerships and cross-cutting networks (Jessop 2002: 76), it is also possible that such organizational formats may acquire a life on their own. If authority making in these circumstances rely on techniques of cooperation, enrolment, inclusion and exclusion, then analyzing the new relationships that are forged by these actors – be they 'transnational networks' or 'multi-stakeholder partnerships' – may provide further insights into how these organizational formats come to be invested with authority through the production of specific forms of action considered legitimate by different sub-publics (Abrahamsen 2004).

Importantly, analyses along these lines may also help us to identify the cases where such action is considered illegitimate, met with apathy or indifference, failing to engage with the identifications and relationships of a variety of different sub-publics, a subject touched upon by Porter, as well as Newman and Clarke (see below). This, we find, will, complement Slaughter's study (2004) of the emerging disaggregated world order, which offers an interesting point of departure for those scholars interested in the analysis of dynamics of elite politics at the intersection of formal governmental domains, but which, as we suggested In Chapter 1, seems to end where the everyday politics of everybody else begins.

Innovation, authority-building, and legitimacy work

Most organizations – state agencies, companies, and other organizational forms – tend to trade on the idea of permanence, as well as on the notion that reality is to some extent manageable and programmatic. Public sector organizations usually justify their activities and projects of modernization with the claim that a domain can be administered better or more effectively, hence the recurrent identification of 'failures' to be corrected and the never ending presentation of new policies and initiatives. Private sector businesses are justified by the ability of their services or products on offer to actually satisfy some kind of demand, which, if it is not already there, must be actively constructed. At the same time, however, these organizations constantly have to renegotiate their relationships, internally and externally. Indeed, there is a sense in which their stability rests on their ability to transform and innovate (Bach and Stark 2005: 37). The success of their aspirations to innovate are increasingly contingent upon techniques of calculation, strategizing, and image and identity work. The precise form of these techniques varies from context to context, as several chapters in this book demonstrate. This reflects the differential and historically shaped nature of the boundaries between the public and the private, including the differential coding of these spheres. Transforming and innovating also involve attending to the broader public's expectations of proper conduct – expectations that are also highly context dependent.

Consider for example the distinctive ways in which private market actors construct and manage their self-representations in Mexico and France, conceptualized as 'legitimacy work' by Blasco and Zølner in Chapter 5. Since the prestige of such actors has always been low in these parts of the world, and the state perceived as responsible for social welfare, some private actors may seek to enhance their legitimacy in the eyes of the public by complying with or exceed the minimum level of public expectations concerning their societal role, for example by voluntarily engaging in social welfare activities traditionally viewed as the preserve of other social institutions, in particular the state. While French firms would have to exceed the minimum legal requirements to acquire greater legitimacy through social welfare activities, Mexican firms, due to profound state deficiencies, would potentially gain significant legitimacy simply by demonstrating compliance with basic legal requirements. Further, in their legitimacy work, private actors may 'borrow' legitimacy from popularly endorsed institutions by expressing their social engagement in ways that echo those institutions. Again, the specific pattern is contextually dependent, since popular endorsement enjoyed by specific institutions will vary, as will the extent to which that support can be successfully 'transferred' from one sphere of activity to another.

This finding feeds into discussions about the difficulty of making broad generalizations across contexts concerning the potentially increasing role and legitimacy of the authority of private sector organizations. The difficulty is not only that their legitimacy may differ due to differences in public expectations, but also that purportedly 'private actors' may themselves fail to identify with the transformative projects of a modernizing state, an issue explored by Newman and Clarke. The core argument in Newman and Clarke's chapter is that public sector modernization in the UK does not, even if authorized by the state itself, engage with popular identifications and relationships. Specifically, the emphasis in British public sector reforms on marketization and privatization of functions previously deemed the province of the state – and on constant attempts to renegotiate the state-citizen relationship through a 'transformative' language and 'innovative' institutional set-ups revolving around the 'citizen-consumer' – is met with mixed feelings. There are certainly signs that it is at odds with 'popular expectations', to use Blasco and Zølner's vocabulary. In other words, when non-state actors – corporations, voluntary associations, and in this case citizen-consumers – are authorized by the state to assume responsibilities or perform the 'role-expectations' inherent in the figure of the citizen consumer, there is no guarantee that popular identifications and meanings change accordingly. This leads Clarke and Newman to stress not only the importance of taking 'meanings' seriously – to view them as 'the site of contested interpretation and translation' – but also the risk of relying too much on 'epochal' views of social transformation: from state to non-state, from public to private, etc. Such views tend to conceal the complex field of relations below the level of binary conceptions.

The New Zealand diaspora strategy analysed by Larner as well as the transnational operations of the local governments studied by Salskov-Iversen and Hansen exemplify the complex ways in which policy initiatives, promoted by different types of state actors, may not only reach into other territories and non-state modes of organization, but also be ploughed back to these state actors themselves to harness their modernization and innovation projects. Larner's analysis shows how the New Zealand government facilitates the making of formal connections with expatriate citizens in order to prompt the insertion of domestic organizations into global economic flows and networks. This, in turn, is premised on the assumption that the international competitiveness of overseas experts can improve national economic performance by fostering greater productivity, creativity, and innovation. Larner argues that efforts at entangling expatriate business, cultural, scientific, and policy networks with national development projects may be seen as an example of how governments have begun to think about their expatriate populations in new ways, mobilizing ideas about the desirability of global markets, entrepreneurial firms, and active individuals. Importantly however, she also emphasizes that it would be misleading to view the new thinking as simply coming out of 'the designs of neoliberal elites'. Nor should it be seen as a mere response to the rise of a 'globalized network economy'. Rather, it is the very idea of 'globalization' that is giving rise to these activities. They are being enacted through an 'iterative process' between government agencies, intermediary organizations, and various expatriate actors.

The idea of 'globalization' and concomitant 'iterative processes' also plays a significant role in Salskov-Iversen and Hansen's study of modernizing and innovating public sector organizations at the sub-state level. Appropriating 'private sector ways' of thinking and ruling, these organizations view the new media technologies as a means and an object of public sector innovation – simultaneously an instrument of direct intervention in specific public sector practices and routines, and a vehicle for knowledge sharing about how best to manage and organize the public sector across boundaries. Importantly, for those who join these networks, the gain may not only be knowledge and contacts, but also identity and reputation – which suggests that being projected and connected across national boundaries is increasingly valued by also subnational government institutions as it allows them to reassert their authority, not least locally.

Building authority and doing legitimacy work by explicitly embarking upon a carefully communicated and seemingly ambitious innovation project is risky business – and, unsurprisingly, perhaps, the risks are often overlooked or neglected as prestigious initiatives are rolled out across organizations, cities, nations or even on a global level. The stories unfolded in this volume give us some idea of the inherently murky nature of most 'innovation' projects; of the tensions and dilemmas woven into any 'bold' move; of the losers and winners of the 'imperative of change' (Clarke and Newman 1997). Thus, a notion like 'best practice', a standard innovation tool (see Salskov-Iversen and Hansen this volume), is fraught with problems because it immediately forces us to ask: best for whom? Likewise, there is rarely a clear-cut division between the past and the future. Even if Berlin's history is sought eliminated in today's branding projects enacted by public-private partnerships, the past refuses to die: the world remembers just as a large percentage of Berlin's population fails to be absorbed by the culture economy (Stöber this volume). In both Old Town and New Town (Clarke and Newman, this volume) we see the new emphasis on the citizen-consumer in uneasy co-existence with multiple, competing, and contradictory layers of paradigms of state-citizen relationships. Blasco and Zølner's analysis, in turn, reminds us how culturally sensitive and potentially counterproductive modernization-cum-branding projects in the private sector can be when leveraged for legitimacy purposes.

More fundamentally, the above studies draw our particular attention to the precarious nature of authority: all rulers – or aspirants to authority – engage to a greater or lesser extent in a process of legitimation, resorting to a wide spectrum of justifications and activities with a view to changing and improving their situation and relationships. These justifications, made in the present, but crucially depending on knowledge and experience of the past – witness the cases of Berlin, Mexico, and France – serve to legitimate the present, and not least, a future configuration of activities and circumstances. While the above studies on legitimation, legitimacy work and the operation of various forms of governmentality give us some important insights about the concrete processes and practices by which legitimacy is sought created and subjects are positioned as self-regulating, they tell us less about how legitimacy and self-regulation is actually achieved, or whether it is lost or eroded. Institutions and organizations may make claims about their moral rightness and their acts may be justified in terms of what is believed to be prevailing societal values. Yet, this alone does not provide a shortcut to legitimacy.

These difficulties obviously hark back to the complexity of the concepts of authority, legitimacy and governmentality mentioned in Chapter 1. In a sense, legitimacy work, legitimation or the attempts to make subjects 'fit' governmentality are the work of governments, corporations, and other associations. This work is not necessarily successful. The subjects may elicit a sense of obligation and comply with these authorities, but compliance may be conditional and calculating. Non-compliance may result from indifference. At any rate, the above studies have taken the study of how organizations try to gain legitimacy into the realms of the 'private', the 'hybrid', and the 'transnational', unravelling some of the discourses, practices, and mechanisms involved when organizations, institutions, and new constellations engage in making themselves visible and distinct to broader publics. Whether these public care to listen is another issue. Further studies are warranted, we suggest, not only into the relationship between the creation of authority, organizational self-promotion, and image-making from both 'public sector' and 'private sector' perspectives, but also into the practical responses to such legitimacy work from various subpublics.

Mediation and the making of authority

One way or the other, most chapters in this volume note the way in which technical devices and media technologies contribute to the production and framing of economic, political, and social issues, relations, and practices, thus stretching them across and reconfiguring established boundaries. Porter focusses on the role of mediation in the disaggregation of public authority towards private, technical, and popular forms of authority. Larner as well as Salskov-Iversen and Hansen in turn emphasize the capacity of the media to facilitate different kinds of global networks and thus enable various modes of entanglement, not least enrolment into new governmental set-ups. Flyverbom and Bislev show how the governance of media and communication technologies, in this case the Internet, stands out as an increasingly important policy field in global governance, just as Salskov-Iversen and Hansen demonstrate how the policy focus in the public sector on e-modernization and e-innovation has become a vehicle for the development of transnational networks of knowledge exchange on these (and other) issues.

Stöber and Chouliaraki examine the media factor and media technologies from somewhat different perspectives and in more detail. Stöber analyses the role of place branding in urban politics and identify a complex and mutually reinforcing relationship between the representations of cities disseminated by various media industries and government agencies, and the efforts made by the same agencies to boost the competitiveness of cities and countries. Here, the media has a double role – simultaneously a key institutional player in the local 'creative' economy and a professional image producer commissioned to instil a new identity into a specific locality. The study reminds us of how the media can function both as a messenger of city images while at the same time operating as a profitable private business which, through its ranking activities and the widespread consumption of these rankings, obtains 'private' authority. In this way, the rise of place branding suggests broader changes in the ways in which local (and state) governments operate: the re-imagination of the city ties in with specific representations of the role of the place in a competitive social order, as well as with the processes of redesigning the ways in which authority, particularly in the public sector, is exercised and managed.

Chouliaraki demonstrates how broadcasting institutions draw on both language and image to tell stories of social phenomena, which are globally disseminated and consumed. Very often, the topics brought up by these institutions in this discursive and mediated space relate to aspects of societal conflict or natural disasters that take place well beyond 'the West'. The result is stories complete with what she terms 'ethical proposals for audiences'. To understand these ethical proposals, their mediated character, and the ways in which they are capable of producing apathy, indifference or socially responsible action among audiences, is important for the simple reason that future cosmopolitan publics and authority recognized beyond established national and international institutions will ultimately have to rely on some sense of social solidarity. The incorporation by the media discourse of voices of authority, in this case 'private moral authority', is important. These voices of authority mediated through television can potentially appear as a cause for socially responsible action on the part of the spectator.

While Chouliaraki's study is specifically concerned with the issue of distant suffering and the role of private moral authority in turning distant suffering into an object worthy of our sympathy and deserving responsible intervention, her findings have a much broader applicability and relevance. For one thing, they illuminate how distant events may come to justify local actions of potentially global ramifications, and the role of the media in bringing about these actions: what happens or is organized at specific locations travels globally and becomes recontextualized in other locations, often, but not always, bypassing whatever controls have been set up by governments. We will argue that we need more studies of how authority making relate to processes of global mediation. Such studies should go well beyond the traditional focus on global governance institutions and pay special attention to the technical devices and media technologies that facilitate new logics of interaction which impinge on the way actors operate, make sense of themselves, materialize or exercise control 'at a distance'. This is not merely a question of communicating faster and perform well-known functions more effectively, but of communicating in entirely new ways and thus making possible new types of activity, and by implication, raising new questions.

If it makes sense to speak of a 'global political space' (Latham and Sassen 2005), this space is shaped by flows of material and ideational artifacts, and by the co-evolution of novel forms of authority, social relations, social practices, and discursive representations that would have been unthinkable without these technologies – precisely because these technologies produce new mechanisms for exercising authority at a distance. Salskov-Iversen and Hansen's discussion (this volume) offers a salient case of this. Here we see the governments of two cities, none of which belong to the league of World Cities, being enrolled into a global web of city governments, all dedicated to the cause of e-modernization. The technical affordances of modern mediation modes add a qualitatively different aspect to the dynamics at play, both in terms of actually enabling contact and communication between geographically dispersed institutions; by disseminating and thus making translation of specific knowledge possible; and, just as importantly, by doing image, reputation and identity work, just as we saw it in Stöber's study of Berlin (this volume).

However, it would definitely be a mistake to regard such processes as smooth and easy. The technical processes involved are always very localized, subject to complex interferences and breakdowns. To actually arrive at anything like 'macro orders' – including the above mentioned global political spaces, in part based on creative application and appropriation of these technologies and their interaction with human beings – is not easily achieved, if at all.

* * *

New arrangements of authority are emerging 'within' and 'beyond' the nation state, be it in the shape of 'private' entities, 'private moral authority' going public, 'public-private' and 'multi-stakeholder' partnerships in local and transnational settings, interlinked 'networks' and criss-crossing 'webs'. These arrangements rely on particular and historically contingent social practices and techniques, material and human. As our focus on the mediation of authority has suggested, technological components of various sorts have both a critical importance to everyday social life and help to mark out new spaces of authority. Future studies of new forms of global politics need to pay more attention to the ways such spaces are created and how, as Larner suggests, not only the categories of local and global but also those of public and private, state, and civil society, citizens and non-citizens, are themselves being reworked through such processes.

In discussing the challenge of researching the spatial dispersion of complex social forms and collective arrangements, their multiple connections and the ways in which they operate on and criss-cross various scales or levels – a challenge that each of the preceding chapters of this collection has had to face – Barry (2001: 22) speaks of being 'empiricist' in a double sense: being focussed on the detail and the complexity of empirical examples so that one gets a sense of the irreducibility, messiness, and contestability of the social; and gets things in perspective, generalizing analytically from specific examples and through the invention of new concepts. We may have come some of the way to achieve this. But we find it useful to add two things. For one thing, being 'empiricist' in the present context is not to reject 'abstraction' nor the need to have a vocabulary for the study of macro orders. Further, this type of analysis can be linked to a particular view of the 'political', which takes more into account the role of 'micropolitics' in what might otherwise be characterized as 'politics without institutions', 'governance' without 'government' (Rosenau and Czempiel 1992), or as 'power conceived not as a matter of imposing sovereign will, but enrolling the cooperation of a chain of actors' (Braithwaite and Drahos 2000: 31) It is important to emphasize that micropolitics is not an issue of the small (Deleuze and Guattari 1987; see also May 2005; Connolly 1991). Rather, it is a politics which social actors exercise upon themselves as they engage with others, responding in this way to 'difference' and 'distinction'. It includes techniques and routines organized and deployed by associations of various sorts, and it serves as the primary vehicle for and feeds into 'macropolitics'. In fact, all large-scale institutions, organizations, and associated spaces of authority are in one way or another nourished by micropolitics (Hoff and Hansen 2006). It is through micropolitics in different settings that alignments are forged between the objectives of different institutions and organizations, and the interests and projects of individuals and groups who are the subject of and recognize the authority exercised by these institutions and organizations.

Approaching the politics of disaggregation and entanglement of authority from this vantage point naturally leads us to consider how the dynamics of micropolitics tie into wider processes. For example, as Porter points out in this volume, disaggregated authority can undermine conventional democratic legitimacy, because some disaggregated processes can be harder for citizens to monitor and hold accountable, and because the private and technical authority involved is not necessarily aligned with the interests of citizens. But, as he adds, disaggregation can also provide new entry points and ways for people to shape the more formalized and institutionalized policy processes, creating new channels for participation and transparency beyond the nation-state. Underlying the ambiguities produced by disaggregation – including the complex and unforeseeable patterns of entanglement, alignment and enrolment of people into specific organizational forms, activities and practices considered authoritative by some but not everybody – is obviously the question of accountability and its role in discussions of democracy. These are discussions that others are invited to pursue, drawing on some of the thoughts produced by the authors of this volume.

Bibliography

Abrahamsen, R. (2004) 'The Power of Partnerships in Global Governance', *Third World Quarterly*, 25(8): 1453–1467.
Bach, J. and Stark, D. (2005) 'Recombinant Technology and New Geographies of Association', in Latham, R. and Sassen, S (2005) *Digital Formations. IT and New Architectures in the GlobalRealm*. Princeton: Princeton University Press.
Barry, A. (2001) *Political Machines*. London: The Athlone Press.

Braithwaite, J. and P. Drahos (2000) *Global Business Regulation*. Cambridge: Cambridge University Press.

Clarke, J. (2004) *Changing Welfare Changing States. New Directions in Social Policy*. London: Sage Publications.

Clarke, J. and J. Newman (1997) *The Managerial State*. London: Sage Publications.

Connolly, W. (1991) *Identity/Difference: Democratic Negotiations of Political Paradox*. New York and London: Cornell University Press.

Deleuze, G. and F. Guattari (1987) *A Thousand Plateaus*. Minneapolis: University of Minnesota Press.

Dicken, P., P.F. Kelly, K. Olds, and H.W-C. Yeung (2001) 'Chains and Networks, Territories and Scales: Towards a Relational Framework for analysing the Global Economy', *Global Networks. A Journal of Transnational Affairs*, 1(2): 89–112.

Hoff, J. and H.K. Hansen (2006) 'Conclusion – perspectives on politics and democracy', in H.K. Hansen and J. Hoff (eds) *Digital Governance:/Networked Societies Creating authority, community, and identity in a globalized world*. Copenhagen: Nordicom/Samfundslitteratur, 329–42

Jessop, B. (2002) 'The state and the contradictions of the knowledge-driven economy' in J.R. Bryson, P.W. Daniels, N. Henry and J. Pollard, *Knowledge, Space, Economy*. London: Routledge, 63–78.

Latham, R. and S. Sassen (2005) *Digital Formations. IT and New Architectures in the Global Realm*. Princeton: Princeton University Press.

May, T. (2005) *Gilles Deleuze. An Introduction*. Cambridge: Cambridge University Press.

Rosenau, J. and O. Czempiel (eds) (1992) *Governance without Government. Order and Change World Politics*. Cambridge: Cambridge University Press.

Slaughter, A-M. (2004a) *A New World Order*. Princeton: Princeton University Press.

Index